# FINANCIAL CRISIS AND THE FAILURE OF ECONOMIC THEORY

## Modern Heterodox Economics

*Series Editor:* *Carol M. Connell*

### Titles in this Series

1 Money as Organization, Gustavo Del Vecchio's Theory
*Gianfranco Tusset*

### Forthcoming Titles

The Invisible Hand of Power: An Economic Theory of Gate Keeping
*Anton N. Oleinik*

The Problem of Production: A New Theory of the Firm
*Per L. Bylund*

The Birth of Economics as a Social Science: Sismondi's Concept of Political Economy
*Francesca Dal Degan*

www.pickeringchatto.com/mhe

# FINANCIAL CRISIS AND THE FAILURE OF ECONOMIC THEORY

BY

Ángel Rodriguez, Jorge Turmo and Oscar Vara

PICKERING & CHATTO
2014

*Published by Pickering & Chatto (Publishers) Limited*
*21 Bloomsbury Way, London WC1A 2TH*

*2252 Ridge Road, Brookfield, Vermont 05036-9704, USA*

*www.pickeringchatto.com*



BRITISH LIBRARY CATALOGUING IN PUBLICATION DATA

Rodriguez Garcia-Brazales, Angel, author. Financial crisis and the failure of economic theory. – (Modern heterodox economics)
1. Economic forecasting. 2. Economics – Sociological aspects.
I. Title II. Series III. Turmo, Jorge, author. IV. Vara, Oscar, author.
330'.0112-dc23

ISBN-13: 9781848935150
e: 9781781444924
ePUB: 9781781444931

This publication is printed on acid-free paper that conforms to the American National Standard for the Permanence of Paper for Printed Library Materials.

*Typeset by Pickering & Chatto (Publishers) Limited*
*Printed and bound in the United Kingdom by CPI Books*

# CONTENTS

# ACKNOWLEDGEMENTS

We started thinking about the issues discussed in this volume some years ago, at the time of our PhD dissertations. We envisaged economic theory from a broader point of view than previous economists had, thanks to the ideas and encouragement of Rafael Rubio Urquía. His intellectual breeding has been present throughout the writing of our book. We want to thank the two referees that made suggestions that have improved our work. The same applies to the series editor, Carol M. Connell, who encouraged us to carry out our analyses in a more concrete and clear-cut manner. Any remaining inaccuracies are our own. We want to also thank Trajan Shipley for his impeccable performance in improving our English.

# ACKNOWLEDGEMENTS

# LIST OF FIGURES

# INTRODUCTION

The financial crisis abruptly disrupted a long period of continuous economic growth and low unemployment levels in developed countries. Along with the outstanding performance of the Chinese economy and the upsurge of Russia, Brazil and India, worldwide economic prospects were brilliant. In addition, inflation was under control, world trade was increasing considerably and many developing countries were escaping from poverty. Moreover, experts did not forecast any serious trouble in the near future, just some corrections of global imbalances through a soft-landing process. The crisis came as a complete surprise.[1] People in developed countries, including experts and economists, were also astonished. Reports on the financial crisis issued by the IMF, the World Bank or the European Union[2] repeated the same mantra: the crisis was unexpected. This approach to the crisis can be resumed as the 'No one saw it coming' hypothesis. In Chapter 1, we will explain that this hypothesis is incorrect, because some experts did see it coming and gave very clear warnings about the devastating effects of the coming crisis, but they were only credited when GDP and unemployment figures were worse than the worst warnings.

The next step was twofold: on the one hand policymakers had to deal with huge, and to a certain extent, new problems, as we explain in Chapter 5. On the other hand, there was a search for something or someone to be blamed for the crisis. There were many candidates. Global imbalances had been considered a dangerous threat because in the long run they are unsustainable. Some countries[3] were experiencing a housing bubble, the consequences of which are very well known. Financial innovations created many sophisticated financial products whose potential dangers were difficult to assess *a priori*, but proved to be harmful. The deregulatory swing since the beginning of the 1980s drove many financial processes out of the reach of monetary authorities. Rating agencies failed to adequately measure the risk of some assets or they did it so on purpose, misleading investors.

In this volume, we envisage the problem from another point of view. We have been working on the study of the allocative process from a non-orthodox perspective. We believe that mainstream economics has been very fruitful in dealing with some issues regarding allocative processes, while others remain out of its reach.[4] Generally speaking, mainstream economics focuses on economic processes that take place close to equilibrium, or it supposes that equilibrium almost always prevails. Keynesian economics, broadly speaking,[5] and Austrian economics are more prone to a perception that the economy is seldom in equilibrium. So, we believe that the dominant economic theory before the crisis was not as complete as it seemed to be. The financial crisis forced us to revise this concern. No one can hold that dominant economic theory had no responsibility in the inability to explain and predict the crisis because policymaking and regulatory activities before 2007 were conducted relying on mainstream economic models. This fact reaffirmed the idea that such models had to be revised. This was the starting point of this book.

Economic theories – and economic paradigms more generally – differ because of their assumptions regarding the three building blocks of every economic paradigm: the principle of economic behaviour, the characterization of the agents and the operational environment. For instance, classical and neoclassical and Austrian economics believe that prices are flexible while Keynesian economics does not. The consequences of assuming flexibility or stickiness determine the explanations and predictions of each model. The same applies to many other key features of each paradigm.

The crisis provoked a strong controversy about the usefulness of each paradigm in explaining and predicting the crisis. We want to go beyond this controversy and pay attention to the particular features of each theory that explain why it has failed. We do not focus on the whole theory, but on some specific parts that have proven to be defective, or on those parts that, in our view, are missing. In our research we have realized that in some cases economic theory was defective because it lacked some parts, namely the functioning of the financial system. It does not matter if the theory is labelled as classical, Keynesian or Austrian. What matters is whether the theory contains an accurate characterization of the agents and the operational environment or not.

In Chapter 1, we briefly review the financial crisis and the forecasts made just before the crisis by the main international economic organizations such the IMF, the OECD and the European Union. We stress that these forecasts failed miserably, adding more confusion to the painful scenario we experienced. Many experts relied on the 'No one saw it coming' hypothesis to avoid being blamed for it. But they were not right because some authors predicted the crisis. Their problem is that the models they were using were too narrow to cope with the scope of the crisis. So, we propose to broaden the focus to be able to understand the crisis.

In Chapter 2 we explain how to broaden the focus by relying on a theoretical framework that encompasses the analysis of the characterization of the agents and the operational environment. We show that we can study neoclassical and new classical economics, Keynesian, neo-Keynesian and post-Keynesian economics and Austrian economics using this approach to ascertain the differences and similarities among them. As a consequence there is a large set of elements concerning the characterization of the agents and the operational environment that can be combined to produce different economic paradigms. So, the analysis has to be carried out from this wider perspective, a kind of meta-theory.

In Chapter 3 we address this point. We stress, following Lakatos, that in every economic theory there are critical and auxiliary variables. If we remove the critical variables or assumptions from the theory its nature changes completely. In addition, we show that if a critical variable proves to be weak or it is falsified by the facts, the whole theory is called into question. As a consequence, the process of theoretical improvement implies the awareness of the criticality of some hypotheses and requires paying close attention to the new facts and data that can switch successful models into useless ones. As an example, we show in Chapter 4 how real business cycle theory almost completely displaced the previous models in explaining aggregate fluctuations and became the dominant theory for many years. The improvements made in the transmission mechanism of the model reinforced its usefulness, but the impulse mechanism remained unchanged. As a consequence this theory has been unable to explain the origin of the financial crisis. Conversely, growth theory has been changing along with changes in available data and including more factors to explain why countries grow at different rates.

In Chapter 5 we focus on a very meaningful fact of the crisis: policymakers were faced with a major challenge because the crisis affected nearly all developed countries and all economic sectors. At the same time they could rely very little on their macroeconomic and microeconomic toolbox. As a result, they improvised. In so doing they brought forward a wide array of issues that economic theory had not analysed and they implicitly established a research agenda for economic theory over the coming years. Many future improvements in economic theory will come from these requirements made by policymakers during the crisis.

To analyse how economic theory can improve, in Chapter 6 we focus on the financial system because we have lived through a financial crisis. We are certain that many other issues in economic theory deserve a more in-depth analysis to be improved, but here we limit our scope to financial issues. The greatest weakness of economic theory in dealing with the financial system is that its size and depth is far larger than the role it plays in economic models. As a consequence, many territories remain uncharted by economic theory. We engage in a tentative chartering of these territories by investigating whether the existent economic paradigms, not only mainstream economics, can enlarge our knowledge about the financial system to avoid future crises. Moreover, we look at the novelties that need to be incorporated into economic theory to prevent a repeat of history. While we believe that these novelties will help to avoid future financial crises, they are not enough. We therefore also propose changes in economic theory and in economic policy to avoid similar financial crises in the future.

# 1 THE FINANCIAL CRISIS AND MODERN ECONOMICS: FROM SURPRISE TO PUZZLEMENT

## Main Figures of the Crisis

One of the most salient features of the current crisis is that there were no warning signs. We had been living through a long period of growth in the majority of developed countries. During the last twenty years economic crises seemed to affect only developing countries. Those who lived in North America and Europe believed that they were immune to crisis. Only Japan had suffered a long period of stagnation and lost its position as a leader among developed countries. At the beginning of the 1990s Japan was the world's second biggest economy and it rivalled the US GDP, but ten years later this challenge had vanished.

The dotcom crisis was temporary because it mainly focused on some technological companies and it affected only these companies. The crisis drove the stock market to a peak followed by a sudden stop and fall. Many investors lost their money, but the overall economy did not suffer a downturn. Unemployment increases only affected workers in the tech companies.

The creation of the euro was a success even though some experts warned that the Eurozone was not an optimal currency area.[1] For many years the euro was beneficial for all its members: some countries could borrow at a very low interest rate while others increased their exports considerably. This success attracted other European countries to join this promising project.

At the same time China was growing considerably and world trade was increasing. China needed raw materials to grow and increased its direct investment in African and South American countries that lacked capital. Now China is a factor of stability and well-being for the whole world economy. The US economy grew and continued to be the largest market in the world, the best place to invest, and the dream of hundreds of thousands of immigrants from all over the world. Thus, on the eve of the crisis we seemed to have been living in what many have considered in retrospect a paradise.

The crisis that started in 2008 has affected mainly developed economies. It has reduced production and has rendered a lot of capital equipment useless. Millions of workers have been laid off and have undergone serious difficulties re-entering the job market. Household income has shrunk and the demand side of the economy has suffered. In addition, confidence has disappeared, making business activity much more difficult and hampering a possible economic recovery. More important still, the crisis has been long-lasting and has caused a lot of distress. The US and Canada have recovered faster while the Japanese economy has stagnated again and the European Union is in a painful situation. Additionally, it is unknown whether we have reached the bottom yet.

The change has been so dramatic that we now have to approach the evolution of our economies in a different way. This is not a normal crisis and we have started to use the term 'The Great Recession' to describe it. In fact, we are witnessing a structural change that exceeds by far the size of an economic crisis and it is reshaping the whole economic system. This is why we have to explain it very carefully. We have to bear in mind that contrary to the dotcom crisis, the current crisis was first a financial phenomenon that afterwards affected production and employment. There has not been a mismatch between the demand and supply side in only one sector: it has been a systemic change, the consequences of which will last for decades.

As a consequence of large amounts of very risky mortgage loans, in September 2007, US bank Countrywide Financial underwent liquidity problems that it could not afford and a bank run took place. The Federal Reserve was forced to intervene and Countrywide was sold to Bank of America. On the other side of the Atlantic, Northern Rock could not meet its obligations and the Bank of England gave it liquidity support. Then, the Bank of England tried to sell it, but no financial institution was willing to take it over and Northern Rock was nationalized.

The problem of Countrywide Financial was the increased number of foreclosures it could not handle, but it was not the only firm that was struggling. The mortgage-backed securities that allowed mortgage loans to increase considerably became increasingly illiquid as foreclosures rose. Facing the risk of more financial entities being affected, the US Treasury opened a new facility in March 2008 to allow banks to obtain Treasury notes with their mortgage-backed securities. But the timing of the solution was too late for Bear Sterns, which was taken over by JP Morgan due to its urgent liquidity problems.

Meanwhile the Bank of England, aware of the same problem, followed the US Treasury by accepting mortgage-backed securities from banks that needed liquidity. Both last resort lenders were facing the same challenge. The step that ignites the process is that a financial institution cannot meet the liquidity demands of its customers because it has committed too much money in medium- and long-term loans. When these loans prove to be less safe than expected and their repayment becomes doubtful the risk of a bank run increases. To avoid it, the monetary authority must inject liquidity to help the bank survive on its own. But in some cases the problem is not one of liquidity but of solvency and the third step is to find a buyer willing to recapitalize and stabilize the bank. If there is none, as in the case of Northern Rock, the monetary authority has to nationalize it.

The measures taken could not stop the process. In September 2008, the weakness of the mortgage-backed loans threatened Fannie Mae and Freddie Mac forcing the US Federal Housing Finance Agency to take control of them. Both are federally owned banks whose aim was to ease the access to the housing market for the US population. They were not obliged to bear a lot of risk to maximize the profits of their shareholders, but just the opposite: it was supposed they would behave conservatively. It is very difficult to explain why they performed so badly before the crisis, unless we suppose they shared the same mistaken theoretical background and incorrect procedures and practices as private financial institutions.

In the same month, Lehman Brothers filed for bankruptcy, dismissing the implicit rule that it was too big to fail. This was a turning point in the financial crisis because the US Treasury refused to rescue it. The US Treasury was intending to send a message of strength, but instead it unleashed a perfect storm. Stock markets plummeted all around the world and the Bank of England and the Federal Reserve injected billions of pounds and dollars into the banking system. Many financial institutions were partly or fully nationalized, although only temporarily. Meanwhile, the European Central Bank was silent and did not act.

The refusal to bail out Lehman Brothers was a disaster for the whole economy and banks realized that they had to merge to survive, otherwise they would be nationalized. Lloyds TSB took over HBOS and Bradford & Bingley was nationalized in the UK; Merrill Lynch was sold to Bank of America; Washington Mutual was controlled by the Federal authorities and partly sold to JP Morgan Chase in the US.

The financial crisis reached the rest of Europe as well. In September the government of Iceland decided to nationalize Glitnir Bank. The decision shed light on the fact that the whole Icelandic banking system was on the edge of a cliff because their liabilities were far larger than their assets. The government was forced to nationalize all financial institutions. In 2006 Fortis carried out the takeover of the Dutch bank ABN and failed to manage it successfully. Thus, in a rescue effort, 49 per cent of its shares were bought by the governments of Belgium, the Netherlands and Luxembourg.

The wave spread to more countries. The German government bailed out Hypo Real Estate, the largest property lender in the country. The Irish government, whose banks had been attracting deposits from all around the world, decided to guarantee all of them. The decision proved to be a mistake, because it converted the private debt of the banks to their customers into the public debt of the Irish people. The consequences of the decision are still with us. The Russian government, whose central bank is not independent, opened a large loan facility to Russian banks. In the US the Troubled Asset Relief Program was put in place, aimed at buying bank assets in exchange for liquidity when required. More examples of the same were Wachovia Bank, which was taken over by Wells Fargo and Sovereign Bank by Banco Santander in the US. Dexia, a Belgian group, was put under control of the Belgian, French and Luxemburg governments. The government of the UK became the owner of Royal Bank of Scotland, HBOS and Lloyds TSB when it bought half of their shares.

The economic policy measures adopted by central banks avoided a systemic banking crisis, except in Iceland in 2008 and Cyprus in 2013, but the cost was very large. The IMF has estimated[2] the fiscal cost of the measures taken by the governments. Its estimation includes capital injections in weakly capitalized banks, guarantees for financial sector liabilities, purchases of assets whose markets have dried up, and central bank support through credit lines to financial institutions. In advanced economies the average has been 50.4 per cent of the GDP. The UK has spent 81.6 per cent of its GDP and Sweden 69.7 per cent. The US has devoted 81 per cent but Canada just 25.1 per cent. In Germany the figure is 22 per cent, in France 19.2 per cent and in Ireland 267 per cent. It is worth mentioning that among the countries that have been rescued since then, namely Ireland, Greece, Portugal and Spain, only Ireland has spent a large percentage of its GDP in helping its financial institutions. We should ask ourselves whether a stronger public intervention in Greece, Portugal and Spain in 2010 could have fared better.

The financial storm, the public money spent on bank rescues and bailouts, and the turbulence generated by the lack of confidence among financial institutions caused severe erosion in developed economies. The GDP figures of 2009 were ugly. Japan decreased by 5.5 per cent, the US by 3.5 per cent and Canada by 2.8 per cent. In Europe, the decrease was 2.6 per cent in France, 3.5 per cent in Spain, 4.9 per cent in the UK and 5.0 per cent in Germany. In sharp contrast, China's GDP rose by 9.2 per cent. Concerns about the crisis peaked and uncertainty spread, but experts were confident that the crisis would be over soon.

In 2010 Germany's GDP increased by 4.0 per cent, the US by 2.4 per cent, Japan by 4.7 per cent and the UK by 1.8 per cent. The growth in France was 1.6 per cent and in Italy 1.7 per cent. It seemed that the worst was behind us and the world economy was recovering. But there was another slowdown in 2011. GDP growth in the UK was 1.0 per cent, in Italy 0.5 per cent, in France 1.7 per cent, in the US 1.8 per cent and in Germany 3.1 per cent. Japan showed a decrease of 0.5 per cent. Experts were not able to predict future events. Some of them believed that the slowdown would be temporary, while others feared a double dip in developed countries. The figures of 2012 have confirmed the worst hypothesis. France has not grown at all, and in the UK the increase has been a reduced 0.3 per cent. The German economy grew by 0.9 per cent, far less than the previous years, and in Italy the GDP has decreased by 2.4 per cent. Only the Japanese economy, at 1.9 per cent, and the US, at 2.2 per cent, have performed well. Many experts believed by the end of 2010[3] that the economy of developed countries was rebounding, but the figures of 2011 and 2012 do not back this assumption. We can say that the US has escaped from the crisis although it is not at full strength yet. The Japanese economy is experiencing ups and downs without a definite trend, while the main countries of the European Union are suffering a double dip recession. The crisis has not finished yet and it may be long-lasting.

The Great Depression started in 1929 in the US and hit Europe in 1930. It ended, depending on the country, in 1934–5. Our current Great Recession started in 2008 and is still with us. The length of both is very similar. The consequences of the Great Depression were large and affected not only economic variables, but society, politics, even literature. One dramatic change was the economic theory displayed in Keynes's *General Theory*. Our discipline changed forever. Will the Great Recession drive a similar change? As we will explain at a later stage, economic theory has exhibited many weaknesses throughout the crisis. We must learn from them and we must review our conventional and widely shared wisdom. The performance of our economic theories must improve.

While output grew slowly or decreased, another problem complicated the situation. In some countries the Great Recession dramatically decreased tax revenues, forcing governments to borrow money in international financial markets. But agents in these markets were very reluctant to lend money because of a deep lack of confidence. The interbank market dried up and banks did not trust each other. Thus, a growing demand for borrowing by national governments facing large public deficits could not be met. As a consequence, several European countries were pushed to the brink of default and asked the European Union for help.

The first was Greece, whose actual public deficit had been masked for years using creative accounting procedures. After the elections in 2009 the new government that came into power admitted the correct amount of its deficit and its public debt. Greece suddenly became unable to service its public debt because the access to financial markets became very difficult. Every Greek bank suffered a severe outflow of capital and the confidence in the Greek economy plummeted along with CDS prices, while the spread of interest rates skyrocketed. The new figures led rating agencies to downgrade the level of the Greek debt by several steps and the financing of public and private Greek debt was driven to a point of no return. The Greek government had no alternative but to turn to the EU and the IMF for help. The European Union led the process and in May 2010 a package of 120 billion Euros was agreed upon. Greece agreed to a very severe adjustment plan that included public expenditure cuts, an increase in the retirement age, privatizations of public firms, salary cuts for civil servants, and so on. Since the Greek economy did not recover, they could not afford the payment of the loans and another rescue package, including a default, was agreed on in 2012. Since then the Greek economy has been under scrutiny and has undergone a painful process of negotiations, riots and a severe downturn in GDP. Three years after, the Great Recession is hurting Greek people and the future is grim. A continuous decrease of living standards is causing widespread social distress.

The second case was Ireland. As we have explained, the government decided to guarantee all the deposits in Irish banks. It was a huge mistake. The banks had earned a lot of money by investing in high-risk products. When risk materialized, the value of the toxic assets in their balances fell to zero and they could not meet their obligations. The guarantee of the Irish government helped the banks survive but it turned private debt into public debt and the fiscal deficit peaked to 30 per cent of GDP. Ireland called for help too. In November 2010 an 85 billion Euro rescue plan was designed to help Ireland. The obligations were very similar to Greece's: wage and expenditure cuts, an increase in the retirement age, etc. The government approved the plan and they were immediately defeated in the general elections that took place in January 2011, among protests and riots. The Irish GDP decreased along with wages and living standards. Many Irish people were forced to emigrate. Fortunately, the real side of the Irish economy was able to adapt to the new circumstances without further decline in production. Two years later Ireland has been able to borrow again in the international capital markets, but the microeconomic consequences of the crisis have not disappeared yet.

The third was Portugal. In March 2011 the government of the Socialist Party tried to pass a law in the Parliament to cut public expenses, civil servant wages and to increase the age of retirement. The population did not accept this and the project was defeated because the other parties did not want to share the burden of the responsibility. Prime Minister Jose Socrates resigned and called for elections in which his party was dealt a severe defeat. The winning Social Democrat Party realized that there were no other options and, like Greece and Ireland, called for help. In May a 78 Billion Euro rescue package was approved. The memorandum of understanding they signed included the same measures that the Parliament had rejected two months before. Two years later, Portugal is experiencing its own Great Recession, its economy is depressed and further sacrifices have been imposed on the population in order to receive European loans.

From June of 2011 on, the Spanish risk premium peaked. International investors believed that debt repayment was doubtful and that there was a risk of default. In addition, Spanish savings banks proved to be very weak and poorly capitalized. The percentage of housing sector assets was very large in their balances. These assets had been very profitable during the housing boom, but they became toxic once the bubble burst. The mergers that took place from 2009 on failed to improve their long-term sustainability and Spain could not afford a bail-out because of public deficit. In June 2012 Spain called for a bank rescue that was approved in July. One hundred billion Euros were available. Spain was obliged to implement the same economic policy measures as the rest of the rescued countries. Once the balance of the banks was externally audited in December 2012, 47 billion Euros were released to clean up their balance sheets.

Finally, the effects of the problems in Greece affected the banks of Cyprus, whose balances became very fragile, and a 23 billion Euro rescue package was designed to prevent them from filing for bankruptcy.

The overall process has been sizeable, long-lasting and very harmful. It has affected many countries and it is ongoing. There has been a financial crisis, output has decreased considerably and unemployment has grown in many countries. Many banks have been nationalized or taken over by other financial institutions. Public deficit and public debt have grown a lot in developed countries and their financing has become increasingly difficult. Some countries have been rescued and are now under close scrutiny by international economic authorities. The economic growth of emerging countries has been slowed down too, as a consequence of the stagnation of the worldwide economy. And we cannot say that the crisis is over.

The first priority now is to find out the best way to help the economy to recover. But we should not postpone the effort to understand how things went wrong and what we can do to avoid repeating the same mistakes. Practical issues, economic policies and economic theories must be revised. We are going to focus on economic theories by explaining the causes of the crisis. Since the crisis was not forecasted, as we are going to show in the third section of this chapter, it implies that the causes could not be found in our textbooks.

## Causes of the Crisis According to Mainstream Economics

When we think about different schools of economic thought we usually refer to neoclassicals, Keynesians and Austrians. These schools have evolved over time, as we will explain in the next chapter, but their intrinsic features have not disappeared. Nevertheless, the neoclassical synthesis that took place after World War II combined neoclassical methods and a Keynesian approach. As a consequence the classification of an economist as Keynesian or neoclassical became more difficult. The same applies to mainstream economics. The term appeared in the late twentieth century as a way to define a widely shared approach to economics. Those that share it can claim to belong to mainstream economics, even though its departure point is not neoclassical, but Keynesian or Austrian. In Chapter 4 we will show that Keynesian economists made relevant contributions to real business cycles theory, a model strongly rooted in neoclassical economics. The reason is that mainstream economics focuses on assumptions like the representative agent or rational choice theory, and it relies heavily on the use of mathematical models. A self-labelled Keynesian economist can agree on these issues and therefore he becomes a member of mainstream economics. As a consequence, mainstream economics evolves over time thanks to the contributions of economists that belong to different intellectual traditions.

Those that do not agree, even if they consider themselves Keynesian, Austrian or something different, challenge this approach and are outside mainstream economics. They can be labelled 'heterodox' because they oppose the 'dominant paradigm' although they may not have more in common than this opposition. From the sociological point of view mainstream economics dominates our profession because a majority of economists agree on its methods, assumptions and topics, even though there is plenty of room for disagreement on other issues. The editorial board of scientific reviews and the members of scientific committees, think tanks and public advisers are usually recruited from the ranks of economists that share the assumptions of mainstream economics. The same applies to members of international economic institutions like the IMF, OECD, World Bank and others. It is difficult to find heterodox economists in these positions because of their basic disagreement on the main approach to economics. The difference in the departure point makes it impossible to establish a common ground. For this reason, to analyse the causes of the crisis, we must first explain the approach of international economic institutions, the International Monetary Fund, the OECD and the EU as representatives of mainstream economics. Then, we will briefly outline the point of view of Keynesian and Austrian economics.

'The global economy is in a severe recession inflicted by a massive financial crisis and an acute loss of confidence.'[4] This was the beginning of IMF analysis on the crisis that had started six month before. The title of one of the paragraphs was: 'How did Things Get So Bad, So Fast?' They pointed towards the subprime crisis in the US in 2007 and the default of Lehman Brothers as the starting point of a liquidity and solvency crisis that spread to an unprecedented level while the interbank market dried up. Even though a general financial crisis was avoided, the consequences battered the global economy through different channels.

The credit crunch and the accelerated deleverage process that took place hurt even the most highly rated borrowers. When the housing bubble burst, a sharp fall in prices reduced the wealth of owners, making them unable to service their loans. As a result, wealthier households underwent a severe income reduction and witnessed a sharp reduction in stock prices. On top of it, due to the increasing interconnectedness of the financial system, the troubles that originated in the US spread worldwide, affecting the real side of the economy in many countries.

The lack of consumer and investor confidence drove a negative feedback loop in which developed economies were trapped. Because of wealth reduction, households cut down purchases of durables driving up firm's inventories and forcing them to reduce production and to lay off workers. Besides, the credit crunch worsened the situation for weaker firms, feeding the process. One of the worst consequences has been that global capital flows have run to safety and have showed a strong preference for investing in their own countries. As such, some countries have managed very well during the crisis because they were believed to be safe harbours. Others have been punished by international financial markets that did not trust them.

The approach of the OECD to the causes of the crisis was quite similar: 'So, what were the causes of this crisis? One way of answering this question is in terms of a metaphor- an overflowing dam. The water behind the dam was a global liquidity bubble or easy access to cheap borrowing.'[5]

Then, the authors explain the root causes subjacent to the global liquidity bubble. First, there were low US interest rates as a result of the dotcom crisis. The Federal Reserve decided to decrease interest rates to fight the crisis and to help the economy recover. But it maintained these low rates for too long. In addition, low interest rates in Japan set by the Bank of Japan to overcome the lost decade of the 1990s led investors to the so-called carry trade. They borrowed money very cheaply in Japan and used it to buy much higher yielding assets in the US or other countries. China was one of the main agents of this process. From the beginning of the decade, China has been running increasing current account surpluses because of the strength of its exports. Since the Chinese government wanted to maintain its currency under control, they invested the surpluses in secure assets like US Treasury Bonds, increasing the available liquidity in the financial system. Many Sovereign Funds owned by oil exporting countries did the same and liquidity increased further.

This amount of liquidity was mainly invested in the housing sector and the stock market and generated a double price bubble that remained unnoticed. Until the beginning of the 1990s banks had always been very conservative in their financial behaviour. Then, they began to engage in the generate-to-distribute model, creating new investment devices. They took advantage of the increasing demand in housing markets in some countries and offered mortgages to new customers at low initial interest rates. Afterwards, they packaged the mortgages and securitized them, offering the package as a new product to investors, the now famous RMBS. That way they did not bear the risk of these mortgages. They securitized different products as well and sold them to investors who were unaware of their risk. When housing prices and assets fell sharply the whole system collapsed and the financial crisis spread worldwide. The point of view of the European Commission is explained as follows: 'the proximate cause of the financial crisis is the bursting of the property bubble in the United States and the ensuing contamination of balance sheets of financial institutions around the world'.[6]

They explain why this happened and why it spread to the rest of the world. First, they mention the Great Moderation, low interest rates and sustained growth that generated a wave of optimism among economic agents that undervalued the risks they were bearing. They mention, like the OECD above, the long period of low interest rates in the US and Japan and the increasing amount of current surpluses of oil exporters and China that were invested in the US. As a consequence, there was an excess liquidity supply in the US that was channelled to Europe in three ways. First, there was the upward pressure on the European exchange rate that reduced imported inflation and paved the way for the reduction of interest rates. Second, the carry trade because many investments were made in the Euro Area offloading the excess liquidity on our continent. Financial firms borrowed in the US, where interest rates were very low, and invested in the Euro Area, where profitability was higher. Third, the integration of capital markets diverted capital flows to real estate markets in several countries, fostering the housing bubble, the bursting of which has hurt these countries considerably. The whole picture includes the same reasoning regarding the behaviour of the banks from the dotcom crisis onwards as we have explained before. There are some additional remarks on the lack of economic policies to take into account the effects of financial markets on the real side of the economy.

The main feature of their explanations is that the crisis has been a financial one whose size and depth has overcome the financial system and has affected the entire economy of many countries. The worldwide global excess liquidity caused by a period of low interest rates and current account surpluses was channelled to several sectors causing bubbles in housing and asset markets. The bursting of this bubble triggered the crisis affecting several economies. They do not go further in their analysis[7] but we have to.

Our analysis focuses on the role of the financial system in the crisis and in economic theory and the mismatches between the former and the latter. In Chapter 2 we present our point of view: every economic theory has three main building blocks, the principle of economic behaviour, the characterization of the agent and the operating environment. We postpone a wide explanation to the next chapter, but here we point out that the financial system belongs to the operating environment. We are going to examine here the approach of mainstream economics to the financial system, its strengths and weaknesses.

In financial markets the dominant paradigm has been the efficient market hypothesis (hereafter EMH). It was proposed by Paul Samuelson in 1965 and Eugene Fama in 1970. The EMH says that the price of each asset that can be bought and sold contains all the relevant information. The price is correct because it reflects the fundamental value of the asset. If the price was above or below this value the agents would correct it by selling or buying the asset. Thus, the market is efficient when the price of an asset conveys all the relevant information about it. Besides, agents are rational because they take into account this information in their decision-making processes.

We have shown that the IMF, the EU and the OECD believe that the amount of global liquidity pushed up the price of assets as well as housing prices. This upward pressure created two bubbles whose bursting triggered the crisis. But if markets were efficient, as EMH takes for granted, they had warned economic agents that a sudden drop was possible. Put differently, if EMH is correct the price of assets before the crisis was correct as well because it was reflecting the fundamental value of these assets. The crisis has demonstrated that those prices were not correct, because after the meltdown they fell considerably, casting a lot of doubts on the credibility of EMH. If EMH did not hold, economic agents were relying on false statements in their decision-making processes.

Another important issue is the credibility of EMH. If before the crisis many agents stood by EMH, after the crisis they realized EMH had failed. Imagine that there is an economic agent observing the upward trend of the price of one asset. If he believes that EMH holds true, he is convinced that this upward trend is mirroring the increase in the value of the asset. As a consequence, it is rational to buy it even though its price had been increasing for months or years. This can be very misleading for an individual, but it is more damaging when a pension or investment fund manager analyses the trend of prices. If he believes that EMH is a good indicator, he will continue buying the asset whose price is rising and he will continue advising his clients to do the same. We are not suggesting that fund and pension investment managers blindly agreed on EMH, but rather that their confidence in this hypothesis led them to bear more risks than they would have been willing to. If EMH holds, economic agents take for granted that their available information is reliable. Otherwise they would be forced to make their own analysis of the assets they are buying and selling and that would be costly. Once they have decided that EMH is correct they use it and may become unaware of the risks they are assuming.

EMH has been criticized in many ways at different times, but we are going to focus only on two of the criticisms. Grossman and Stiglitz[8] pointed out the contradiction between the hypothesis and the cost of the information. If EMH is true, agents have no incentive to pay for information concerning prices, while if markets are inefficient, they are willing to pay for it. Thus, if EMH is correct and information is costly we face a paradox we may encounter many times.

Many years ago F. Hayek explained that markets are efficient only if information is without cost or its cost is very low. Otherwise agents must pay for it and it would not be incorporated into market prices. One of Hayek's main ideas was that economic agents were in a continuous search for wider and more detailed information than that provided by market prices. Hayek's approach to the analysis of the functioning of markets has been neglected by mainstream economics for decades. We can say that mainstream economics has been blind and we will explain why in the next chapter. Now, the effects of the financial crisis we are still undergoing are pushing it to the forefront again and we are regretting our blindness.

Another issue that is worth mentioning is that EMH favours deregulation processes. If markets provide us with all the necessary information, we need not regulate them. If we lack information or it is highly asymmetric, regulation is required to assure that markets perform well. Many experts have said that the derogation in 1999 of the Glass–Steagall Act fostered risky behaviour among banks by eliminating firewalls between commercial banks and investment banks. If EMH is correct, the Glass–Steagall Act was unnecessary and its elimination was a step in the right direction. But if EMH is not correct, firewalls are necessary and its derogation was wrong.

Another source of criticism arises from the type rationality of each agent. During the boom it was supposed that agents were fully rational, despite Greenspan's comments on the 'irrational exuberance of markets'. EMH implicitly takes for granted that agents are able to use the information conveyed by market prices. Besides, mathematical models of asset prices rely on the rational expectation hypothesis, assuming that agents are rational and make their estimates about future values of fundamental variables and prices in a consistent way. That entails that they know and use the model proposed by economists. The type of rationality of agents is a feature of the characterization of the agent, the second building block of each economic theory. The assumptions about the type of rationality of agents shape and determine the kind of economic theory that is created. EMH takes for granted a very demanding type of rationality of economic agents.

But many leading economists did not agree with the assumptions that follow from the rational expectation hypothesis. Nobel Prize winners, Daniel Kahneman and Amos Tverski,[9] developed the *behavioural finances or behavioural economics theory*. They state that the behaviour of some of the agents in financial markets exhibits a bounded rationality. They are rational but not fully rational, because there are cognitive limitations that divert them from being fully rational. They believe that bounded rationality is more usual than the kind of rationality assumed by EMH and it can explain a large part of the observed behaviour in financial markets. They stress that bounded rationality increases with uncertainty. Since uncertainty prevails in financial markets agents seldom exhibit full rationality as EMH implies. If they are not fully rational the information conveyed in market prices may be useless for them. The information that prices convey can be good or bad, but if economic agents are unable to take advantage of it, their behaviour will not be optimal. They will not behave in the way predicted by the theory.

Thaler and Sunstein[10] say that Greenspan and many other financial experts could not forecast the arrival of the crisis because they believed that EMH performed well. As a consequence, they believed that the economic agents were acting the same way. They did not take into account more realistic features of the agents and the possibility of people acting irrationally or at least being rationally bound. Financial institutions and financial contracts have changed a lot during the last twenty years and they are increasingly complex. Many agents may simply be unable to understand them and mistakes are unavoidable. Mainstream economics believed that EMH was a suitable framework of analysis, but it was not. Economists that share their ideas managed our economies, taking for granted that markets were efficient and agents were fully rational. But the economic environment was not one of efficient markets and the economic agent was not fully rational either, and so, the crisis came about.

## The Causes of the Crisis According to New Keynesian Economics and Austrian Economic Theory

The first issue we want to address is to what extent this approach, namely Keynesian economics, can explain the crisis. Since mainstream economics has been unable to explain it, we have to look elsewhere. It is worth mentioning that Keynes's work was his answer to the consequences of the Great Depression and the reasons that led to it. It was also a sharp criticism of the equilibrium approach of the economic theory and its poor performance in explaining the causes of the Great Depression and in finding the correct recipe for recovery. Keynesian economics has evolved from this departure point. From World War II onwards, the success and failure of Keynesian economics is well known, so we will refrain from reviewing it. New classical economics has been dominant over the last thirty years and is still the backbone of the models we are using.

Keynesian economics stresses that economies do not run smoothly because there are large and persistent price and wage stickiness and markets do not clear. Keynesian economists state that monetary issues matter, because money is not neutral in the short run, but they seldom pay attention to the financial system as such. They stress the importance of the demand side of the economy against the prevalence of the supply side in mainstream economics. Nevertheless, they share a common ground: the real side of the economy is much more important than the monetary side, not to mention the financial system. As a consequence the usefulness of Keynesian economics to explain the causes of the crisis is small, but deserves a closer look.

Keynesian economics has been a weak challenge to the dominant paradigm over the last thirty years for theoretical reasons. Keynesian economics has acknowledged its main flaw, the lack of micro foundations, and has improved it considerably. In fact, new Keynesian economics, as we are going to explain in Chapter 2, has made a great effort to set the microeconomic foundations of their models. So, there has been a convergence between the dominant paradigm and new Keynesian economics in some fields, while maintaining the differences in others. For instance, new Keynesians have been able to modify original RBC[11] theory by including monetary issues[12] and no competitive price setting.[13] These are the dynamic general stochastic equilibrium models, DGSE thereafter. DGSE models have been used by central banks and other experts to analyse the economy of a country or a group of strongly-linked countries, such as the Eurozone. They have been used in short-term forecasting, substituting former structural models whose main features were unsatisfactory. That way, to a certain extent new Keynesian economics has mixed new classical economics by adding new elements to mainstream economics.

Mainstream economics' failure to explain the crisis applies to new Keynesian economics as well since DGSE models also failed in their forecasts. Even though there are still clear differences between classical and new Keynesian approaches, they now share DGSE as a framework of analysis. And this framework has been blamed for not having predicted the crisis.[14] As a consequence, new Keynesian economics also suffered from the same failure.

Nevertheless, there are Keynesian economists more focused on explaining the roots of economic instability than in introducing some Keynesian features on DGSE models. They are labelled post-Keynesian economists. A salient difference between new Keynesian and post-Keynesian is the way they envisage financial issues. Keynes focused on the effects of agents' expectations in macroeconomics, and price and wage stickiness, but he did not pay so much attention to the financial side of the economy. But nowadays there are post-Keynesian economists much more concerned with the role of financial markets and their effects on aggregate fluctuations. The most important is Hyman Minsky, whose financial fragility hypothesis[15] has been set aside over the last twenty years. In our opinion it is worthwhile to revisit it because it contains the main elements that explain and help us to understand the financial crisis. The backbone of the hypothesis is that in advanced economies the financial system exhibits strong pro-cyclicity. Firms can rely on their own profits for investment or in borrowing money and increasing their level of leverage. When sales and profits increase, firms that rely on their profits to invest fall short of demand while leveraged firms can meet demand and succeed. As a consequence there is an increasing tendency among firms to borrow money to keep pace with their rivals. The overall leverage level rises and so does the overall risk level. Thus, the financial system is pushing the whole system towards instability.

When interest rates are below profit rates, firms continue borrowing. Sooner or later, the increasing borrowing demand drive interest rates above profit rates and some firms fail to roll over their debt because they have become insolvent. A credit crunch happens and other firms are affected as well. Firms engage in fire sales to reduce their indebtedness but they are in excess supply and the process pushes down prices, making the repayment of the debt more difficult. The financial fragility hypothesis explains the financial crisis very accurately and Hyman

Minsky deserves much credit for it. But before the crisis, even though its theory was well known among experts, few of them believed that it was a good description of the economy. We will come back to this point later. In Chapter 2 we will show that some critical features of the building blocks of new Keynesian economics are very different from post-Keynesian economics. This is the reason why post-Keynesian economics can contribute to explain the financial crisis, while new Keynesian cannot.

The Austrian approach is different.[16] Austrian economists believe that economic agents are far more complex than depicted by mainstream economics. We will explain this idea in the next chapter. They also agree that radical uncertainty in the operating environment is the rule because information is scarce and costly and because novelty plays a large role in economics. As a consequence, they believe that aggregate fluctuations are driven by internal factors, which are unavoidable and they will produce a downturn sooner or later. The Austrian business cycle theory, or ABCT,[17] explains this and we are going to look at it shortly.

Production is a roundabout process and the timing of each step of the process is not interchangeable. It is not reversible either. Mainstream economics focuses on production factors and productivity but does not take into consideration the intertemporal dimension of production. This approach diverts mainstream economists from analysing the intermediate stages of production and the effects of possible mismatches among them. ABCT states that there are roughly speaking two different types of goods. High-order capital goods belong to the initial stages of production. Low-order consumer goods are the culmination of the productive process. Intermediate stages can be defined if necessary. Both require production factors and inputs, but some of them are not interchangeable either. Most important, the use of every production factor and input is time-dependent. The temporal dimension of all of them is not just a matter of a subscript in the notation. No matter how productive an input is, if it is not supplied in a timely manner, it becomes useless.

ABCT focuses on the medium term, when problems arise. In the short term the structure of production cannot be modified. In the long term all the errors are rectified and the structure of capital is correct. But in the medium term, erroneously made investments have consequences and the decisions made are impossible to change because of the heterogeneity of most capital goods. Besides, there is room for new decision-making processes about where and when to invest that will prove correct or not in the future.

If roundaboutness increases, instead of producing consumer goods, new and more efficient capital goods are produced that will increase the amount of consumer goods in the future, provided these goods meet the expected demand. Conversely, if roundaboutness decreases, firms shift from the production of capital goods to produce consumer goods, but productivity does not increase.

That implies that the period between the initial investment in capital goods and its return when consumer goods are sold increases along with roundaboutness. Long periods imply that it takes a lot of time to know whether investments are profitable or not. As a consequence, the rectification of bad investments is more difficult and more costly. Short periods allow investors to rectify when they realize they are wrong.

What led investors to increase the roundaboutness of the processes? A lowering in interest rates levels. ABCT assumes that there is a natural rate of interest that depends on the intertemporal preferences of agents. If agents have a strong preference for the present, natural interest rates are high. They are lower when their preference for the present is less strong. Market interest rates are influenced by monetary policy of central banks. When market interest rates are driven below natural interest rates, investors believe that there is a strong willingness to save, so they can rely on this tendency to invest in very roundabout processes. The low market rate of interest along with the abundance of credit led firms to lengthen the production process. The prices of intermediate goods rise relative to the prices of consumer goods prices and the structure of production becomes unsustainable.

Since consumer preference for the present remains unchanged, when they reassert their preferences by demanding more consumer goods, the amount of savings fall short of the required investment. Production processes in intermediate stages cannot be redirected. The mismatch between the wishes of firms, namely more capital goods, and the wishes of consumers, namely more consumer goods, cannot be managed and it drives the economy into a recession.

We have shown in the second part of the chapter that international institutions (EU, IMF, OECD) point to a long period of low interest rates and easy credit conditions as one of the main reasons for the financial turmoil in developed economies. They do not take a closer look at the underlying processes because their experts do not endorse ABCT, but their explanations are quite similar. Both agree on the key role that low interest rates play in the unleashing of the crisis. Both stress that low interest rates led firms to increase their investment by borrowing large amounts of money. Both explain why prices rise for some period beyond sustainable levels. And both point out that when agents become aware that these levels are unsustainable, the crisis begins. ABCT performs much better than any other theory in explaining the current crisis. If experts from international institutions had paid attention to ABCT they could have forecasted the crisis. Unfortunately they strongly disagreed with its fundamentals, so as a result ABCT was not in their toolboxes.

## Failures of Mainstream Economics and Failures to Pay Attention to Those Who Forecasted It

### *The Crisis was not Predictable*

One remarkable feature of the current crisis is that many professional forecasts failed because either there were no warning signs before it or the signs were misunderstood. The *IMF World Economic Outlook* of October 2007 explained that:

> the baseline projection for 2008 global growth has been reduced by almost ½ percentage point relative to the July 2007 *World Economic Outlook Update*. This would still leave global growth at a solid 4.75 per cent ... Risks to the outlook however are firmly on the downside, centred around the concern that financial market strains could deepen and trigger a more pronounced slowdown.[18]

And, in October of 2008, the Executive Summary of the same document stated that:

> The world economy is entering a major downturn in the face of the most dangerous financial shock in mature financial markets since the 1930s. Global growth is projected to slow substantially in 2008, and a modest recovery would only begin later in 2009.[19]

The IMF forecasted a modest growth in the US (0.1 per cent), the Eurozone (0.2 per cent) and Japan (0.5 per cent) while the UK GDP would decrease by 0.1 per cent. Emerging and developing countries would not be affected and would continue at the same pace. In the first part of this chapter we have shown the GDP figures in developed countries thorough 2009. The difference is huge and the trend is just the opposite. This IMF World Outlook forecasted a slight recovery in 2009 while real figures showed a deepening of the crisis.

The economic forecast of the European Union, in Spring 2008, said that US GDP growth was projected to be 0.7 per cent in 2009, while the Japanese growth was 1.1 per cent. They forecasted a 1.8 per cent GDP growth for the EU27 and 1.5 per cent in the Euro Area.

As in the second part of the chapter, we have used forecasts of the IMF and the European Union because they are very meaningful. Both documents were written by teams of economists whose expertise and technical qualifications are not in doubt. No one would question the raw information they are using. They would not question the statistical procedures either. Their reports are supposed to be the best macroeconomic forecasts available and the most reliable as well. Other institutions issue analyses on specific sectors and/or countries, but they are more locally focused. If the CEO of a multinational company wants to take a glance at the evolution of the economy, he should read the Executive Summary of the IMF. The EU forecasts are the practical and short guidance for those interested in the evolution of the EU economy.

In addition, prominent economists and businessmen declared that it was unpredictable. In an article published by the *New York Times* in November 2008, Henry Paulson, Secretary of the US Treasury, said: 'We are going through a financial crisis more severe and unpredictable than any in our lifetimes'.[20]

When Queen Elizabeth II visited the London School of Economics in November 2008, she asked why nobody noticed the credit crunch in advance. In July 2009, nine months later, the British Academy presented its answer:

> So in summary, Your Majesty, the failure to foresee the timing, extent and severity of the crisis and to head it off, while it had many causes, was principally a failure of the collective imagination of many bright people, both in this country and internationally, to understand the risks to the system as a whole.[21]

As a consequence over the last five years there have been plenty of complaints about the failure of international organisms to predict the arrival of the crisis. The same applies to rating agencies that have rated AAA assets that afterwards have proved to be toxic, and to international finance advisors that have misled investors. A wave of sharp criticism against experts has arisen in many countries, mainly because none of them was able to predict the crisis. Then, criticism increased because of their inability to pull us out of the crisis. Policymakers of many governments have been discredited in the same way. As a whole, the failure in recognizing that a crisis was coming and the extent of its size has diminished the credibility of experts.

Many questions remain unanswered. If our best experts were unable to predict the crisis, can we trust them? Can those who failed before the crisis help us to get out of it? Since their models and theories have proved to be useless in explaining and predicting the crisis, is it worthwhile to use them to overcome the crisis? Can we trust these models and theories to conduct economic policy once we recover from the crisis?

The answer to all these questions is not straightforward because they are intrinsically very difficult. In addition, there were economists that predicted the crisis. So, we have to address the question of why those that predicted the crisis were not heard. Besides, the kind of arguments of those that were right can shed light on the reasons why a large majority was wrong.

## *It was Predictable and it was Predicted*

We are going to explain the predictions of economists that were able to foresee the coming financial crisis. We limit ourselves to experts that explained the theoretical reasons of their predictions and that were able to date the crisis in advance. Dating is important because it is a type of commitment. An author can foresee the evolution of the economy if he understands its dynamics. If he believes he is right, he should commit and tell us when the crisis will start.

This section is partly based in an article of Dirk Bezemer (2009) that reviews the predictions of several economists before the crisis.[22] We focus on the mechanisms of the crisis to stress why authors were able to predict it. Then, we will examine why those mechanisms were not taken into consideration by the majority of experts.

We are going to group the authors that predicted the crisis according to their main theoretical reason for saying that a crisis was coming. It is very important to bring to the forefront issues that they were able to see some years before the onset of the crisis to analyse why other people were not able to see the same.

The first is the housing bubble in the US and other countries and the effect that the burst bubble had on the economy. Dean Baker, co-director of the Centre for Economic Policy Research in Washington predicted in his article in 2005[23] that asset prices will fall in the medium term. He explained that the positive wealth effect of the housing bubble would be followed by a sudden downturn that would reduce consumption spending and would push the economy into recession.

Wynne Godley warned from the beginning of the century that the US housing market growth was unsustainable in the medium term and that the consequence would be a recession. He depicted an accounting framework of the US economy to explain that part of its economic growth was fuelled by debt growth. In the housing sector, prices increased steadily and fostered capital gains. When capital gains stopped, prices would decline and a recession would start before 2010.

Jakob Madsen, a Danish economist, pointed out that growing housing prices in his country alongside unprecedented mortgage levels were unsustainable. He explained that Danish economic growth was too heavily based on the housing sector. In 2007 he predicted a fall in housing prices that would drive the Danish economy into recession.

A second group focused on internal and global imbalances that were the source of future threats for the economy in many countries. Eric Janszen, a professional investor, explained before the dotcom crisis that the market value of technological companies was far beyond their fundamentals and he warned about the coming bubble in this sector. Since 2006 he wrote many times that private and public sector in the US had built up too much debt. Its level was too high and unsustainable, so an economic crisis was very likely to happen. In 2006 he predicted that the crisis will hit the US economy within some years and in December 2007 he warned investors to be ready to deal with falling US stock markets.

Stephen Keen, an Associate Professor in Sydney, wrote in 2008:

> in December 2005, almost two years before the crisis hit, I realized that a serious financial crisis was approaching. I was so worried about its probable severity – and the lack of awareness about it amongst policymakers – that I took the risk (for an academic) of going very public about my views.[24]

In 2006 he pointed out that the overall debt-to-GDP ratio in Australia was 147 per cent and that it would exceed 160 per cent of GDP the next year. Both were unsustainable and the expansion would come to an end. The downturn would be severe and the economy would plunge into recession.

The third group focused on the effects of the US loose monetary policy. Fred Hudson, in a paper presented in 2006,[25] warned about the unsustainable 'growth of net worth through capital gains' fostered by US monetary policies after the dotcom crisis. Decreasing interest rates and a large amount of credit flows led households and firms to borrow beyond any previous limit, and they fuelled a process of asset prices increase. More precisely, in 2006 he published an article in *Harper's Magazine* entitled 'The Road to Serfdom: An Illustrated Guide to the Coming Real Estate Collapse'. There he wrote:

> The bubble will burst ... America holds record mortgage debt in a declining housing market ... For those who bought at the top and who now face decades of payments on houses that soon will be worth less than they paid for them, serious trouble is brewing ... Taken together, these factors will further shrink the 'real' economy, drive down those already declining real wages, and push our debt-ridden economy into Japan-style stagnation or worse.[26]

Kurt Richebächer had warned against the technological bubble before 2000 and against the housing bubble from 2002. In 2006 he wrote:

> the recovery of the US economy since November 2001 has been dominated by an unprecedented consumer borrowing-and-spending binge ... wealth creation trough soaring asset prices has been driven by ultra-cheap and loose money and credit, and not by saving and investment.[27]

Then he said that real estate prices will certainly decrease. In August 2006, when prices began to fall, he wrote that 'a recession and bear market in asset prices are inevitable for the U.S. economy ... This will not be a garden-variety recession, in which monetary easing unleashes pent-up demand, as it used to do in past business cycles.' And he insisted in the causes of the coming turmoil: 'The U.S. liquidity deluge of the last few years has had one single source: borrowing against rising assets baked by the Fed`s monetary looseness ... all hinging on further rises in asset prices. But they are going to plunge.'[28]

The fourth group point to financial developments. Raghuram Rajan[29] explained that financial development along with deregulation increased the efficiency of the financial system by widening the number of agents and products. But he pointed out that the originate-to-distribute framework had a strong pro-risk bias because banks made profits by generating risky assets and distributing them to other agents that bear the risk. Some years ago he warned that banks were bearing low-probability tail risks associated with assets prices. If asset prices eventually plummets, this low probability materializes and losses may be large. He advised us to implement and enhance prudential regulations without further recommendations.

In a paper in 2006 William White asked if price stability was enough, taking into account that the financial system had changed considerably:

> The structural changes in the financial sector in recent decades have been profound. Some combination of technological change and deregulation has led to a quickening process of disintermediation from banks, growing reliance on market processes, globalisation and institutional consolidation. In short, we now have a liberalised financial system which seems much more likely to show boom-bust characteristics than the previously repressed one.[30]

He goes on to describe the risks associated with this process, stressing that before the financial crisis in South-East Asia in the 1990s and the debt crisis in Russia in 1998 there was an environment of price stability. There were no warning signs of a downturn. As a consequence, he states that price stability is not enough to avoid economic downturns and that the experts should pay attention to other variables as well.

> As noted above, the arguments used are that bubbles are hard to identify and that 'pricking the bubble' would demand interest rates so high as to damage other, unaffected parts of the economy. Yet a convincing counterargument is that the indicators considered by policymakers should extend well beyond asset prices.[31]

From a different point of view, Robert Shiller published a book on the bursting of stock-market bubbles in 2000. In the second edition of the book, he wrote in the preface:

> further rises in the stock and housing markets could lead, eventually, to even more significant declines ... a long-run consequence could be a decline in consumer and business confidence, and another, possible worldwide, recessions. This extreme outcome ... is not inevitable, but it is a much more serious risk than is widely acknowledged.[32]

Shiller had been researching for years on bubble creation and bubble bursting, and had stated many times that consumers were not as rational as they were supposed to be. This is one of the keys to understanding why the warnings of the economists we have mentioned in this section were ignored.

## *Why was it Predictable but was not Predicted?*

Some experts warned us that a crisis was very likely to happen in the near future. But their warnings did not prevail against the conventional wisdom. There were a lot of arguments to avoid acting. There were a lot of theoretical weaknesses too. The size of the hypothetical crisis was unknown and unforeseeable. The mechanisms that could trigger it were unclear. Even though the experts whose predictions we have outlined belong to mainstream economics the majority of economists either did not pay attention to their warnings or they believed a crisis was very unlikely to happen. We are going to explain why.

First, we should address the housing bubble in the US and other countries. In 2006 and even 2007 a soft landing of prices was the widely shared prediction. For instance, in Spain there was a large leveraged buyout in 2006 and only one major sector firm had decided to leave the Spanish housing sector because it foresaw the coming crisis. The reasons behind this behaviour are the assumptions about how the market was working and how rational the agents were. Shiller warned that agents were showing an irrational exuberance, but the majority of experts did not agree with him. We will elaborate further on this.

What about internal and global imbalances? Janszen and Keen state that they were unsustainable. They wonder whether any experts paid attention to them or were aware of their dangers, even though the statistics were publicly known. The problem was that internal imbalances were linked with global imbalances. China and oil-exporting countries were running current account surpluses that were channelled mainly to the US and generated a large amount of cheap money. The Chinese government decided to invest in the US because its asset markets were larger and safer than any other. The same applied to the sovereign funds of oil-exporting countries. The current account surplus of China was a consequence of their exports' strength and the artificially low value of the renminbi. Oil-exporting countries took advantage of increasing oil and gas prices and growing worldwide demand. Chinese and oil-exporting surpluses were due to the normal running of markets. China was a great export-led economy and the demand for oil and gas was fostered by world GDP increase. As a consequence, investment of the Chinese government and sovereign funds in developed countries financed their debt-to-GDP ratio increase. We had never before experienced the negative consequences of global imbalances and our economic theory approached them as an equilibrium phenomenon. There were concerns about the size of the global imbalances, but they were focused on the effects of the unavoidable correction process. There were also concerns about the sustainability of the current account deficit in the US in the long run. Some experts explained that a sudden withdrawal of Chinese money would generate an economic crisis in the US. But the effects of global imbalances on assets and housing sector prices were outside the scope of the analysts. The underlying economic theory was too narrow.

One of the effects of global imbalances was a large amount of cheap money invested in different sectors and countries that pushed down interest rates. After the dotcom crisis the interest rates were low for many years in developed economies as we have explained in the second part of this chapter. Many authors have stressed that the Chairman of the Federal Reserve, Alan Greenspan, decided to reduce the US interest rate to help the economy recover after the dotcom crisis. His economic policy succeeded and US interest rates were low for many years while GDP was growing. Hudson and Richebächer explained before the crisis that this growth was artificial, because it was based on debt growth and capital gains instead of a saving and investment process. Consequently, they predicted the crisis but their warnings went unheeded.

The main concern about the effects of a long period of low interest rates is inflation, but it was kept under control for many years. Since prices did not rise experts took for granted that monetary policy was correct. This belief has proven to be false, but before the crisis they seldom questioned it.

White's article was an exception because he believed that price stability was not enough. His article went beyond the conventional wisdom, pointing out that price stability could mask a bubble formation in the stock market and the housing sector. Sovereign funds were clearly in excess supply and, following the assets shortage hypothesis by Caballero,[33] pushed up the price of assets without affecting consumer prices. Besides, household wealth grew along with the price of assets, including home prices. As a consequence, worldwide liquidity inflated a bubble that remained unnoticed.

Mainstream economics theories and models focus on inflation abatement because inflation harms economic performance. Central banks have implemented a toolbox to fight against inflation that has performed quite well over the last twenty years. And there has been a widely shared agreement on the effectiveness of these measures. There have been some exceptions, among them the criticism of how monetary policy has been conducted in the US as we have explained in the previous section.

Besides, it was taken for granted that additional measures were not necessary, that early warning systems were useless. They may have helped to know in advance what was going on. But the major limitation is that models and theories could not explain the relationship between growing asset prices and economic downturns. They could not explain it because this relationship was absent from models and theories. Mainstream economics has proved to be myopic in dealing with it. Additionally, and more important still, there was a theoretical gap of which theorists were unaware. Mainstream economics has been blind to its own theoretical narrowness.

Rajan and White pointed at deregulation and financial innovation as one of the engines of the crisis. Why did mainstream economics believe that their advantages exceeded their shortcomings? There have been two major reasons to support deregulation. On the one hand, the world economy has experienced a period of unprecedented growth since the beginning of this century, in spite of the dotcom crisis and the terrorism that afflicted New York in 2001. Developing countries have grown a lot and China is now the second largest economy in the world. Brazil is leading economic growth in South America, while other countries like Ecuador, Colombia and Chile exhibit very good figures. India is starting to grow, lifting more than two hundred million people out of poverty, and many countries in South-East Asia are improving their living standards as well. Deregulation has played an important role in these processes, fostering economic growth. As a consequence, financial markets' deregulation has been considered a step in the right direction towards making them more efficient.

On the other hand, models and theories have a marked pro-deregulation bias. Microeconomic models stress the advantages of free markets and perfect competition that are the ideal. We study deviations from perfect competition to establish their welfare losses and to put into practice economic policies to reduce their disadvantages. Macroeconomic models are equilibrium models in which rational agents make the correct decisions taking into account their preferences and the constraints they face. If agents are rational and can manage all the available information, regulation is useless and harmful. Free markets outperform public intervention in virtually all circumstances.

The analysis of the effects of financial innovation and securitization were still more difficult because of their novelty. Besides, their mathematical complexity places them out of the reach of many economic agents. It is well known that some financial products were not fully understood by the managers of the banks that were distributing them. They only knew that these products were profitable, so they decided to bear the risks. But their decisions were not based on a sound and careful analysis of their fundamentals and the full range of possible outcomes. Less informed economic agents were just making a bet.

The preferential shares that were sold by the Spanish savings banks are a good example of this. It is not a particularly complex financial product, but the majority of its buyers simply did not understand its main features. Some of them were misled by sellers, but others were not. It is worth mentioning that some office managers sold preferential shares to their relatives, believing that it was an absolutely safe product. When entities filed for bankruptcy, many customers lost all their money. Their advisors had been directors of the branch offices, and also their cousins and brothers. The customers trusted them and this is why they bought the preferential shares. Much more complex financial products, such as the residential mortgage-backed securities, the RMBS, have had much more devastating consequences which were very difficult to predict in advance.

From a broader point of view the reasons why a majority of experts did not pay attention to the predictions of a coming crisis lie in their characterization of the operating environment and the main features of economic agents. The first has been dominated over the last twenty years by the EMH, despite the criticism it has received. To explain this we have to recall that some experts did show the internal flaws and incoherences of the theory, but the theory performed well for many years. Investors that relied on EMH in their decision-making process found it useful and easy to handle. It only proved to be wrong after the onset of the crisis. At this moment investors realized that companies were not as valuable as market prices reflected, banks could not ascertain if their overnight partners were reliable or not and owners of Greek public debt believed that the risk they were bearing was different from the risk of German public debt.

Before the crisis they trusted market prices in each case, and they shared their trust with all their partners in the financial markets. The functioning of financial markets before the crisis relied upon an agreement on EMH. If a sizeable number of agents had abandoned EMH in 2005 because they believed that the hypothesis was not trustworthy anymore, there would have been an earthquake-like movement in financial markets that would have shocked them. This earthquake might have prevented the crisis from occurring. But it did not happen because economic agents were confident in EMH.

In addition, EMH simplifies considerably the calculations required for the decision-making processes. If market prices do not convey all relevant information, analysts and managers must engage in a time-consuming process of searching, identifying and structuring information. Besides, if all agents share the same general framework, EMH in this case, each agent can easily predict the behaviour of the rest. Last but not least, mathematical algorithms have to be fed with clear-cut specifications. Nuances and differences do not fit well into mathematical models. Practical and operational reasons to use EMH and other hypothesis should not be forgotten. These hypotheses have been devised to help models run smoothly, to discard corner solutions or indecisiveness.

Economic agents were using EMH as the best available approach to a fully fledged model. They assumed that there were some minor deviations between the values supplied by EMH and real values, and they were willing to bear that risk. The main problem is they believed that deviations were small and affordable and the crisis showed that deviations were in fact large and unaffordable. The advantages of EMH were evident before the crisis while the disadvantages were not. Taking into account all the above arguments the best course of action for economic agents up to 2008, or maybe 2007, was to rely on EMH. But this course of action led economic agents into a dead end. They were unable to predict the arrival of the crisis because the consequences of EMH precluded it. The theory was blind to its own limits and so were theorists that relied on it. Since they trusted EMH because it had performed well for some years, their predictions could not envisage a sudden economic downturn. Economic agents that agreed on EMH by theoretical or practical reasons could not forecast the crisis. Only economic agents trained in a different theoretical framework would have been able to do so.

A meaningful consequence of our reasoning is that economic agents have not been fully rational, as they are supposed to be. If economic agents fully agree on EMH they are implicitly discarding that the hypothesis could be wrong or at least partially wrong. EMH is very useful in easing calculations and avoiding time-consuming processes of information searching. It is a very good device but is not the correct answer to all questions. Just as with any other device EMH has its limitations, and there are processes that are out of its reach. Thus, a fully rational economic agent should be aware that EMH may have flaws and may fail to explain current and future events. If an economic agent believes that EMH can be used in any circumstances and at any moment, this agent is not fully rational. Criticism of EMH explains not only the main EMH failures, but its main incompleteness as well. It stresses that we should not rely on it without a previous analysis of its adequacy to the problem we are dealing with. It is not rational to use a tool without knowing its applications and whether it is suitable for a specific problem or not.

The characterization of economic agents is another issue that is at stake. Many standard macroeconomic models assume perfect rationality and the rational expectation hypothesis. This entails a very narrow characterization of the economic agent. We have shown above that these assumptions have been criticized as well. The point here is to ascertain to what extent assuming perfect rationality has helped or hindered economic agents before the crisis. Perfect rationality is necessary for the understanding of all the available information in financial markets. If agents cannot manage it properly markets do not run smoothly, because many agents make mistakes and the overall efficiency is not assured.

Thus we are facing two general problems. On the one hand, if agents are not fully rational the functioning of markets will be disturbed. Part of the information is correctly interpreted while another part is not. The behaviour of the former helps the economy, but the behaviour of the latter harms it. The former makes sound allocative decisions while the latter just increases the noise in the system. The overall system will run into trouble, sooner or later. Economic theory is myopic if it takes for granted that all agents are fully rational.

On the other hand, if theorists assume that perfect rationality holds, but in truth it does not, further problems arise. When they observe the overall outcome of the economic system they are sure that equilibrium prevails. As a consequence, further research is unnecessary and a more in-depth examination is useless. They do not engage in the kind of research required to check whether the theory performs well or not and this assumption makes theorists blind. If the theory is wrong, perfect rationality does not hold and more accurate information is needed, but we are not aware of it. Just the opposite, we believe we can do without it. Many experts were averted from considering the probability of a crisis from happening because they believed that agents were rational and that the economy was running smoothly. For them, the crisis was a bitter surprise.

## The Urge for a Wider Approach

At this point we can answer the question we posed before: why did we not listen to those that predicted the crisis? The answer is not straightforward, but some parts have already been unveiled. First, it has been a financial crisis. A careful look at the models we are using shows that the financial side of the economy is virtually absent from general-purpose models. There are a lot of detailed analyses of the financial sector and how it runs. The microeconomic approach to the banking sector is a dynamic field of study. Game theory has proven to be useful in dealing with some financial issues. But macroeconomic models lack a correct characterization of the financial system and the functions it performs. RBC theory, the main tool used to analyse aggregate fluctuations, provides little room, if any, for financial issues. DGSE models include only very narrow descriptions of the financial system. The same applies to Overlaping Generations (OLG) models. The kind of detailed analysis of the financial system that is currently being undertaken to avoid a meltdown is absent from macroeconomic models, because they are unable to cope with them. We are going to show in Chapter 5 why policymakers were forced to start afresh in dealing with the financial crisis. The available models and theories fell short of their needs. Thus, they improvised.

Second, economists have strongly relied on hypotheses about the characterization of the agent and the operating environment that have proved to be defective. They have assumed implicitly or explicitly that they were correct and they have used these hypotheses. They knew that large deviations from their assumptions threatened the usefulness of the models, but they believed that such deviations were very unlikely. The models did not show that this crisis could happen. The forecasts made using these models misled economists. They believe that a soft landing was probable while a sudden stop and a dramatic downturn were ruled out.

Mainstream economics models depicted some future scenarios. None of them was as pessimistic as our current situation. A wave of deep recessions in developed countries followed by private and public debt difficulties in an environment of unprecedented unemployment rates could not have been forecast using our models. In 2010, Solow stated that he was a mainstream economist but that mainstream economics did not fare well in explaining the crisis.[34] A large number of economists would agree with him. Mainstream economists used models that were intrinsically unable to predict the crisis. Someone could say that the solution implies discarding mainstream economic models and substituting them with a different group of models. We do not agree on this point. We believe that the correct way is to analyse all economic models from a wider point of view to identify their main building blocks and the role they perform. That way, we will be able to detect their critical and auxiliary variables and to determine which parts of each model are better or less well suited to deal with a specific problem.

# 2 A DIFFERENT LOOK AT ECONOMIC THEORY: THE ANTHROPOLOGICAL APPROACH

## Widening the Focus: Economic Theory and Philosophy

As with any other scientific branch, the content of economics is not only the corpus of actual economic theories. To a certain extent, economics also includes every single word written about economic issues in the past. All this knowledge is available to us now but it does not mean that it is competing today to explain the economic phenomena. Part of it is obsolete and we study it only for historical reasons. Today, when we talk about contending theories in economics it is necessary to first establish the ones that are more relevant and that deserve to be taken into account.

A suitable criterion of demarcation is provided by history. At the end of the classical period, the three major economic traditions of our times, the neoclassical, Austrian and Keynesian, developed over a sixty-year period. For this reason, we will not treat economic theories of the classical age (even if they are still active, as in the case of neo-Marxists theories).

There is another important reason. We are especially interested in focusing on cooperation among theories, more than in stressing their mutually exclusive characteristics. However, we face some difficulties which arise from two aspects. On the one hand, neoclassicals, Keynesians and Austrians are rooted in different philosophical and epistemological bases. As a consequence, they apply different methodologies in their model building. On the other hand, their respective evolutions over time have been rich and complex. Can we study these theories as if they were homogeneous in themselves and among themselves? In our opinion we can, provided two conditions are fulfilled: all these theories should deal with the same object of study and all of them should share the same internal structure when dealing with that object of study.

From neoclassical microeconomics to the definition of economics as catallactics by Mises, we will hypothesize that economists have focused on the same 'economic problem'. Lionel Robbins observed this very coherently in his famous definition of the subject matter of economics:[1] 'Economics is the science which studies human behaviour as a relationship between ends and scarce means which have alternative uses'. According to Robbins, economic theories explain those processes in which economic agents allocate scarce resources to alternative ends. As it can be easily shown, these 'allocative processes' have been the object of study in the work, for instance, of Jevons, Menger and Walras, but also of Keynes, Hayek, Simon and Lucas. This does not imply that all economists had treated the problem exactly in the same way. Not all of them had fully understood its implications either. However, the point we want to emphasize is that the 'allocative approach' is connatural to the field of economics.

We realize that 'allocative processes' are in themselves a specific kind of human action. When someone allocates scarce resources to alternative ends he or she is acting deliberately. The outcome of this allocation can be explained as a consequence of his or her actions. The object of study of the economic science, then, is at the same time the object of study of the wider theory of human action. Here we find a common ground of those schools of economic thought. In this sense, these 'allocative processes' extensively studied in economics can be included and defined inside more general processes that explain the human being just because they are processes generated by real human beings.

This connection between economics and the theory of human action sheds light on the importance and influence on economics of other sciences, whose subject is the human being. Philosophy, anthropology or psychology have much to say about human beings and can provide invaluable help in understanding economic phenomena. In fact, as we are going to explain, there is a close relationship between different definitions of economic agents in economics and the philosophical approaches that inspired them.[2]

Let's consider now the second condition of possibility. Do these three theories share a common inner structure because they share the same object of study? We are not talking about their mathematical methodology to gather and analyse data. We want to know if they approach the explanation of 'allocative processes' as if they were human actions. If they do so, they must analyse three elements: who the agent of that kind of action is, how this agent behaves when it carries out the actions of a personal plan, and what the environment where the actions are carried out is like.

According to Rubio de Urquía,[3] it is quite easy to ascertain this common structure in models of different economic theories. Though this will be demonstrated in more detail in the following sections, it is necessary to make a brief presentation of this 'meta-theory' of economics. Rubio de Urquía states that this common structure is formed by three basic building blocks:

First, the conception of the person who acts, that is, the definition of the economic agent, which implies a specific anthropology based on a specific philosophical doctrine.

Second, a principle of systematic behaviour present in every action. All economic theories affirm that people always try to get what they want in the best possible way, taking into account what they know (or they think they know) and what they have (or they think they have).

Third, the environment or locus where the economic agent acts. The environment is variable, depending on feature of markets, goods, information, number and type of agents involved, etc.

When these three elements are defined in a clear and specific fashion, they constitute a concrete theory of human action and, when this theory is applied to the explanation of allocative processes, we have a specific economic theory. It is straightforward to realize that these three elements have a different status in the construction of an economic theory. The definition of the economic agent has the primacy because its object of study is economic human action.

The diversity of economic theories in the twentieth century do not rely on the different explanations of how means and scarce resources relate to each other. The radical separation among those theories lies in their different approaches to what is a suitable representation of the 'human agent'. For instance, when we analyse the consequences of the acting of the same economic agent on different economic environments, as neo-Keynesian and neoclassical models actually do, they arrive at different state predictions, but methodologically both are the same kind of theory. However, the outcome is very different if we analyse the consequences of the acting of different economic agents on the same economic environment. In this case, not only the state predictions will be different (as it can be verified comparing Keynes's model with any other economic model), but the whole character of the state predictions will diverge as well. Let us analyse the main economic theories using this rather simple meta-theory.

## *Neoclassical Theory*

### Origins

The founding fathers of the neoclassical school were strongly influenced by utilitarian and positivist thought, which were both very popular in the nineteenth century in Europe. Positivism asserts that only empirical knowledge deserves the status of real knowledge. From this statement they concluded that there is only one valid method for acquiring knowledge, that is, the empirical method.[4] This thesis, which we know as methodological monism, drove many thinkers to test the capability of the method of natural sciences in the realm of social sciences. With this objective in mind, many studies were launched with the aim of using the research methods of physics (Newtonian mechanics) in all kinds of social sciences (e. g. sociology, history or economics).

Authors such as William S. Jevons, Leòn Walras, Francis Y. Edgeworth, Vilfredo Pareto, Luigi Amoroso and Irving Fisher, just to name the most prominent, were involved in this endeavour. The project was extremely ambitious because, ultimately, it implied transforming economics into an exact science, next to physics, while keeping intact its own peculiarities.

The statements we find in the foreword of their first works are candidly honest in this sense. Walras talked about the elaboration of a 'pure political economy' with ideal types that abstract reality and permit the use of mathematics.[5] Edgeworth suggested the analogy between the principles of maximum happiness and maximum energy, defending the cooperation between the methodologies of physics and utilitarianism in a conception of the human being as a pleasure machine.[6] Irving Fisher[7] organized the comparison between economic and mechanical concepts in a two-entry table, a method also used by the Italians Pareto[8] and Amoroso.[9]

One outcome of this intellectual endeavour was the *homo oeconomicus*. With the aid of utilitarianism, the neoclassical economic agent is represented by a mathematical utility function, that is, the relationship between each element in the consumption set of possibilities and the level of utility (or pleasure understood as an intensive and physical sensation) they produce. In this fashion, the human action is restricted to choosing the highest suitable level of utility subject to certain restrictions faced by the agent (for instance, budgetary restriction).

The loss of realism inherent to this approach to the economic problem is, at the same time, a limitation and an advantage. It is a limitation because this specific economic agent is far removed from the real acting person of the real markets. But it is also an advantage for its operability that allows mathematical modelling of many different circumstances and phenomena.

### Evolution

(a) The General Equilibrium Model

Conversely to what could be expected, the conception of the economic agent has remained very stable to that of the founding fathers, despite neoclassical economics' long history. The major advance was provided by Kenneth Arrow and Gerard Debreu with their mathematically consistent solution to the Walrasian general equilibrium.[10] In the 1950s, the challenge for neoclassical economics was to develop a sound theoretical framework for the problems of time and uncertainty in economics. They found a simple and easy solution to do this without altering the inherited conception of the economic agent. The key concept was the contingent-state commodities that considered different not only those commodities that are physically different but also those dated in different moments of time or located in different places in space (that is, commodities in different states of nature) even when they are physically equal.

> We suppose *I* individuals, and *S* possible states of nature. In the *s*th state, amount *xsc* of commodity *c* (*c=1 ... C*) is produced. It is assumed that each individual acts on the basis of subjective probabilities as to the states of nature.[11]

The individual utility function is now defined as a vector in a SC-dimension space (*S* states of nature and *C* commodities) of greater magnitude than the usual utility function *C*.[12] Once the commodities are differentiated by the time and place of their consumption or delivery, it is possible to consider decision making under uncertainty in the same fashion as it is considered under certainty. As Debreu pointed out, the concept of state contingent commodities 'allows one to obtain a theory of uncertainty free of any probabilistic concept and formally identical with the theory of certainty'.[13] This approach was seen as a technological revolution in the late 1960s and the beginning of the 1970s.[14]

In this new kind of model, the representative economic agent has preferences over consumption (eventually over leisure also) represented by an inter-temporary utility function as:

$$V(c) = \sum_{t=0}^{\infty} \beta^t U(c_t)$$

where $0<b<1$ is the discount rate. The utility function is strictly concave with $U'>0$ and $U''<0$.[15] As can be seen, if the commodities are state-contingent, the maximizing problem is, in essence, the same as the static one.

(b) New Classical School

Keynesian economics momentarily eclipsed the development of neoclassical theory, but it did not destroy it. After Milton Friedman challenged Keynesianism with its own weapons and restored some of the neoclassical elements on monetary theory, economists such as Lucas, Sargent and Wallace came back to neoclassical origins, utterly defying the Keynesian tradition. The Arrow–Debreu framework and the discussion about expectations mechanisms by Friedman, Cagan, Muth and Sargent paved the way for the change of economic paradigm. In the early 1970s new classical economics helped to restore and modernize the neoclassical heritage bringing back the assumptions of:

(i) Sound microfoundations in a Walrasian framework
(ii) Flexible prices and market clearing
(iii) Dynamic analysis
(iv) Rational expectations
(v) Neutrality of money.

The movement in this direction have continued almost unchallenged until today, the real business cycle theory (RBC) being its most fruitful expression in recent times. The main features of RCB models are the following: (i) there is a representative agent (household or firm) that maximizes an objective function (utility or profit) subject to some intertemporary consumption or technological constrains; (ii) price flexibility and rational expectations hold in order to assure market clearing and the equilibrium of the economy; (iii) business cycles arise from random technological shocks, but never from any kind of monetary disturbances; (iv) there exist several transmission mechanisms of the shocks as intertemporal labour substitution, smooth consumption over time or lags in investment.[16]

(c) New Keynesian Economics

Finally, we are going to introduce a controversial point of discussion. Starting in the 1970s and during the 1980s, several economists tried to reproduce the successful strategy of the neoclassical synthesis, that is, to build a 'neoclassical' economic model with Keynesian flavour.[17] Keynesian was identified with disequilibrium, downward sticky prices and imperfect markets. Blanchard, Stiglitz, Summers, Akerlof, Barro and Grossman, just to quote a few names, made the effort of adding new hypothesis to the new classical models. They accepted dynamic optimization, expected utility functions, rational expectations and all those methodological aspects of the theory that were not in contradiction with what they understood as Keynesian. Their new hypothesis did not threaten the core of neoclassical methodology, they only stressed that the economic environment had to be understood and modelled differently. For that reason, new Keynesian theories are, in our opinion, so close to the neoclassical school than they are sometimes difficult to distinguish from it. In fact, new Keynesian economics has been severely criticized by post-Keynesians such as Roy Rotheim, Paul Davidson, Jan Kregel and Assar Lindbeck.[18]

## *Keynesianism*

### Origins: *The General Theory*

*The General Theory* (*GT*) is still the basic source for Keynesianism in economics. However, *GT* is a book that avoids lineal interpretations due to its different thematic levels. Besides, its line of argument starts from the consideration of individual economic agents and finishes by studying the economy as an organic being that exceeds its parts. In our opinion, the former analysis appears in the *GT* in the core of the book and the latter is part of the conclusions that advance the solutions to, for instance, the problem of unemployment.

At the core of *GT*, Keynes proposes a conception of the economic agent that makes abundant use of anthropological assertions originally contained in *A Treatise on Probability*.[19] He set forth that knowledge is formed through two different kinds of judgements. The agent gets the first type of judgement through intuition, that is, by a process that is non-mediated and exempt from error, and allows a direct knowledge of reality.[20] This simple knowledge produces propositions and logical relations, in such a manner that the agent is able to form arguments containing two intuited propositions and a logical relation that holds between them. The logical relation is a degree of rational belief or a subjective probability that establishes how the two propositions are connected in the agent's perception. With propositions A and B and the logical relation $\alpha$, the agent builds an argument or indirect knowledge of the type: If A, then B, with a degree of rational belief (or subjective probability) $\alpha$.[21]

The second type of judgement measures the completeness of the knowledge contained in the empirical evidence at the agent's disposal. This 'weight of the argument' points to the amount of ignorance or the amount of knowledge agents think they have about a concrete reality.[22]

Keynes used this theory of knowledge in the *GT* to explain how economic agents make their decisions and, principally, how they decide to invest their savings in the long term. His theory of knowledge served the purpose of explaining the weakness of human expectations about the future. Because, if decision making depends on the relation between a probabilistic judgement and a confidence judgement (the weight of the argument), it is not clear at all when the knowledge we collect will be enough to be sure about the probabilistic judgement. As Keynes himself said, this is a very confusing matter. From this fact, he concluded that human action is always intermingled with an inerradicable or fundamental uncertainty not related to mathematical probability but to ignorance. This is crucial to understand the conception of the economic agent in Keynes's *GT*. He rejected the neoclassical approach and tried to explain the general equilibrium problem in a completely different setting. In Keynes's theory, decision making is affected by this kind of uncertainty that cannot be reduced to frequentist probability, which implies a more conservative behaviour of the agents. In fact, the agents are unable to foresee what the future will bring, so they are forced to adopt uncertainty reducing strategies. In the *GT*, Keynes presents two of these strategies: falling back on conventions or acting on animal spirits.

Keynes calls conventions those patterns of action people adopt when they distrust their own knowledge. Sometimes, conventions are understood as a belief in the future continuity of the ongoing conditions. In any event, they serve to clear up any psychological concern due to uncertainty,[23] but they do not provide any solid ground. Conventions can be abandoned and adopted rapidly and are subject to violent and sudden variations.[24] Conventions are 'market place idols', 'a substitute for the knowledge which is unattainable'.[25] Animal spirits, on the other hand, are a different way to explain human actions. For Keynes, animal spirits are 'a spontaneous urge to action rather than inaction, and not as the outcome of a weighted average of quantitative benefits multiplied by quantitative probabilities'.[26]

In Keynes, the economic agent has a twofold characterization as passive (when acts are based on conventions) or active (when acts are based on the spontaneity of animal spirits). In any case, this conception is more complete than the neoclassical one because this economic agent projects his/her imagination toward the future and distinguishes between plans and achievements. Not surprisingly, the dual behaviour of agents corresponds here with the consideration of a free market where consumers and entrepreneurs interact without the intervention of a government or the state. Keynes is trying to explain how, if consumers always act based on conventions and entrepreneurs always act subject to animal spirits, the final result of a free market economy will be sub-investment and unemployment.

These hypotheses on decision making under uncertainty are a distinctive landmark of Keynes's theory. In the case of consumers, the Keynesian theory describes their behaviour ex-post as dependent on exogenous psychological reasons. The marginal propensity to consume determines the proportion of the consumer yield that will be allocated to consumption. The remaining yield, the part not consumed, will be the object of a different decision: how much will be devoted to acquiring bonds (that is, how much will be saved) and how much will be maintained as liquid money. This decision is explained with the liquidity preference theory and its related three motives: transaction, speculation and precautionary. Money may be used to acquire goods and services, to take advantage of our pretended better knowledge of the future but, also, to protect ourselves from the uncertain evolution of the forthcoming events. This precautionary motive is behind the liquidity premium consumers demand as part of the interest rate they demand in exchange for their savings. 'The liquidity premium, it will be observed, is partly similar to the risk-premium, but partly different; the difference corresponding to the difference between the best estimates we can make of probabilities and the confidence with which we make them.'[27]

In this sense, the precautionary motive is clearly related to the epistemological theory of *A Treatise on Probability*. At the end of p. 240 in the *GT*, Keynes refers to a footnote on p. 148 where he relates uncertainty to ignorance and the weight of the argument: 'By "very uncertain" I do not mean the same thing as "improbable". Cf. my *Treatise on Probability*, chap. 6, on "The Weight of Arguments"'. But there is a closer relationship between the concepts of liquidity preference and weight of the argument:[28] in situations of uncertainty, consumers are heavily influenced by the 'weight of argument' and use conventions as guides of action.[29] For instance, agents alleviate their doubts by increasing their demand for money, because money

> takes charge at the moments when the higher, more precarious conventions have weakened. The possession of actual money lulls our disquietude; and the premium which we require to make us part with money is the measure of the degree of our disquietude.[30]

The influence of uncertainty on the interest rate of bonds is extremely important to determine the aggregate level of employment, because the volume of investment depends on the relationship between that rate of interest and the entrepreneurial expectations of future revenue of the investment, what Keynes called the marginal efficiency of capital. Due to the influence of uncertainty on consumer behaviour and to the nature of money,[31] the rate of interest will tend to be excessively high, discouraging entrepreneurs and producing an insufficient level of aggregate demand.[32] The consequence is involuntary unemployment and the question to be answered is: how can effective demand be raised up to the point when full employment is reached?

While he is explaining these issues, Keynes jumps from the micro level to the macro level and back again. Uncertainty is borne by individuals but it is solved at the collective level by means of conventions. Decisions are taken by individuals but their consequences are made evident in the aggregate. In conclusion, the problem is the effective demand, as the majority of Keynesians and post-Keynesians have accepted. As a consequence, the level of research must be macro and not micro even though the microeconomic analysis is an unavoidable step before the macroeconomic analysis.

**Evolution**

Keynes's *GT* was really offering an alternative and sophisticated economic theory that challenged neoclassical models. The impact of *GT* on economic theory was huge, not only because Keynes departed from the prevailing tradition, but for the variety of topics and possibilities had it suggested. From the very beginning, and due to the extent of issues raised in his book, the heritage of Keynes became a hotchpotch of mixed theories, lively theoretical discussions and extensions of *GT* theory. But there also were several attempts to confine Keynes's theory to textbooks, for example in James Meade's *Introduction to Economic Analysis and Policy* (1936) or Joan Robinson's *Introduction to the Theory of Employment* (1937).

Among the mixed theories, the most important was the so-called neoclassical synthesis, the integration of certain selected Keynesian elements and issues with the neoclassical theory that was successfully achieved very soon by J. R. Hicks (1937) with the IS–LM model. Hicks opened the path for the coming of the 'Keynesian era' that, as Brunner and Meltzer reminded us, was not going to be the 'Era of Keynes'. Other authors who found strong links between *GT* and Marx's *Capital* were Michal Kalecki, Joan Robinson, Piero Sraffa and Luigi Pasinetti.

But the core of post-Keynesian economics was devoted to the extensions of the *GT* and the exploration of those issues that Keynes did not develop enough. The capital and its accumulation, the theories of distribution and the role of money in the economy were the main elements of progress for post-Keynesians, as well as of dissent. The Cambridge controversies showed the vitality of the school in its confrontation with the neoclassical and the Austrian theories of capital until the denial of mainstream economists consigned the discussion to oblivion.

Monetarism redirected the attention of post-Keynesians towards monetary issues, with Paul Davidson and Hyman P. Minsky leading the way. Davidson had returned to Keynes's monetary theory and the importance of the finance motive in the liquidity preference theory. He attacked the classical dichotomy, the idea that only the real sector of the economy matters because the monetary sector only mirrors what happens in the other. The non-neutrality of money was also stressed by Minsky with his famous financial-instability hypothesis. In his opinion, capitalism is inherently instable for institutional reasons. The evolution of prices of capital assets depends on the way economic activities are financed. Commercial banks change their behaviour during the cycle from prudence to boldness producing a movement from 'hedge' to 'speculative' and then to 'Ponzi finance'[33] that leads the economy to default and to the collapse of financial activity.

## *Austrian School of Economics*

### Origins

The Austrian School sprung from the talent of Carl Menger. When he published his *Principles of Economics* (1871) there were two competitive schools of thought in economics: the Classical School and the German Historical School. Roscher, a salient member of the latter, strongly opposed the individualistic tradition of Adam Smith and he provided the framework for the organicistic comprehension of societies and their primacy over individuals. Conversely to Smith's spontaneous emergence of social institutions, German Historicists envisaged the interrelation between individuals and social environment the other way around.

Menger found a way to overcome the difficulties of historicism and classical economics. He proposed analysing economic problems and explaining the appearance of social institutions with a new approach 'on man, viewed as a creative actor and the protagonist of all social processes'.[34] He stressed the role of time, limited knowledge and subjectivity in human action. He also explained social institutions as patterns of behaviour spontaneously adopted by a community as the most suitable solution to a specific problem of social coordination (for instance, money).

Other authors such as Böhm-Bawerk or Frank Wieser followed the theoretical road opened by Menger, applying this subjectivistic methodology to the theory of value, capital and roundabout production of goods. But it was Ludwig von Mises who codified the disperse knowledge generated under the auspices of Menger subjectivism. He provided, with all kinds of theoretical novelties and not without controversy, the first textbook of the School. In *Epistemological Problems of Economics* (1933), he distinguished two branches in the sciences of human action, namely praxeology and history. The first branch applies the concept of action and its categorical conditions to the deduction of praxeological theorems about human action in different circumstances.

> The starting point of our reasoning is not the economy, but economic action, or, as it is redundantly designated, rational action. Human action is conscious behaviour on the part of a human being. Conceptually it can be sharply and clearly distinguished from unconscious activity, even though in some cases it is perhaps not easy to determine whether given behaviour is to be assigned to one or the other category.[35]

This undeniable reality of human action led Mises to state the aprioristic character of praxeology and economics. The logical-deductive reasoning must be complemented with experience to narrow the realm of problems the economist must consider relevant. Experience is the basis of the theoretician's suppositions and the theorems so built are the tools to understand what we experienced. History, the second branch of the sciences of human action, simply consists in the 'systematic gathering and study of the facts of experience concerning human action'.[36]

In the process of understanding the essence of human action, Mises recognized the influence of Kant,[37] especially with reference to the acquisition of human knowledge. Kant noted that, for knowledge to be possible, there had to exist some *a priori* categories of thought that should precede sensory experience.[38] But, if thought and action are co-generic realities, then the Kantian formal theory of knowledge can also be applied to the theory of human action. Mises took Kant's argument to state that certain *a priori* categories should exist in the agent's mind in order for him/her to be able to act.[39]

There are only two categories: first, there is causality, because the human mind is always searching for constant cause–effect relations among phenomena;[40] second, there is teleology, because human action is always intentional. This theory has an interesting implication because Mises thought he had built a whole axiomatic theory of human action, apodictic or true in itself, on the basis of those two *a priori* categories.

Intentionality also explains the asymmetry of time in human action. Past, present and future are not homogenous, because past is embedded in the agent as knowledge; present is the elusive moment where actions are performed; and future will be in part created by action. In this sense, the conception of an irreversible arrow of time is opposed to the physical conception of time usual in neoclassical models.[41] The passage of time is inherent to human action and it is introduced as a category of it.

This Kantian theory of knowledge emphasized the subjective aspect of knowledge and the limitation of human ability in knowing the essence or nature of external reality (for the agent). Each agent possesses a set of knowledge and information that has been acquired through his vital experience during his life. Those fractions of knowledge are responsible for as many particular visions of the world as there are agents. According to this, social coordination, the process that reconciles the plans of action of all the agents in a discrete period of time and space, can only be achieved if agents profit from privative knowledge they own. Besides, these interactions entail the creation of new information that permits the social coordination of the people involved. The market, the Law, money, etc. are complex solutions to complex problems of social coordination that can only be discovered through a spontaneous process of interaction driven by the agents' needs. This is also the stronger of the Austrian arguments provided in support of their liberal creed.

**Evolution**

The third great name of Austrian School of Economics is Hayek. The influence of Hayek's thought lies both in the diversity of issues he dealt with and, also, in his in-depth analysis of every one of them. He was authoritative in his studies of such different matters as business cycles, theoretical psychology, the economic calculation problem, politics and the nature of the monetary system. In all these topics he took the Austrian School of Economics to new fields and possibilities.

His conception of the economic agent was also subjectivistic and, in this sense, close to that of Menger and Mises. But it was much more sophisticated. In his psychology book, *The Sensorial Order*, Hayek developed a novel theory on the functioning of the brain that enabled him to support, on the one hand, the existence of a previous logical structure of the mind and, on the other hand, to provide the foundation of his theory of spontaneous order and evolution of social institutions. This theory is coherent with the realism of the hypothesis that Austrian economics advocates. It is also an answer to the criticism against Austrian economics' apriorism. As we have seen in Mises, the whole edifice of catallactics is built over Kantian *a priori* categories of thought and action. The theory of human actions, then, is axiomatic in essence. Hayek's psychological theory offers a possibility to escape from apriorism and to root the theory on scientific grounds.

After Hayer, other authors have enlarged the study of different topics of the school. Ludwig Lachmann developed a 'radical' subjectivistic theory of expectations and Israel Kirzner reconsidered Hayek's knowledge problem and role that performs the 'entrepreneurial function' to discover and take advantage of profit opportunities.

Despite differences among authors there are important features in their works that permit us to state the existence of an Austrian school of economics: economics (catallactic) is part of a more general theory of human action (praxeology) understood as a dynamic process; its study requires methodological individualism; economic agents never have complete information but only partial and subjective, the knowledge is disperse and changing; mathematical formalism is rejected in favour of verbal formalism; economic theory is aprioristic and deductive; etc.

> Austrian theorists conceive economic science as a theory of action, rather than of decision, and this is one of the traits which most distinguishes Austrians from their Neoclassical colleagues ... Moreover, what concerns Austrians is not the fact that a decision is made, but that it is embodied in a human action, which is a process (that may or may not be completed) involving a series of interactions and acts of coordination. It is precisely these which Austrians view as the object of research in economics. Thus, for Austrians, economics is not a set of theories on choice or decision at all, but instead it is a theoretical corpus which deals with the processes of social interaction, processes which vary in their degree of coordination, depending upon the alertness actors show in their entrepreneurship.[42]

## Complementarities among Economic Theories

As we have seen, each economic theory is based on a specific characterization of the economic agent that is heavily influenced by concrete philosophical and anthropological conceptions. In many cases, the evolution and success of a theory overpowers their philosophical origins and the theoreticians continue with the advancement of the theory without being aware of them. The progress of a scientific field cannot be completely sound in the absence of this exercise of retrospection. Principally, the point of departure adopted is a limiting factor from the beginning of the research and scientists ought to be conscious of the limitations of the tools they are using. These limitations affect the field of definition of the theory as such, that is, the problems the theory will be able to deal with or understand. This very fact is not surprising and can be found in any branch of knowledge, from physics to sociology. Boundaries can be ignored as long as we stay inside of them; the problems appear when we try to move outside the limits we have established with our thought.

In economics, the treatment of the economic agent ranges from the extreme simplification of neoclassicals to the complexity of Austrian. Any of these conceptions has its own pros and cons in the understanding of economic phenomena. Although we have only revised the work of three prominent thinkers, there are some valuable lessons we can learn from the three instances we have highlighted due to their relevance and influence in the history of economics.

In neoclassical modelling, the agents are deliberately characterized in a very simplified way. Vilfredo Pareto maintained that since we cannot know any phenomenon in its entirety, the scientist must rely on a method of 'successive approximations'. Probably, the *homo oeconomicus* was understood in this fashion at the beginning, as a raw version that will be perfected upon completion of the understanding of human beings. But unfortunately, *homo oeconomicus* has proved to be less flexible than Pareto thought. Due to the intermingled nature of positivism and mathematics, the neoclassical consumer is ontologically mechanical, a device conceived to choose passively among predefined alternatives. Its function is to carry a given structure of preferences that, in combination with the principle of optimization, determines its behaviour. That structure of objectives is given in the structure of preferences and only provides information about how certain elements of reality are preferred to others. Its actions, then, are limited to arranging means to ends, with the objective of reaching the most preferred combinations of ends. Differently from what is common in human beings, the *homo oeconomicus* does not project its future in its actions because it knows (or is able to gather the necessary information to know) all that is needed to achieve the best option. Preferences are always consistent and it never prefers realities incompatible among them. Correspondingly, the neoclassical theory is unable to explain what happens when people tend to prefer incompatible realities, or when the plans of action are not feasible, or when the knowledge about the future is absent even in the form of frequentist probability, or when means and ends values cannot be expressed in terms of money. Something very similar can be said about the neoclassical producer. The weight of the mechanical origins of neoclassical thinking is visible in its theoretical development, also mechanical on all of its levels. Economic agents are mechanical devices that relate to each other in mechanical ways. Obviously, this extreme degree of simplification is, at the same time, the reason for its success. The neoclassical model provides the least problematic approach to the study of the allocative processes. The difficulties depend more on the mathematical complexity that is needed to comply with the method of 'successive approximations'. There is a huge elasticity of mathematical complexity due to small changes in the 'realism' of the neoclassical models.

In *GT*, Keynes made a major effort to overcome the shortcomings of neoclassical theory in several aspects but especially with respect to the realism of the economic agent conception. In his ideal world, entrepreneurs and consumers interact freely and carry the whole economy to a stalled situation with involuntary unemployment and insufficient aggregate demand. The main reason for this permanent disequilibrium lies in how Keynes characterizes the cognitive traits of the economic agents. The way they process the information and imagine the future explains how they behave. In this sense, Keynes defined his economic agents as persons, not as mechanical devices, for whom ignorance is an impediment to act. Keynes found the solution to this problem in the strategies that agents can adopt to minimize the sensation of incertitude and ignorance about the future. In the case of consumers, conventions are the way they encounter to deflect the fear and consume. This theory was not as important for the explanation of consumption as it was for the justification of the levels of savings. Keynes conceived consumption as a stable behaviour that rarely exceeds the amount of the earnings of the agent but savings were part of the decision about what to do with that part of earnings not spent on consumption. The consumer could keep the savings as money demand or could lend it to entrepreneurs, increasing the amount of effective demand. Here, conventions operate an important role in explaining why savings could not be enough to assure full employment as well as explaining the volatility of the economy in the environment of an economic crash.

In the case of entrepreneurs, a personal tendency, namely animal spirits, drives them to act, but not totally irrationally because they translate their expectations into the marginal efficiency of capital, that is, the expected marginal income of the investment. Curiously, Keynes ascribes a greater capability of calculating this efficiency to the State than to the entrepreneurs. The conception of agents, consumers and entrepreneurs is richer than the neoclassical one but it also has its own limitations. In synthesis, Keynes affirms that persons acquire by intuition a true knowledge about reality but, also, that the experimental and inductive origin of that knowledge makes it incomplete and uncertain. Being conscious of this circumstance, the agents never get rid of the uneasiness and fear of the uncertain tomorrow and prefer to trust irrational strategies for action. In our opinion, this theory places an excessive emphasis on the fundamental character of uncertainty and the inability of the agents to circumvent it. Probably Keynes wanted to point out the problems of the economy of his times and, for that reason, preferred to define a cognitive dynamic for which the agents are unable to learn from experience and seem to stay always in the same state of ignorance.

The anthropological traits drawn by Mises in his theory of action are also remote from those of the neoclassical. As we have stated, Mises conceived human thought as formed by *a priori* mental categories through which sensations acquire significance. These categories, that are part of the concept of action, help to interpret the elements of experience through 'some information about the reality of the universe',[43] never arbitrarily. Therefore, this primary element of the categories of thinking is the first step down the long road of understanding.

His theory of knowledge leads Mises to defend a deep subjectivism in the study of praxeology. First of all, Mises states the conscious and deliberate character of human action that is opposed to unconscious behaviour.

Three prerequisites are necessary to feel the need to act:

> [First] Acting man is eager to substitute a more satisfactory state of affairs for a less satisfactory. [Second] His mind imagines conditions which suit him better, and his action aims at bringing about this desired state. The incentive that impels a man to act is always some uneasiness. A man perfectly content with the state of his affairs would have no incentive to change things. He would have neither wishes nor desires; he would be perfectly happy.
>
> He would not act; he would simply live free from care. But to make a man act, uneasiness and the image of a more satisfactory state alone are not sufficient. [Third] A third condition is required: the expectation that purposeful behaviour has the power to remove or at least to alleviate the felt uneasiness. In the absence of this condition no action is feasible. Man must yield to the inevitable. He must submit to destiny.[44]

Mises brings out two essential subjective elements: human beings pursue definite objectives with their actions; human beings are 'purposeful' and human action is 'purposive'. Their objective is to achieve a different reality from the one they are experiencing. Second, they are actively searching for those new and different realities. As Kirzner expressed it, 'human action ... contains within it an essential entrepreneurial element'.[45] Human beings imagine the future and try to adopt the most appropriate courses of action in order to convert them into reality. The actor judges the different eligible plans of action according to a subjective valuation of the final goal. Hence, though the problem of individual choice apparently could be similar to the neoclassicals (the agent has to choose among different allocations of means to ends related to different courses of action), at least there is a radical difference between them: in the neoclassical case, the sets of means and ends are *a priori* given but in the Austrian case, the economic agent has to discover or create them in his or her mind.

This coexistence of different theoretical proposals for the explanation of economic phenomena is a perplexing reality for many economists. How is it possible after so many years of research? For many, there is no problem of any kind: they simply judge their approach as superior. But, things are not so simple. Not so long ago, only the field of neoclassical microeconomics was considered as 'solid' while Keynesianism was reigning over macroeconomics. It is true that neoclassic economists recovered prestige in their macroeconomic models but, after the last financial crisis, our confidence in them cannot be the same. Unfortunately, the pre-eminence of one economic theory over the others does not seem to be related to its ability to explain the economic phenomena. There are sociological elements mixed with the resilience to the obsolescence of theories. Anyway, the real problem remains: are we really explaining the economic phenomena with our theories, old or new?

We must recognize that economics is not an easy field of study. Human beings are difficult to understand and to forecast, but the understanding of the interaction among human beings is even trickier to comprehend. To shed some light on human action requires too much knowledge coming from too many different branches of the human sciences. Obviously, we can try the easy way and pose the problem in a neoclassical fashion: let us suppose that the agent has already solved the complicated part of forming his or her personality that includes all the knowledge relative to ends and means. But, if the agent has perfect information about means and ends and about the technical capacity of means to satisfy the ends, we are not talking about human action but of something completely different. There, we only find a mechanical reaction.

On the opposite side, we can try to imagine how things would be if, instead, we decide to choose the hard way. If we imagine the economic problem in its greatest imaginable complexity, the research would demand too much knowledge about relevant processes which take place within the human being but, also, too much knowledge about how human interactions create social structures and produce social novelties. The starting point should be to understand how human beings constitute the sets of means and ends, how they decide the hierarchy of ends and how all these elements change over time. Only for the sake of argument and to clarify the arduousness of this task, will we sketch a summary of some basics elements of this research. For instance, we would need to define the meaningful mental contents relevant for the human action. Elements such as beliefs, values, attitudes and theoretical and technical representations of the world should be defined and understood. It would be necessary, also, to explain how this 'stock' of meaningful mental contents changes over time, which are the dynamics associated with that change. It seems plausible to speak of three dynamics in this context: cognitive dynamics (including learning and knowledge acquisition processes that explains the way we actually process the information we gathered from the world); ethical dynamics (arranging and rearranging – sequentially – the hierarchy of ends we pursue); and, finally, cultural dynamics (consisting, mostly, in the social framework of beliefs, values, attitudes and representations of reality).

Surely, none of the economic theories we have named as 'contemporary' are fully adequate in providing the suitable framework for this comprehensive study, but it is also true that they are not equally well equipped to give the first steps towards it. If we take any human being (even ourselves) as representative of what we aim to explain, it is easy to observe how the field of definition of these three theories grows in complexity from the neoclassicals to the Austrian. This does not imply that the most simple are contained in the more complex, because their fields of definition are equal. Perhaps, the main difference between the neoclassical, on the one hand, and the Keynesian and Austrian, on the other, resides in the fact that the economic agent of the former is not a person at all, while it is in both the Keynesian and the Austrian. This is a real handicap of mainstream economics in its task of dealing with the high-level complexity of the economic model. The interconnection of markets, institutional frameworks and human environment of beliefs and values needs a better and more realistic approach to the human being. The utility of neoclassical models in the consideration of simple allocative processes or in the management of quantitative data and constructs (macro magnitudes as GDP or inflation) is obvious, but there are many real and empirical problems impossible for them to understand. They are simply outside its field of definition. This financial crisis has made this incapacity clear.

Keynesian conception of the economic agent is especially useful in understanding the sudden movements of demand and investment that precipitates a crisis, but it is too pessimistic about the cognitive capabilities of human beings. *A Treatise on Probability* contains a richer theory of knowledge than the version of the *GT*. Maybe, Keynes only wanted to explain the peculiarity of the great depression of 1929 but, in any case, he raised the question as to what extent the unrealism of hypotheses could limit the usefulness of theories in understanding the failure of a whole economic system.

The insistence on the subjective character of knowledge by Austrian economists, most notably Mises and Hayek, had as its final aim the study of the process of self-coordination of markets. For a proper understanding of that kind of process, Mises built the most realistic conception of the economic agent of the three we have revised, but it also has its drawbacks. From the beginning of this school of thought, Austrian economists have had the perception that the 'invisible hand theorem' was true. Indeed, they have been mainly interested in the coordinating aspects of the economic process. The Misesian economic agent is a pro-market human being whose only social bindings come from the entrepreneurial and exchange activities he or she establishes with other agents. In the absence of state intervention, economic agents driven by the entrepreneurial function (the capability to locate and exploit profit opportunities) produce a virtuous process of dynamic social coordination. The possibilities of social failure in the Austrian theory come from the interruption of the spontaneous order created by the agents, as conspicuously happens in the case of financial crises. But it is never produced by the action of the agents, contrary to Keynes's doctrine.

Whilst the three perspectives are quite well separated and have their own shortcomings, there is a potential advantage in the use of their complementarities. But there is also a potential for growth in the definition of the economic agent that has not been used yet. In the next chapter, we study in more detail both their weaknesses and strengths to prepare the way for our proposal for an improvement of economic theory.

# 3 THE 'BUILDING BLOCKS' OF MODERN ECONOMICS: WE DO REALLY NEED A META-THEORY

## Modelling Agent's Economic Behaviour: The Choices that Theorists Face

In the previous chapter, we have seen that all economic theories or models rely upon a specific anthropology, that is, upon some more or less explicit ideas of human beings as economic agents. There we classified theories and models under three large headings, neoclassical, Keynesian and Austrian. Setting aside historical issues, this classification was made taking into account the kind of 'statements' about the economic agent and the environment they create. We saw that there are specific statements that made a model 'Keynesian' and not 'neoclassical', and vice versa. It is also true that 'mixed' or 'hybrid' models can be found, but ultimately they rely upon a critical statement or assumption which allows classifying them into one of these broad categories. This classification is useful in itself as we can arrange the literally thousands of models and theories according to their underlying assumption. But this will be of limited interest if it does not help to improve our understanding of economic processes.

The question here is whether a *systematic* research on the structure of models and theories is possible to make them more reliable and closer to reality. Or, more precisely, if it is possible to appreciate the differences and commonalities of economic theories from a point of view that includes all of them simultaneously.

In this chapter we are going to draw the main lines of this research, which has been carried out by Rubio de Urquía, and others, such as Rodríguez, Muñoz et al., and Muñoz and Encinar.[1] This will be done mostly in the first section of the chapter. Section two and three will deal with the methodological issues raised by the structure of theories and models developed in the first section. Finally, we will deal with the thorny issue of distinguishing between regular and disruptive science, linking it to the kind of statements we make about economic agents when we are modelling a specific type of process.

## *The Structure of an Economic Theory or Model*

In the three most important traditions of economic thought, the central problem of economics as a science is how agents allocate scarce means to alternative ends. They arrange this research in different modes (studying the logic of decision making or how plans of actions are selected or the psychological strategies for minimizing uncertainty in clearing for decision making, etc.); but they all study the problem of allocating scarce means to alternative ends and the results of that allocation. In general terms, economists aim to understand and predict decision making (why the economic agent selects a specific plan of action and no other) and, the consequences of that decision (consequences for the economic agent, consequences for the environment where he or she acts, and consequences of the interaction of that decision with the decisions of other homogeneous or heterogeneous economic agents that share the same operational environment or in terms of the emergence of organicistic properties in societies). The elements that shape the basic and common structure of any contemporary economic thinking (the economic agent, the principle of economic behaviour and the operational environment) are the rational way to understand how the plan of action and its consequences are causally connected.

Economic theory deals with this research through different ideal characterizations according to the scientist that is explaining the allocative process. This is, in fact, what economists usually do: they define abstract theoretical pieces that explain the allocative processes under a concrete specification of the realities idealized.

However, if such a thing as a general structure of economic theory exists, it must remain open and free of analytical constraints. If we are certain about the existence of a common theoretical structure for contemporary economic theories, then, the meta-theory that this implies would be like a set of empty and open 'containers' of the basic elements of any economic theory: the economic agent, the principle of systematic behaviour and the operational environment. These are the buildings blocks of the 'meta-theory': all the models and economic theories can be abridged into these analytical categories. When we create models about the economic behaviour of a single agent or a country as a whole, we do it through specific representations of those elements. So, it can work very well as a sorting device of theories and models. But, it is also a 'theory' in itself, because it can provide additional insights about how we can improve the existing models and theories.

Nevertheless, a wholly comprehensive theoretical expression of the allocative process, taking into account all the physical, chemical, biological, psychological, cultural, ethical and sociological factors which shape the working of an allocative process is impossible. A meta-theory should not be taken as a *full theory*. Quite the contrary, it should be regarded as a *theory of theories*, with the aim of improving them. Basically, it helps us in *planning* that improvement. We can get from it guidelines for further research work by signalling the kind of changes that should be made on a specific model or theory. But, how does this meta-theory define its constituent parts, that is, the economic agent, the principle of behaviour and the operational environment? Well, it must define them in the more general terms of a theory of human action. First of all, because the allocation processes are human actions in themselves. Second, because we wish to advance a schematic version of the meta-theory but also that the economic agent could be easily recognizable.

## *The Economic Agent*

Further difficulty arises when we try to fill the abstract theoretical constituents or 'containers' of the meta-theory with specific definitions of each 'container'. For instance, economists have tried to define the economic agent from very different perspectives: data, concepts, ideas or insights that lie outside the scope of the model. They do it in several ways and it cannot be said that there is a standard practice here. From experimental economics and agent-based computer economics through insights coming from cultural anthropology or even philosophy, we use a wide range of sources to fix these elements. Current contemporary macroeconomics still relies upon sophisticated versions of utility and production functions, which are nineteenth-century concepts developed from procedures such as 'introspection', among others. And although it is true that they have proved to be useful in some instances, when we look at the developments in psychology, marketing, behavioural sciences and so on, we quickly realize how out-of-date they are.

In terms of a meta-theory, however, we are not limited to the constrictions of any of these approaches. We need a definition of the economic agent so general as to cover the definitions of the economic agent of, at least, Austrians, neoclassicals and Keynesians. According to Rubio de Urquía, this definition or open 'container' of the economic agent could be understood as an assembly of different general elements that would define what the agent is in a determined instant of time. This 'assemblage' would integrate all those elements that would define who the agent is in that instant of time in the sense of being a producer of plans of action. A tentative exposition of those elements, just for the sake of exposition, would include such human traits and knowledge as beliefs, values and attitudes towards reality or theoretic and technical representations about different external and internal realities. This shows us how complex the definition of different 'containers' could be and, also, that there is a precedence of the 'assemblage' with respect to the decision-making process. In mainstream economics, for instance, the version of the 'assemblage' is the easiest possible, with the good and bad implications that this has, and what the agent must know before acting is given in advance. As we will argue later on, this is not an invalid way to proceed but it could be severely limiting.

But we have not finished yet with the exposition of the assemblage, because human beings are far from being static entities. We need to define the dynamics of change of this economic agent. The assemblage must change over time and it seems reasonable to think that two different dynamics are operating here: the dynamic by means of which agents set specific sets of ends and means, and the dynamic by means of which agents choose a specific arrangement of means and ends among other alternatives. We will call the former the cognitive dynamic and the latter the ethical dynamic.

> The ethical dynamic consists, in general, in the ordering of "what ought to be" and, in particular, in the dynamic of constitution of the sequences of action goals; the cognitive dynamic consists of the dynamic of constitution of theoretical representations. Both dynamics are fundamental and linked to each other.[2]

From the point of view of the meta-theory, it is especially interesting to see how the economic agent creates the knowledge about the means and the ends. Economic agents build sequentially mental representations of the bundles of means which supposedly are available to them, the bundles of ends they pursue, and the alternative arrangements linking ends and means which can be labelled as *plans*. These mental representations are 'produced' from cognitive, ethical or cultural deposits, which usually are labelled as 'subjectivity'. Among these deposits we can find expectations about future events, ways of organizing and ranking ends or partial *Weltanschauungs* inherited from parents or relatives. These deposits can evolve over time, and we generally label their change as cognitive, ethical and cultural *dynamics*. But although we are well aware of the dynamical character of the bundles of means and ends, we have to fix them at a time *t*, if we want to understand the working of the allocative process. From a broad point of view, those dynamics belong to the realm of psychology, ethics and sociology and cultural studies and must be considered as 'given' by economics. That does not mean that they do not affect the economic processes, quite the contrary. That means that we must consider them as *data*.

The anthropological foundation of economic theories also discovers an inner and often ignored source of theoretical progress. Obviously, the *cost* of closer representations to real economic agents will be a growing complexity and intractability of the models and theories. On the other hand, the simpler the representation is the greater the probability of misunderstanding the problem as we can miss a key feature. And here lies one of the most important fault lines among the several schools, as each of them claim that their representation of economic agents is better and more comprehensive than the other ones.

## *The Principle of Systematic Behaviour*

But the definition of the economic agent, of the 'assemblage', is not enough to express how the agent selects one plan of action from his or her bundle of plans. We need to know how the agent acts, not which actions it takes, in each moment. There must be some principle of systematic behaviour that fixes what we can expect from the decision making of the economic agent. Because, in the absence of stable criteria of behaviour, the agent's decision making could be random and incomprehensible. So, in the selection of the plan of action, the agent must always aim for his or her goals with the same ambition. If this principle of behaviour could be assigned to every person, then, it would be, in itself, an anthropological trait. This is what economists have unanimously supposed, that there is always a constant principle of behaviour operating in decision making and that this principle is the principle of economic behaviour: no matter what is inside the ends and means sets, the economic agent invariably always chooses the 'perceived' plan best-suited among other alternative plans. The *principle of economic behaviour* works automatically. That is, the *outcome* is *given* by the structure of those sets. Agents simply pick one plan because it 'seems' to be the best suited to them. Regular economic practice has been represented as an optimization programme, which has taken diverse forms throughout history. Here, one must carefully distinguish between the optimization programme in itself and the *outcome* of the programme. The specific mathematical technology employed is 'neutral' about the outcome, once we have defined the structure of the sets, yet it is not neutral about how these structures are defined, as we shall see later. But now we must first focus on the *outcome* of the working of the principle of economic behaviour. Its 'neutrality' simply means that it has *no* influence on the internal structure of the specific arrangement of ends and means. It simply informs us that an agent picks up the *preferred* plan, whatever it entails.[3] In its simplest form, the principle says that every agent facing two options, A and B, and preferring A, he/she always chooses A. No matter what A and B contain, the systematic character is that he/she *always* selects A. Even if A implies being an altruistic being like Mother Theresa or a greedy financial tycoon, the systematic principle will tell us what he/she is going to choose *once means, ends and plans are known.*

Troubles come when we try to model this process, i.e., when we try to represent specific processes regarding how agents make their choices, for we have to give shape to the ends and means sets. And here not only do the schools of thought collide, they also disagree about the specific deductive technology used. And troubles grow when we realize that these issues are closely linked.

Let's first state that S1K, S1A and S1NC are representations of the ends-means sets. Each of them contains statements about the ends pursued, how they sort them, the means perceived as available and how they arrange them, always referring to the specific issue under focus. Some of them are quite similar. For instance, mainstream macroeconomics, both new classical and neo-Keynesians, are still working with utility functions as a regular device to model consumer preferences. Others are not, such as wage setting processes. The fault lines among them are debates about the likelihood of these statements as reliable representations of the agents' behaviour. Nevertheless, both of them agree in using dynamic optimization as a deductive technology to achieve insights about the performance of the economy. The mathematical optimization techniques are simply representations of the working of the principle of economic behaviour. Again, some schools agree on that and some others do not, as is the case with the Austrians, which reject the use of mathematical technology. And it was the Austrians who opened the debate about the suitability of maths and statistics in this process. For, as they rightly argued, it imposes hard constraints on the *representations of the ends and means ends* themselves. According to the Austrians, the use of maths is not neutral in the sense that it requires specific assumptions about the ends/means sets which are, they argue, false or at least not relevant. Here is where the likelihood of the statements and assumptions about allocative processes mix with the problem of the deductive technology used. To illustrate this point let's turn to another research programme, that of evolutionary economics. It has been developing as a separate programme under the alleged analogy between evolutionary biology and economics. Its core assumption is the use of replicator dynamics as a way of modelling economic performance, and more specifically market processes. As replicator dynamics models come from the theory of population dynamics, there is little room here for maximizing behaviour over time because agents can only be equipped with *routines*, which are equivalent to *genes* in evolutionary biology. Routines lack the elective character of neoclassical 'preferences' or Austrian 'purposefulness'. But they work fairly well when we want to represent market dynamics, for instance.

## *Operational Environment*

All that has been said about the complexity of the economic agent conception can also apply to the problem of defining the operational environment of agents. Traditionally, economics has focused on just one kind of interactive environment, the market. And when it faces an interactive allocative reality that cannot be modelled as a market, it proceeds *as if* it was a market, as is observed in many cases as the study of externalities or the microeconomics of family show. Besides the troubles in dealing with non-market allocative relationships, and as happens with the representation of agents, here there are harsh debates about how the market works and how to model it. From the Walrasian auctioneer and the market clearing assumptions on the neoclassical side, we can move to the sticky prices modelling of the neo-Keynesians, stopping at the Austrian's market process theory and ending with the replicator algorithms of Schumpeterian evolutionary economics.

For instance, in the study of the market as an operational environment, it is convenient to distinguish some of its characteristics such as the external relations of the market, that is, the conditions fixed by politicians; the internal shape of the market that establishes the relationships among its members; the real elements of the market, that is, the characteristics of the good or merchandise that is the object of transaction in the market; and the personal elements of the subjects participating in that market.[4]

As exemplified in the case of the market, the operational environment refers to everything outside the economic agent that affects his or her decision making and the consequences of it. In this sense, we are not only talking about what exists independently of the economic agent. We are also making mention of how the agent receives the information from the environment. This is what Rubio de Urquía describes with the concept of theoretical and practical representations of reality. Every human being possesses representations about how the world functions that permits a better adaptation when new information is gathered. This implies a dynamic of absorption of the information coming from the environment that also operates in changing and generating the economic agent, that is, the assemblage and its parts.

## *The Meta-Theory*

While it is easy to identify the elements that theories share, it is more difficult to give a complete account of what this theory of theories should be. In what follows, we will present schematically the basic structure of the meta-theory we have been talking *supra*. The reader must keep in mind that this meta-theory is presented only as a unit of measure of the contemporary economic traditions. We do not pretend to present in this point a whole new proposal for rewriting economic theory. Our goal is to see how complex the economic research can be and where the economic theories are placed *vis-à-vis* each other. The usefulness of this exercise, we believe, resides in obtaining a *tertium comparationis* that, at the same time, would be able to indicate the complexity of the economic theories' respective anthropological conceptions.

Every economic theory begins with the definition of the economic agent. Then, let $E_{it}$ be a definition of an economic agent understood as a personal assemblage of a person $i$ in an instant $t$ of time. This assemblage is understood within some anthropological conception, as we have explained before (philosophical or scientific) and it is evident in economic theories.

If in the case of a particular economic theory we are interested in simplifying the analysis in order to express a meta-theory we will look for the opposite, that is, the more general expression of this economic agent. So, one element we have to consider is how this assemblage has come to be, expressly, what dynamics operates on its transformation and evolution. We talked before of the cognitive (which is responsible for what the agent acquires as knowledge) and ethical dynamics (which is responsible for what the agent wants, prefers and, in general, is related with the 'ought to be'). We will denote both dynamics as $\delta^c i$, $\delta^e i$. Hence, the actual assemblage is the product of a biography. It also constitutes a system of perception of his or her inner self and surrounding reality and also defines the sets of means and ends of the agent.

The operational environment influences the agent because it is a source of constraints for the assemblage and, also, it is perceived as information. We will denote the environment as *ut* and the dynamic of transmission of the information about the environment to the agent, as $D^{INF}$. This social dynamic would include the culture of a society, its legal system, the political organization, habits, the media and all the ways of transmission of social information, etc. The environment *ut* is also subject to its own and extremely complex dynamics of change that includes the actions performed by the agents.

Once the assemblage, the operational environment and the dynamics have been established, one particular agent or assemblage $E_{it}$, in interaction with a concrete operational environment, will produce a bundle of feasible (at least in his or her imagination) alternative plans of action $H_{it}$. The process of selection of one plan consists of selecting one from the bundle of alternative plans. This selection will be governed by the principle of economic behaviour $\pi$ that is independent of the moment of time because it is systematic. The execution of the plan selected will transform the assemblage and the operational environment (according to the operation of the dynamics of change – cognitive, ethical and of the environment) as new information will be created and, in this fashion, new possibilities of action will appear.

For instance, in Friedman and Savage's utility analysis of risky choices, there is a good expression of a specification of the meta-theory. They defined an assemblage in the form of a function of expected utility that contains the sets of means (goods) and ends (utility). The probability of occurrence of every event is subjected to a process of re-evaluation (cognitive dynamic) that rearranges the ordering of preferences (ethical dynamic). This process is the Bayes theorem, in itself an algorithm, that recalculates the probabilities of events when the agent has acted and new information has been created. The objective of the agent is to maximize his or her utility function (principle of economic behaviour) subject to a budget restriction (that, in this case, plays the role of the operational environment). The theorist can change and vary the content of each of those elements, producing different models and theoretical devices.

This scheme of the meta-theory can become more and more complicated if we introduce more elements such as the states of other agents or the dynamic of change of the environment. But we think it is enough to see how far we can go in the study of allocative processes and how much there is still to be done by economics.

## Explanatory and Predictive Costs of Choices

In the definition of the economic agent or the operational environment, each theorist has to choose how deep it must be and what utility it has for modelling purposes. But they do that in the commitment that their models have to be efficient for purposes of explanation, prediction or both. Though none of the economic traditions cited here thinks of themselves as being more pro-prediction or pro-explanation, it is true that there seems to be a trade-off between these two objectives in social science. The more explicative model is usually the less predictive. This is also related to the realism of the theory and its complexity: the greater the realism and complexity of a model, the lesser its predictive ability. In other words, their choices have costs in terms of prediction or explanation.

Heuristically speaking, the existence of a meta-theory leads us to wonder if the progress of economics did not lie in improving our definitions of the constituents or 'containers' as we have called them. Notwithstanding, there are huge methodological discrepancies among neoclassicals, Keynesians and Austrians that prevent us from reaching quick, meaningful conclusions. In fact, one of the major difficulties for the mutual understanding and cooperation among economic theories lies in their respective methodological approaches to the economic science in which the different philosophical origins we presented in the previous chapter are responsible for these divergent approaches.

In order to see the explanatory and prediction costs of the theories, and because methodological positions seem to be one of the fault lines among the different schools, it would be useful to put them under the scrutiny of the philosophy and methodology of science as a way of rationalizing the divides.

### *A Quick Review of the Philosophy of Science*

The contemporary milestones of the philosophy and methodology of science (hereafter PhMS) are in the works of Karl Popper, Thomas Kuhn and Imre Lakatos. Popper's 'critical rationalism' framework fits especially well when we come to think about the nature of economic theory or modelling. As he argued that all scientific theories are abstract hypotheses about the world, driven by a 'problem solving' drift, we can avoid the kind of problems that empiricism poses for social science. Due to this abstract character, they can be tested only indirectly, as happens with economic modelling: most of the tests are done on the ability of theories and models to explain or predict specific economic phenomena. According to Popper, positive contrasts of the theory never fully confirm it as valid or *true* knowledge. Because when a single counterexample appears, we can consider the theory as false – the falsification problem. Here lies also a demarcation criterion, as a theory should be considered scientific if, and only if, it is falsifiable. So, Popperian scientific progress comes from making abstract theories which could be proven false. Once a counterexample appears, the theory should be improved to explain the counterexample or simply discarded as useless.

The point outlined later by Kuhn is that this kind of scientific progress hardly exists in the history of science. Rather, science is a rather conservative process in which there is a strong resistance to changing the *status quo*, marked by the mainstream *praxis* or *paradigm*. The scientific paradigm is organized around a *core* which marks the works of the 'normal science'. *Regular praxis*, simply applies the *core* to related or new issues never before seen under the prism of the paradigm. It took a lot of time from the seminal works of RBC (1982) until its full development in international macroeconomics, for instance, as the authoritative *Handbook* by Obstfeld and Rogoff was published in 1996. It is only when a new disruptive paradigm appears that real change happens. But this is not as radical or creative as it seemed to be in the Popperian tale. In fact, it is usually preceded by a massive accumulation of empirical evidence that challenges the established paradigm, so the process of scientific change is slower and much more idiosyncratic than what Popper described. Quite correctly, Kuhn pointed toward the sociological bias of the process, which tends to keep working within the *status quo*.

A more workable hypothesis was made by Imre Lakatos, who was able to synthesize Popper's and Kuhn's insights into a full account of scientific logic and sociological issues put together in the concept of a *research programme*. Lakatos saw scientific progress as a competition between research programmes, which is a concept less overwhelming than *paradigm* and closer to the idea of 'theory' or 'model'. These research programmes consists of a *hard core* of basic hypotheses, and *auxiliary hypotheses* which are usually *ad hoc* assumptions and, as such, not fundamental for the research programme development. The idea of scientific progress for Lakatos is very simple: its ability to predict new phenomena. If it does so, refutations of auxiliary hypotheses do not need to be considered. Here lies the critical difference between a *progressive* or a *degenerative* research programme: if the latest auxiliary hypotheses have been introduced to deal with new data or phenomena or, on the contrary, they have just been used to protect the *hard core* against a growing body of empirical refutations.

Returning again to economics, the research programme framework fits very well into the classification we can make in economic modelling using the meta-theory. We could think of broad branches of literature simply as research programmes with *hard core* hypotheses, which give them the neoclassical or Keynesian character, and auxiliary hypotheses designed to deal with specific phenomena. But a historical example can best illustrate this.

In Chapter 4 we are going to review in some detail RBC and contemporary growth theory from the point of view of the meta-theory. So it will be helpful to explain the change in growth theory from the Harrod–Domar model to the latest developments in endogenous growth literature as a way to exemplify how scientific progress works in practice.

From classical economics, labour and capital have been identified as the sources of economic growth. From Smith and Ricardo to Marx, there had been attempts to explain the growing economic activity that started in the late eighteenth century. But we have to wait until the first half of the twentieth century to see the initial attempts of serious mathematical modelling of economic growth, in the seminal works of Harrod and Domar.[5] This early research programme was based on the role of saving and accumulation of capital, but closely intertwined with the Keynesian aggregate demand programme. This research programme, along with other post-Keynesian developments, share the common outcome that economic performance may lead to a stationary state of chronic depression and growing unemployment rates. The disruptive change comes from the neoclassical reaction of Solow and of Swan,[6] which marked the contemporary research programme on economic growth. From a historical point of view, the Solow–Swan challenge was the use of an aggregate production function which has become the standard for all further modelling on economic growth until now. Progress from their works has been made by expanding that initial insight, but does not come from a clear-cut departure from their aggregate production function specification. And this is the point for us: the aggregate production function is the *core* hypothesis of contemporary growth theory, and the quality ladders or extension to international economics issues are mere auxiliary assumptions suited to dealing with a specific problem, but that do not challenge the hard core of the research programme.

## *The Philosophy of Science and Methodology in Contemporary Economics*

Every economic tradition is built upon some methodological thinking but methodology has not been a main concern for all of them. Currently, mainstream economists feel perfectly comfortable within their scientific practice and they do not usually get involved in methodological discussions. Back in 1938, Terence Hutchison was not very preoccupied with the intricacies of philosophy and its implications for scientific method and insisted that the propositions of science should have empirical content and be testable,[7] and it still seems to be true in recent times when neoclassical economists naturally identify the progress of its theory with the progress of economic science itself. An instance of this can be found in the attitude concerning the evolution and progress of Economics as V. V. Chari expressed in his celebration of Lucas's Nobel Prize:

> Scientific progress arises from the interaction between theory and data and the desire to have one unified theory to account for the observations at hand. The search for such a theory proceeds by developing specific abstractions, or *models*, to understand specific observations. These abstractions then lead to the development of a more general theory, which in turn leads to discarding models which are inconsistent with data and the development of better models.[8]

Indeed, the victory of positivistic thinking has been complete in terms of researchers, staff, funding and media impact, and not only in hard sciences such as physics or biology, but also in social sciences such as economics. This extension of natural science methods to the social ones is made easier by the common mentality all positivists share that is prone to accepting that the methods of gathering information from reality (data) and understanding these observations (knowledge) must be similar, *mutatis mutandi*, in all sciences. All in all, methodological monism has always been one of main corollaries of positivism.

The disagreement with this vision of economic science is evident among the dissidents or heterodox economists such as the Austrians and Keynesians, as is their need to justify their alternative proposals from the methodological standpoint. Keynes's theory was born in direct conflict with the neoclassical paradigm because its aim was to occupy its place. The case of the Austrian School is slightly similar to the Keynesian one because it was also born fighting a methodological war, the so-called *Methodenstreit* (method dispute), between Carl Menger and the forerunners of the German Historical School, Roscher and Knies. The historicists of the German School were convinced that it was impossible to obtain 'a theory' from historical facts because every historical event is unique and must be understood or comprehended in its individuality. The pretension of explaining history with general and abstract theories was absurd and unobtainable. In response, Menger published his *Untersuchungen*,[9] with the aim of defending the suitability of abstract economics for the study of history.

But the consolidation of their respective methodological views came from the success of neoclassical economics, which pressured the heterodox schools to explain why their methodological alternatives were superior. Nevertheless, as we have identified a common structure in economic theories, it is possible to find common grounds for methodological praxis. Or, at least, it serves to identify a common path.

In the end, neoclassical economics' pre-eminent position has centered on the methodological debate on the realism or unrealism, 'realisticness' or 'unrealisticness' of assumptions and theories. We have talked before about the transference of methods between physics and economics in the works of the *founding fathers* of marginalist revolution, Jevons, Walras and others. That is why simplification, and hence unrealism of assumptions, is so radical in neoclassical economics. The accommodation of economics within the discipline of natural sciences was arduous and the extent of the simplification needed for the job was enormous. It is not an easy task to insert society into equations. The talent and years of hard work of people like Wald, von Neumann, Debreu and others to mathematically prove the possibility of the general equilibrium are symptomatic of this difficulty.

This deep reductionism took its toll on neoclassicism much later. It was not till the end of the 1940s and the beginning of the 1950s that there was an upsurge of dissident voices against the aprioristic character of many assumptions in neoclassical models and the Marshall–Pigou theory of the firm came under attack for its unrealistic assumptions.[10] The criticisms showed a contradiction, because neoclassicals left out of their theories important empirically observable elements of the economic system. There was an evident cost in terms of explaining the economic phenomena. Milton Friedman raised his voice to defend the methodological practice of the Neoclassical School[11] in his famous 1954 essay entitled 'The Methodology of Positive Economics', which still stands as the undisputed methodological reference for mainstream economics.

For Friedman, the decisive element of theories was not their realism or explanatory power, but how they deal with the empirical reality in terms of prediction. Additionally, he emphasized that there were only two selection criteria suitable for discriminating among hypotheses: simplicity and fruitfulness. Furthermore, he pointed out that the realism of generalizations was not only unessential for theoretical modelling in his judgement, but 'truly important and significant hypotheses will be found to have "assumptions" that are wildly inaccurate descriptive representations of reality, and, in general, the more significant the theory, the more unrealistic the assumptions (in this sense)'.[12] Finally, hypotheses would only be maintained if they survived the rigours of empirical testing, that is, if they could not be falsified.

The academic community expressed a lively interest in the essay with numerous reviews published in the most relevant journals.[13] Friedman's essay was interpreted in subsequent critical readings in many different ways from the methodological point of view and alternatively defined as a kind of Popperian falsificationism, as a piece of verificationism and, even, as having a real connection with the conventionalist interpretation that Lakatos made of Popperian falsificationism.[14] In our opinion, Boland's instrumentalist interpretation would have most likely prevailed as the most authoritative interpretation, as authorized by Friedman himself in the essay.[15]

Regardless, the importance of 'The Methodology of Positive Economics' resided in Friedman's courage to speak on the most controversial topic of epistemology: the question of the 'foundation of knowledge' in which philosophy lives since David Hume put his finger on the 'problem of induction'. How can we say that our theories are true, that they accurately explain the real world? Friedman accepted the basic tenets of Hume's criticism and tried to solve the problem for economics, arguing as follows: if it is impossible to affirm a conjunctive argument[16] from its premises, that is, if it is impossible to arrive to true conclusions using the *modus ponens*,[17] then, it must be at least possible to affirm provisionally, or definitely deny, some or all of the premises of a disjunctive[18] argument using the *modus tollens*.[19] To state it more clearly, if deductivism is doomed to failure, inductivism still gives us a good chance to produce provisional tools for predicting the future. In this 'sort of Popperianism', the predictive success of an argument would be enough to maintain it and its failure would be, accordingly, reason enough to reconsider or refute any or all of its premises. Hence,

> theories are convenient and useful ways of (logically) generating what have turned out to be true (or successful) predictions or conclusions. Instrumentalism is the primary methodological point of view expressed in Friedman's essay ... Thus, theories do not have to be considered true statements about the nature of the world, but only convenient ways of systematically generating the already known 'true' conclusions.[20]

Hence, assumptions must be considered irrelevant to falsify a theory, only predictions can do that job.

Obviously, if this statement is taken rigorously, in its strongest version, it leads to the absurd conclusions that we could trust more in magic and sorcery than in science and discard many useless economists and replace them with successful soothsayers. Clearly, Milton Friedman did not want to imply that. More likely, he was defending that theoretical assumptions must abstract as much as is possible from reality. That is, hypotheses must describe the performance of reality 'as if' only the essential elements of it were operating.

Of course, this exercise in reductionism is not exclusive to neoclassical theories. We would not be able to express with completion anything we like to understand if the contingent was not separated from the essential. But, what happens when we put together Friedman's 'as if' hypotheses with prediction as the only falsifying instance of theories and the use of mathematical formalization? In this case, we have to carefully separate the role of abstraction in science from the specific abstraction that mathematical methods produce in economics. Abstraction in sciences is a necessity. Without abstraction it is impossible to conceive and contain the complexity of reality in mental categories. For this reason, it is hard to criticize the use of reductionism and simplification in any theory of any kind, because all make use of it.

In some sense, Friedman dispelled the doubts about the positivistic and empiricist programme of research that the Neoclassical School represented. We cannot say for sure that it constituted a kind of license for the empiricist practice in economics, but it was important in strengthening the theoretical, academic and institutional processes already at work at prominent universities, and in the relation between them and the US government, in favour of neoclassical economics.[21]

In the end, methodology, which never was a real concern for mainstream economists, disappeared over the horizon more or less completely thanks to Friedman's essay.[22] However, every heuristic choice implies the opening of specific possibilities for modelling and comprehension and the closure of others. Every methodology establishes limits and constraints not only for modelling but also for the comprehension it helps to achieve from reality. In addition, the use of mathematics, utterly indispensable for providing a quantitative account of reality, demanded additional simplifications as it is not able to express any reality we encounter or, at least, not without incurring serious decreasing returns. So, the problem with neoclassical methodology is not really 'abstraction' as such, but the abuse of abstraction due to the desire of using 'as if' hypotheses that must be mathematized. This is the explanatory cost that neoclassical economics has to pay.

Verbal formalization is less strict and more flexible. What Austrians and Keynesians offer as an alternative is a kind of modelling which is less abstract and reductionist than the neoclassicals. In the case of the Austrians, the rejection in using the mathematical formalism and their voluntary restriction of the verbal formalism allowed them to define their economic agent keeping more elements of an observable human being in it than what neoclassical methodology permits. To neoclassicals, the economic agent is a device that reacts automatically and passively according to the principle of economic behaviour (in this case the principle of optimizing behaviour) to an already given factual situation provided by the utility function and the budget constraint. Neoclassical economists, then, voluntarily exclude many observable elements of human beings in their models, for instance, the imagination of the future or the weight of subjective behaviour in decision making.

This is not the case with the Austrians, whose economic agent acts in real time according to the knowledge that, to a great extent, he/she only possesses. In line with this factual situation, he/she selects from his/her action plans the one that *a priori* promises the best result but that, *a posteriori*, can be mistaken. For that, the Austrian insist heavily on the importance of entrepreneurial error and how the new relevant knowledge acquired through it facilitates the reinterpretation of reality and the redesign of the action plans. Hence, subjectivism is a fundamental assumption for the Austrians. The economic agent possesses a subjective knowledge acquired through his or her vital experiences and in the interaction with other agents. To a great extent, this knowledge is personal, non-formal, practical, loaded with feelings, beliefs, values, etc., in such a fashion that it is only *at the disposal of anyone but* those that own them. Besides, it can activate peculiar answers to concrete situations that the concerned agent is able to perceive and, therefore, use for generating a profit. The characteristics of the production of human knowledge allowed the Austrians to affirm that it is being actively generated in a continuous process. It is not already present for the observers, scientists and politicians. That is why Austrians only dare to make 'pattern' or qualitative predictions about the future, because the market process is always changing and evolving so complexly that, even if the economists are equipped with the best theoretical tools, the exact prediction of its future is simply impossible. Their criticism of mathematical and econometrics methods is in line with this comprehension of the object of study and justifies the use of a verbal formalism.

Keynes, for his part, preferred to go to extremes and paid more attention to the problem of induction that explains why the uncertainty is greater and fundamental when the agent has long to wait for the results of an action. Conventional and animal spirit behaviour would appear for the agent to be a necessity in minimizing this feeling of uncertainty in order to make the best decision. In both cases, the consideration of ignorance and uncertainty is excessively intense from the ontological point of view. It is too hard to state such an ontological status of reality and human knowledge because they imply the inability of human knowledge that impedes having a clue of the future trends of human events. In some sense, these behaviours are pathological. While they must not be true in the generality of cases, they suddenly emerge in certain moments of time when, in fact, uncertainty increases due to the collapse of the stability of a precedent state. In this case, if Keynes's position is conceptualized as a particular case and not a general one, Austrian and Keynesian discourses could be made highly compatible as being two faces of the same coin. In summary, they are freer to propose more 'realistic' definitions of the economic agent, definitions that permit the incorporation to the analysis of empirically observable human traits that are potentially important to explain and predict certain economic events.

The same could be said about mathematical formalism. There is no good reason to avoid the use of mathematics to understand the relationship or the functioning of specific behaviours in decision making if there exists a clear understanding of the limits of the use and the reach of the metaphors that formalism presupposes. For Keynes and post-Keynesians, mathematical formalism is instrumental and dependent on the specific reality that is the object of scientific attention. From the very beginning, neoclassical authors have regarded their models as tools for generating quantitative predictions even if the premises of their theories were not supported on empirical grounds. For instance, Vilfredo Pareto used the deductive method to discover the laws governing certain abstract or simple events. But, in accordance with positivism, he devoted a great part of his efforts to statistical analyses in order to corroborate these theoretical laws. Of course, there is a great difference between the way in which Pareto carried out his empirical contrasts and the way they are made today by new classical economists, but the approach remains the same and it is clearly oriented towards quantitative prediction. The evolution of neoclassical models has benefited from 'technological' advances thanks to the progressive perfection of mathematical formalism and the growing quality and number of statistics reinforcing the confidence in its scientific method.

Austrians are at the other extreme of the methodological spectrum. Specifically, Mises defended that introspection can provide such a solid premises as to unfold axiomatically the whole body of the logical science of human action (or praxeology, as he called it).

> Economics is not about things and tangible material objects; it is about men, their meanings and actions. Goods, commodities, and wealth and all the other notions of conduct are not elements of nature; they are elements of human meaning and conduct. He who wants to deal with them must not look at the external world; he must search for them in the meaning of acting men.[23]

This point of departure was not an arbitrary choice; Mises understood there was no other practical way to obtain the praxeological categories of causality and teleology that explain human action. Besides, their properness could be demonstrated by *reductio ad absurdum*, because denying these premises would imply denying the very fact of the human action itself.

Keynes was not very prone to the use of mathematics in economics if we judge how much he used them in the *General Theory*, but he certainly was not a beginner in that science. His position on this topic usually has been related to his controversy with Tinbergen, where Keynes attacked the econometric studies on the basis of the principle of limited independent variety, which is quite a technical issue.[24]

According to R. M. O'Donnell, 'His hostility was directed not at the use of mathematics per se, but at (i) "pseudo-mathematics", or the illegitimate application of mathematical analysis, and (ii) the elevation of mathematics to the highest form of economic reasoning'.[25]

Keynes's philosophical vision of human knowledge and probability led him to place more emphasis on uncertainty and its influence on decision making. In fact, uncertainty is the door of entry for his organicistic theory of society. It is interesting to note how that philosophical approach implied a verbal formalism in the treatment of the human agent but facilitated the mathematical formalism of the behaviour of society. Through uncertainty the conventional behaviour takes the command of decision making and produces the differentiation between the parts and the whole in society. Post-Keynesians are not against the use of mathematics in economics,[26] but there are strict conditions for its application: 'It is important, therefore, to keep in mind that formalization is only methodologically legitimate when analyzing some material that displays regularity and that is homogeneous over the time frame relevant for the analysis'.[27]

Notwithstanding, the heterodox schools have been undermined for their methodological defensive position. They should have done more in developing their own paradigms more thoroughly. There is a lack of progression in their work since much of the characterization of their models is stuck in the time of the pioneers and they are losing the battle of empirical evidence and prediction even when their models explain economic phenomena more convincingly and more accurately. And it is not only their aversion to scientism and social engineering; Austrians, also, have reasons to complain about statistics. In general, they are suited and designed to cover the theoretical inquisitions of neoclassicals and new Keynesians and do not provide information about the value of all intermediate capital goods that are fundamental to the Austrian business cycle theory.[28]

## *Critical and Auxiliary Features of Economic Theories in the Light of the Meta-Theory*

The methodological path chosen is important in understanding what is critical or auxiliary in terms of assumptions and hypotheses. In Lakatosian terms, critical hypotheses belong to the realm of the core of a theory while auxiliary hypotheses form part of its protective belt. If the hypotheses contained in the core change, the theory turns into a completely different one. This does not occur when we discard some of the auxiliary hypotheses. The specific model is different, even new, but the essence of the theory remains.

We have revised some of the differences and similarities of the three contemporary economic traditions. Some give more importance to prediction and emphasize the quantitative features of their models and others prefer to foster explanation, lending more weight to the qualitative aspects. Some are more inclined to methodological individualism and others to the study of the organic behaviour of the whole economy. Of course, these differences are important but cannot hide the fact that, fundamentally, they share a similar approach to the economic problem. Underlying each we find the 'allocative process' and the structure 'economic agent–principle of behaviour–operational environment'. This sameness happens for one reason: because it is ontologically clear that agents lie behind economic phenomena (micro or macro).

However, the truth of this statement is independent of the practicality of it. Aggregation presents technical problems, for instance, for mainstream economics. The use of the representative agent is an elusive solution to the problem. But jumping to the macro level as post-Keynesians defend cannot be done without the 'permission' of the micro level, as Keynes showed, unless we agree with Hoover that macroeconomic aggregates are similar to physical structures.[29]

But which hypotheses can be found to be critical for an economic tradition and which are auxiliary? As long as allocative processes are the common ground for all economic modelling, the most basic critical hypotheses in economics are that someone is acting when she/he allocates resources to ends and that someone is acting according to a systematic principle of behaviour when she/he allocates resources to ends. From this very fact, the different traditions have been building sets of 'core' hypotheses or anthropologies. An Austrian theory always includes a hypothesis about the imperfect knowledge of market participants which can only be improved through entrepreneurship. These core hypotheses are usually surrounded by protective or auxiliary hypotheses which act as specifications of the core anthropology of the process under research, but also as a defence against competing modellings.

From this point of view, those who consider that well-established competing research programmes have nothing to say about a specific topic, are incurring a non-scientific, idiosyncratic defensive strategy. Cooperation among programmes could enhance the progressive character of all of them. Usually this cooperation works through the borrowing of working and auxiliary hypotheses from other programmes, but there is no reason to expect that it cannot work for core hypotheses. What we are looking for is how significant aspects of human behaviour, such as historical time and subjective knowledge, can be integrated into formal models and how the interaction between economic agents and the operational environment works. And, even more difficult, how all these elements can serve the purpose of predicting, even qualitatively, the path of future events.

## How Theories Can Improve

Using the meta-theory scheme and the Popper–Lakatos insights, we can easily identify two kinds of scientific progress. The first one is the *regular praxis* within a progressive or a well-established research programme, i.e., what Kuhn and Lakatos described as the unfolding of a set of core hypotheses throughout scientific fields. The second one is the *disruptive* progress, which challenges a whole body of well-established programmes through modifying some of the core hypotheses. We can transfer this to economic theory and modelling using the meta-theory approach. The *regular praxis* will be done from a specific *anthropology*, a set of core hypotheses about economic agents, which is systematically applied to a broad field of economic phenomena using the deductive technology prescribed by the programme. The disruptive progress is done when we modify the *anthropology* or change the deductive technology regularly used till that moment. It will be useful to see some examples of how this works.

Dynamic general stochastic equilibrium modelling (DGSE) has been, up to this point, the most regular and well-established research programme in mainstream macroeconomics. From the seminal works of Ramsey, and later Cass, Koopmans, and Brock and Mirman,[30] today the problems of dynamic optimization are the cornerstones of most macroeconomic models. The use of this deductive technology joined with specific characterization of economic agents not present in other modellings has been applied to most of the branches of macroeconomics, from the original work in growth theory to international macroeconomics and business cycle theory. *But*, when we look at the evolution of macroeconomic thought over the past seventy-five years, we realize that most of these phenomena were previously modelled by Keynesian, neoclassical, monetarist and new classical economics, although through different core hypotheses about economic agents and deductive technologies. In most cases, they have been working upon more or less the same hypotheses regarding economic agents, and they simply changed some of them, *not all*, to unleash a fully fledged new research programme. Once the research programme is established, the *regular praxis* phase begins, which is featured by an attempt to find out new results consistent with empirical regularities, if possible.

The path of alternative research programmes shows the same route. Evolutionary economics follows a very similar evolution than that of mainstream economics. From early Schumpeterian insights, the seminal work of Nelson and Winter[31] has been developed around two core hypotheses: that the economy is driven by innovation both technological and organizational, and that it can be explained using the neo-Darwinian modelling of biological selection. That was the disruptive point from mainstream economics, and it has been of limited success as a well-established research programme. Since then, people involved in the programme have been developing a rather consistent *regular praxis*, although mostly focused on innovation and growth theory. We will deal with this programme in more detail, because it is a very good example of how we can gather insights from other disciplines to improve our theories.

Our point in the following chapters will be that the RBC research programme was a disruptive change within the neoclassical mainstream. The use of intertemporal substitution and the representative agent hypotheses are the hard core of the programme. The programme has been developing *regular praxis* by extending auxiliary hypotheses to other fields of economics. What we will show in the next chapter is that the RBC research programme was not able to predict the 2008–9 financial crisis and the subsequent Great Recession. That is, there is a strong case based on empirical evidence which undermines the predictive power of the research programme. In the next chapter, we will offer several hypotheses about the financial system which are needed to predict this kind of systemic financial crisis. We will see that critical changes must be made in the representation of the financial operational environment in macroeconomic modelling to deal with these situations. Our point is that the RBC research programme is currently unable to do the job. But before that, we must rationalize how these kinds of changes can be made.

We have seen before that changes in the major 'containers' of each economic model come from two sources: direct observation of economic behaviour, as in the case of experimental economics, or through borrowed concepts from other disciplines and sciences, as in the case of evolutionary economics. The next two sections will be devoted to exploring the possibilities of these two ways. We will not review in full the possibilities that could potentially open each one of them, but we will select one of them so that the reader may see how this cooperation among sciences and research programmes could be made.

## *Through Direct Observation of Economic Behaviour: The Case of Experimental Economics*

Both disruptive and regular progress is done by modifying assumptions about economic agents – anthropologies – or deductive technologies. The way we gather information about human behaviour in order to suggest and test hypotheses is rather diverse. Here we are going to focus on what we can label as 'direct observation'. This consists of relying mostly upon economics itself in the formulation of hypotheses without any reference to other fields. We can find several examples of this way of doing things: the DGSE programme is a good instance of that, as the core hypotheses rely heavily on refined versions of traditional utility and production functions. Most of the improvements have been made to fit these functions into the dynamical optimization technical specifications, so there is little direct observation here, but there are no attempts to approach other social science fields to see if these hypotheses are more or less plausible. This is rather consistent with Friedman's methodological programme, provided that the DGSE modelling is able to deliver predictions that will be sufficient for its scientific standards.

But during the last fifty years there have been other developments with this 'inward-looking' profile which are, nevertheless, committed to the realism of the assumptions and, at the same time, consistent with a positivistic view of scientific progress. That is the case of experimental economics, a programme whose origins can be traced back to the 1950s, and that began with the use of the experimental methods of psychology in gathering experimental data about economic processes. It is quite interesting to see that Vernon Smith (2008), perhaps the key figure in these programmes, is quite conscious of the methodological issues raised by a disruptive programme such as this. The inward-looking orientation of this approach begins with a strong methodological statement:

> the data of astronomy are painstakingly gathered by professional observational astronomers for scientific purposes, and these data are taken seriously (if not always non-controversially) by astrophysicists and cosmologists. Most of the data of economics has been collected by government or private agencies for non-scientific

> purposes. Hence astronomers are directly responsible for the scientific credibility of their data in a way that economists have not been. In economics, when things appear not to turn out as expected the quality of the data is more likely to be questioned than the relevance and quality of the abstract reasoning. Old theories fade away, not from the weight of falsifying evidence that catalyzes theoretical creativity into developing better theory, but from lack of interest, as intellectual energy is attracted to the development of new techniques and to the solution of new puzzles that remain untested.[32]

This experimental approach to economics put in the hands of the scientific *regular praxis* the gathering and verification of data, a task which in other fields is carried out by researchers. Smith claims that according to scientific standards, we should be directly responsible for the source of scientific data, and we should use controlled processes that can be replicated by other experimentalists. From that programmatic statement, the research programme has been carrying out experiments which cover almost all the traditional fields in economics, from supply and demand market processes, auctions, bargaining behaviour, decision making and so on. Perhaps one of the most challenging works was that of Kahneman and Tversky,[33] a critique of the expected utility theory using experimental techniques, and indirectly of the rational behaviour hypothesis. And although this work and others were carried out by psychologists or using experimental techniques coming from psychology, the use of computational methods from the late 1980s has made the programme less and less dependent on psychological issues and more focused on strictly economic issues.

The point is that, far beyond the empirical findings and the soundness of the results, the whole programme is built around an inward-looking, pure economic research aiming to improve our knowledge about the economic agent. The aim is to *improve* the *core anthropology* of economic theory in order to gather more reliable predictions and explanations of economic processes.

## *Through Other Social Sciences or Instrumental Modelling*

Another pathway to improvement in economic theory and modelling is usually done by borrowing hypotheses or methods from other scientific fields. Here, instead of looking inside the field at new and more accurate findings, we look at successful theories or deductive technologies elsewhere in science and try to adapt them to ours by means of scientific analogies. We not only borrow techniques, as is the case with dynamic optimization. We can also borrow 'alien' hypotheses and rewrite them in a way suited to our purposes. Evolutionary economics is a good example of this way of doing things, because from the very beginning it relied upon a double analogy, a mathematical natural selection modelling and a gene-like routinized behaviour.

Evolutionary economics claims that it was Schumpeter who first considered entrepreneurial innovation as the source of economic change, in a kind of theory quite close to modern population biology, as Metcalfe has pointed out.[34] They regard the evolutionary character of Schumpeter's theory as more 'neo-Darwinian' than other Austrian theorists of that time, including Hayek. According to this analogy, innovation plays the same role in economics as genetic mutation does in biology. Once the novelty has been put into the market, the forces of 'creative destruction' explain the change. Contemporary evolutionary economists have pointed out this original character in Schumpeter's work:

> The broader connotations of evolutionary include a concern with processes of long-term and progressive change. The regularities observable in present reality are interpreted not as a solution to a static problem, but as the result that understandable dynamic processes have produced from known or plausibly conjectured conditions in the past- and also as features of the stage from which a quite different future will emerge by those same dynamic processes.[35]

In addition to its Schumpeterian foundation, in evolutionary economics the market process is modelled by the replicator dynamic, the R. A. Fisher mathematical representation of the natural selection process. The gene pool is substituted by routinized behaviour, a concept taken from Herbert Simon's bounded rationality. Some authors have tried to go further in the development of a more ambitious programme, such as Geoff Hodgson and Ulrich Witt, but they have had to use enlarged versions of Darwinism in order to deal with the economic and social dynamics. Hodgson in particular is trying to develop a kind of 'generalized Darwinism'[36] as the basic benchmark for social and economic theorizing. This analogy has been used to replicate classical problems of biological theory, as in the case of altruism and group selection which are far from being completely understood even in evolutionary biology. So, evolutionary economics, with all its flaws, is a good example of how a good analogy can provide the theoretical basis for a disruptive improvement, as it brings well-tested modellings and hypotheses to economics.

This type of progress can be systematically carried out by borrowing concepts and hypotheses from social sciences, as we are all studying human behaviour and its outcomes. For instance, there have been interesting and parallel developments in theoretical psychology which resemble some of the elements of the meta-theory here proposed.[37] If there existed a psychological theory of personality compatible with the 'theory of human action' character of economic theories, it would be very useful when filling-in the 'containers' of the building blocks of economic meta-theory. Daniel Cervone's approach to personality and his so-called KAPA model (knowledge-and-appraisal personality architecture) and Mishel and Shoda's CAPS model (cognitive-affective personality system), conceive personality as a 'complex, dynamic organization of cognitive and affective elements'.[38] Two elements are important in the KAPA model, knowledge and appraisals:

> knowledge consists of mental representations of current or prospective features of oneself, others, or the environment. Appraisals, in contrast, are not beliefs about isolated features of oneself or the world. They are relational judgments, that is, evaluations of the relation between oneself and occurrences within particular encounters. Specifically, appraisals are relational judgments that concern the meaning of encounters for oneself; they are 'continuing evaluation[s] of the significance of what is happening for one's personal well-being'.[39]

Variables of personality related with knowledge make reference to durable mental representations about the characteristics of personality or of the environment. Those related to appraisals refer to dynamic processes that enable the person to give a personal meaning to the 'encounters' or events occurring to him/her. That meaning puts the event in relation to his/her objectives and capabilities, in sum, with his or her concerns. There is a clear correspondence between Cervone's definition of knowledge and appraisals and Rubio de Urquía's cognitive and ethical dynamics. The hypothesis of the existence of appreciative aspects in permanent structures of personality justifies, in our opinion, the hypothesis of a hierarchy of goals with respect to which plans of actions are ordered (which implies as well some criteria or moral categories to inform that order). Cervone's specific theoretical approach emphasizes how that hierarchy is intimately related to the particular history of each person as well as their capacities to obtain new knowledge and to value the surrounding reality. That is just one way of proving that a multiple and fruitful exchange of ideas can exponentially foster our knowledge of economic phenomena.

In this chapter we have shown that not only a systematic research on the structure of models and theories is possible, we can also more accurately target the way we can improve them, either by *regular praxis* or by *disruptive changes*. It will always be done by relying upon representations of economic agents and operational environments increasingly better suited for our purposes. This allows us to take further steps in the next chapters in trying to deal with the troubles the 2008 financial crisis created for mainstream macroeconomics and find ways to solve it.

# 4 THE META-THEORY AT WORK: A CASE STUDY IN GROWTH THEORY AND REAL BUSINESS CYCLE THEORY

In this chapter we are going to examine growth theory and real business cycle theory (RBC theory) to apply the general framework we have outlined in the preceding chapter. We want to stress which variables are critical and which are not in both theories and in the model as well. As we are going to explain, there are differences between the theories because there is not a single model of growth theory, while RBC theory is a unique model. In addition, we are interested in showing the characterization of the agents and the operational environment of the models.

Thus, we are going to look at the critical variables in a set of economic growth models and to distinguish those from the auxiliary ones. In this manner, we will explain why the process of improvement has shifted the focus from one critical variable to another. The critical variables in RBC theory have not changed over time, so we will focus on the improvements. In addition, we are going to show that both theories share some features concerning the characterization of the agents and the environment, while others are very different.

The starting point of RBC theories is well defined whereas the starting point of growth theory is not. We have decided to start our analysis with Solow's model.[1] The preceding models[2] are interesting as well but to a certain extent can be subsumed into the former. There is a wide consensus which considers this model as the departure point for modern growth theory and we share this consensus. We are not going to analyse models that belong to the Keynesian tradition.[3] They are interesting, but they have not influenced growth theory. It can be said that mainstream growth theory has no neo-Keynesian features, while RBC theory has incorporated some of them. In addition the model of Solow can be considered a disruptive paradigm in the sense of Lakatos, as we have explained in Chapter 3. Previous models, for instance Harrod and Domar's, belonged to the Keynesian paradigm. Solow's model was pathbreaking because it was based on a new set of assumptions and its critical variables were different. Thus, we are going to analyse the development of this new paradigm. Once established, this paradigm nearly completely displaced the previous one. Growth theorists after Solow departed from its model and developed a stream of 'normal science', following their guidelines.

## Critical and Auxiliary Variables in Growth Theory

Growth theory as we have defined it before is not a single model that has evolved over time but a set of several models and approaches aiming at explaining the growth of the world's economies and the differences among them that the data show. The common ground of nearly all models is its logical dependence upon Solow's model. As we are going to outline in the second part of this chapter (pp. 81–6), the ability of a model to fit the data has been a key criterion to decide whether a model is good or not, and to what extent. Because of that, scarcity or paucity of data has deterred researchers from checking their models using world-wide data samples. Instead, they have focused on countries or areas where data was abundant and reliable. As long as additional data has been available, theories have been forced to take it into account and to become more sophisticated. But the general structure of the models has not changed very much and the same applies to their critical and auxiliary variables.

Therefore, in this section we are going to focus on the main models starting with the seminal papers of Solow and of Swan and moving to the model of Aghion and Howitt.[4] Additional models will be studied in the second part of this chapter because they have improved growth theory and have helped to achieve a better understanding of the data. We are not going to enter into the technical details of every model. We take for granted that they are generally known and, if required, they can be reviewed by sourcing the original articles referenced in the endnotes at the end of this volume.[5]

Solow's model[6] cited above is based on an aggregate Cobb–Douglas production function that exhibits diminishing returns. The kind of returns of the aggregate production function is a topic being discussed in growth theory. Solow's assumption was the conventional approach in the 1950s and is widely shared among economists today, though some experts still have reservations. The mathematical tractability of functions exhibiting diminishing returns and its intuitiveness are its main advantages. There is just one good that can be either consumed or saved to invest. The savings and depreciation rates are considered exogenous. Population grows at a constant rate and each person supplies inelastically one unit of labour per time. Per capita output growth depends on per capital stock of capital, which in turn depends on the savings rate.

Diminishing returns implies that regardless of the level of population growth rate, depreciation and savings rate, the economy reaches a steady state where per capita growth stops. Diminishing returns are the critical variable in this model. If we remove it the outcome is different. Savings rate, depreciation and population growth rate determine the output level, but not per capita growth. Output level is important, but less so than growth rate. If you substitute capital and labour with other variables the outcome still depends on diminishing returns that lead the economy to a steady state. One salient feature is its simplicity and tractability. It can be easily computed provided we know the values of variables and the effects of a change in one variable can be calculated as well.

Solow's second model[7] includes in its framework an exogenous rate of technological change. If technological change does not exist, each economy reaches its steady state and per capita growth stops. But technological changes increase productivity so the economy escapes from its steady state, or, more precisely, the economy exhibits per capita growth at the rate of technological change. Diminishing returns still hold, but their effects are offset by technological change. In this model the interplay between diminishing returns and technological change is the key feature. Technological change cannot be taken for granted and therefore diminishing returns may prevail and per capita growth stops. In addition, the rate of technological change can vary from one period to another and as per capita growth. More important still, it is exogenous in a way that RBC theory adopted as a key feature of its model. The exogeneity of the only source of per capita growth has been an ongoing source of discussion among theorists since Solow's paper appeared. Technological change is the engine of growth in this model but it is quite unsatisfactory.

Both models assume that there are any number of agents in the economy whose behaviour is the same and is not explained in any way. It is actually an aggregate model of the economy. Solow was aware he was building a model based on 'heroic' aggregation, but it was the only way to make it workable. These types of models have been labelled 'exogenous growth models' because of this feature. Regarding the environment, it includes only the two production factors of the Cobb–Douglas function but there is no interplay between the environment and the agents because they are not addressed by the models as such.

The next model we are going to explain is exogenous as well, but it includes human capital along with labour and capital as a production factor. It was described in a paper in 1992[8] by Gregory Mankiw, David Romer and David Weil. The aggregate production function has two different types of capital: physical capital and human capital that both depreciate at the same rate. There is labour as well, and the technological change that affects labour productivity. Savings can be invested either in physical capital or in human capital using the same production function. Both types of capital exhibit decreasing returns. Thus, we can envisage this model as Solow's 1957 model with human capital.[9] The model points out that the contribution of labour to overall production is based not only on raw labour, but on specific skills of manpower, its human capital, so the same labour force can be much more or much less productive, depending on its skills. Thus, Mankiw, Romer and Weil take a closer look at the finer details of Solow's model. Output per capita depends on accumulation of physical capital and human capital. The effects of physical capital on output are the same as in the original model, but the effects of human capital are not. Human capital depreciates but its level has a strong influence on per capita output growth. Physical capital fosters growth depending on the rate of investment, but human capital fosters growth depending on the rate and on the level as well. Therefore, there is a clear spillover of human capital on the model: the more human capital in the economy, the more economic growth, and vice versa. From another point of view, it can be said that the level of human capital exerts a strong influence on the productivity of physical capital, an external effect that data supports.

The running of the model is very similar to the previous, but the additional critical variable is human capital. If we withdraw human capital from the model we are back to Solow's model. Technological change is included in the model as well but is not critical to explaining per capita growth. It can increase per capita growth but the level of human capital contributes as well. One important consequence of the model is the need for new and more accurate data to back its specification. Raw labour is easy to define and data about it is available, but data on human capital is not and the authors devoted a lot of time in showing that there were data that supported their statements. But the most important thing is the shifting of focus. In Solow's 1957 model, human capital was absent while technological change was the key feature in explaining per capita growth. In the model of Mankiw, Romer and Weil technological change has a limited role while human capital plays a dominant one. In addition, the discussion about the exogeneity of the engine of growth diminishes because the level of human capital is not, in any way, exogenous. The authors do not engage in explaining how and why a part of aggregate output is devoted to producing human capital, so it is not a properly endogenous variable, but the spillover effect of human capital on per capita growth makes the technological changes less important as an engine of growth.

Human capital is the key feature of Robert E. Lucas's model[10] from 1988. In his article, the first version of which was written for the Marshall lectures in 1985, he explores the engine of growth too. He wanted to show that there can be per capita growth without technological change and he eliminates it from the model. The model of Mankiw, Romer and Weil had shifted the focus from the technological change to the levels of human capital to explain per capita growth. Lucas showed that it could be eliminated. His model is based on physical and human capital, like the previous one we have examined. Physical capital and individual human capital have decreasing returns, but aggregate human capital exerts positive spillover effects. Therefore, depending on the aggregate human capital there is per capita economic growth. As long as aggregate human capital increases, so does its external effects on physical and individual human capital. Individuals split their non-leisure time between working and accumulating human capital depending on their preferences.

In this model, the key feature is the external effect of aggregate human capital on the productivity of physical and individual human capital because they counterweight and offset the decreasing returns of both factors of production. Another important issue is that economic agents choose their level of human capital by deciding to work less in the present to increase their stock of human capital that in turn will increase their future income. By so doing they are increasing the stock of human capital in the economy and fostering the productivity of human capital of other agents. The decision to devote more or less effort to acquiring human capital is endogenous. Lucas wants to stress that economic growth in his model is not exogenous, as in Solow's. It is the outcome of individual choices that are micro-economically grounded. Thus, his model gives more room to individual agents because they decide how much to invest in their own human capital.

Lucas's model does not rely on exogenous events to explain per capita growth. He proves that economic growth can be explained endogenously. But this statement only holds if positive spillovers arising from aggregate human capital exist. To establish if Lucas is right or wrong it is necessary to explain how and why those spillovers are present and to show that they are large enough to offset the decreasing returns of physical and individual human capital.

Since the first model of Solow we have shown that per capita growth cannot be accommodated with the usual assumption of aggregate diminishing returns of the production functions. To solve this, Solow's second model relies upon external technological shocks, while Mankiw, Romer and Weil point out that the level of human capital influences its productivity and Lucas stresses the external effect of individual human capital endogenously chosen. The three models are capable of explaining per capita growth but their engines of growth are quite different.

The endogeneity of economic growth that arises from Lucas's model is stronger and more defined in the model of Romer, which we are going to explain. His title is very meaningful[11] because Romer wanted to highlight that economic growth arises from endogenous phenomena as a consequence of purposeful decisions and activities of economic agents. He wanted to eliminate any trace of exogenous technological change and to stress the microeconomic foundations of economic growth. Aggregate production depends on labour, human capital and physical capital. He assumes that labour and human capital are fixed and focuses on physical capital.

There is only one final good, but many intermediate goods, so there are two sectors in the economy. Each set of intermediate goods are different and are not close substitutes. Intermediate goods are produced using human capital, forgone output and designs. Designs or instructions to produce intermediate goods cannot be kept secret. As a consequence, each producer of an intermediate good can use them without cost. The producers of intermediate goods are the only ones that manufacture them and they charge a monopolistic price, while the final good is produced in a competitive price setting. The monopolistic price of each intermediate good fosters innovation by adding new intermediate goods and the overall production of the final good depends on the size of the former, which increases continuously because designs can be used freely and without cost. In this case, as in the case of Lucas, agents can choose, so their characterization is broader than in Solow's models. Romer explains how profit-driven agents engage in the production of new designs to earn the monopolistic rents of a new intermediate good while for Lucas the expectations of large future earnings drive agents to increase their human capital.

The aim of Paul Romer is to explain that technological change driven by knowledge is the engine of growth. But he wants to stress that technological change is endogenous, not exogenous. The critical variable in this model is the assumption that designs, once produced, become a public good that enhances the production of intermediate inputs. They are partially excludible, non-rival inputs. Because they are partially excludible, firms that produce intermediate goods can earn monopolistic profits which encourage companies to engage in research. Because they are non-rival, other companies can take advantage of them to produce new intermediate inputs that increase their size and the final output. Thus, the critical assumption is that the number of intermediate inputs is important, and not only its overall amount to explaining output growth.

There are undeniable links between Romer's model and the model of Aghion and Howitt.[12] They both rely on technological change as the source of growth and they both believe that technological change is strictly endogenous so it can be explained through careful analysis of the behaviour of agents involved in research and production. But there are differences as well. Romer relies on the production of intermediate inputs while Aghion and Howitt rely on vertical innovations that are generated by a competitive research sector. The final amount of research determines growth rate.

Aghion and Howitt are mainly concerned with explaining growth rate. In their model, research intensity is ruled by a Schumpeterian creative destruction process. Every innovation is vertical, so the pre-existing ones become outdated and are displaced from the market. The owner of the latest vertical innovation earns the monopoly benefits while the pre-existing owners disappear. Innovation depends on the amount of resources devoted to it but the monopoly rents of an innovation, however, depend on the lapse of time until a new innovation takes place and displaces the incumbent from the market. The solution of the model implies that firms exhibit perfect foresight in that they can forecast the length of the abovementioned lapse of time to choose the optimal amount of investment in research.

The critical supposition in this case is that every single innovation affects the whole economy and increases final output. The consumption good is produced using unskilled labour and the intermediate good. So, the intermediate good is produced just with skilled labour and its quality increases along a quality ladder. The higher up the ladder, the more productive the intermediate good is and the more final output grows. The rhythm of the innovation race is ruled by the Schumpeterian creative destruction process explained above.

Reviewing more models of economic growth is beyond the scope of this chapter. In the next section, we will show that many other models display the same set of critical variables we have analysed up to now, even though other features are very different. This brief review of the models highlights an important fact: economic growth models rely on several, sometimes very different, critical variables. As a consequence, the criterion to assess whether they are better or worse is to what extent they fit the data and if their critical variables are more or less trustworthy.

## The Evolution of Growth Theory: A Process of Improvement. Exogenous and Endogenous Growth Theory

Solow's first model,[13] or more precisely the model that was outlined independently by Robert Solow and Trevor Swan,[14] was a success because of its simplicity and tractability. Solow chose a path of drastic simplification even though he was aware of the complexity of economic growth. Thus, the obvious line of improvement is the inclusion of more hypotheses and variables into his model to cope with the true complexity of the phenomenon.

Solow's second model[15] addressed an evident weakness of the previous: per capita growth. Data showed per capita growth in the majority of developed countries and the model could not explain it. In the initial model, before an economy arrives at its steady state there can be per capita growth, but it ceases to exist once the steady state has been reached. Solow added an exogenous technological change to explain per capita growth and his model improved. Using the model, many experts engaged in growth accounting exercises that clarified many issues though this cast some doubts about the model as well.[16]

The exogenous technological change explained per capita growth but at the same time pushed forward the topics under discussion. Economists were not at ease with exogeneity, while recognizing that the model was very useful and easily tractable. Some attempts were made to explain economic growth endogenously such as the AK model[17] and the learning by doing model[18] but they were not as complete as Solow's. In addition, growth accounting was impossible using these models and theorists seldom used them.

At this point we have to stress the importance of data in the development of growth theory. Growth models aimed, and still aim, at fitting the data. Data was scarce in the 1950s because good national accounts were only available in developed countries, while developing ones lacked the adequate statistical apparatus to gather information. In addition some variables were not homogenous across countries. As a consequence models were tested using these data. Over time, the effort of gathering information and organizing it was fostered by economic policy requirements and the amount of economic series increase along with their accuracy. New and different data posed new challenges to growth theory as we are going to explain. But at the same time the novelties allowed experts to engage in more in-depth analysis and to enter more into details that were out of reach in the 1950s. The evolution of growth theory has been partially determined by data availability.

The data set collected by Maddison[19] and Summers and Heston[20] took to the forefront the cross-country convergence controversy. Previously, to a certain extent, the available data backed the fact that there was convergence across countries, as Solow predicted. The new data incorporated more countries and more periods and it clearly showed that convergence failed to happen. Backward countries did not catch up with the advanced countries. This was not consistent with Solow's model and it fostered new theoretical approaches. The majority of them are classified as endogenous growth theory. They are different from AK and learning by doing models because they establish the rationale for agents to act. There was much evidence of the fact that many markets are not competitive, that technological change is an intentional activity and that general purpose knowledge can be used freely. But it was impossible to accommodate these facts into a workable model for technical reasons, because the introduction of increasing returns or oligopolistic competition was difficult. So, the next step in improving growth theory was made by building completely different models to take into account the new facts and the explanatory needs for new data.

In his 1986 model,[21] Paul Romer enlarged the classical production function by adding the results of the research and development of each firm. This activity exhibits individual decreasing returns but there are spillovers so firms can freely take advantage of them to increase their own output without cost. The spillovers generate a stock of knowledge that behaves as a public good. Departing from this point he wrote another article in 1987.[22] In it he showed that there were technological spillovers because of purposeful research and development activities of individual firms whose rewards they could not capture. Thus, the output of single firms depends on their own amount of factors and the overall amount of labour and capital in the economy that determines the size of the spillover. Making simulations, Romer showed that this specification matched the growth rates of different countries fairly well and explained why catch-up processes did not happen: less developed countries could not benefit from technological spillovers that arose from research and development activities.

The next step was to properly endogenize the engine of growth. To do so, Romer describes the functioning of a two-sector economy in another article in 1990[23] which we have examined in the previous section. Here we want stress that this third article was the logical consequence of the two we have mentioned before. On the one hand, Romer wanted to correct the failures by explaining the data on convergence. On the other hand, his intention was to accomplish the first task using a model where growth was an endogenous phenomenon. The way in which he attained his goal is very meaningful in explaining the process of improvement in growth theory. The first aim was the adequacy for the data. Models that do not fit the new data must be reformed or abandoned. This is a main tenet of growth theory and one that continuously improves it. The second aim is the effort to provide sound microeconomic foundations in explaining economic growth. This has been a general trend in macroeconomics from the beginning of the 1980s, as we are going to show in the third part of this chapter (pp. 86–9), and growth theory has led the way. In our opinion, modelling macroeconomics with good microeconomic foundations is necessary even though in some cases it is not straightforward because the most suitable microeconomic foundations are not as workable as we would like.

Romer was not the only one to use microeconomic foundations to explain economic growth. On the contrary, the articles spread a wave of microeconomically grounded models. We have explained Lucas's model in the first part of the chapter (see pp. 78–9).[24] Agents decide their level of human capital by devoting more time to invest in it instead of producing and consuming. Thus, their microeconomic decision to consume less in the present in order to increase their individual human capital stock is key. The aggregate level of human capital generates spillovers that offset the decreasing returns of each production factor so the economy does not exhibit a steady state. Both models rely on microeconomic foundations to explain economic growth even though the type is different.

From the late 1980s on, virtually all models of economic growth are based on microeconomic foundations. A salient feature of economic growth models after Romer is that they stress the meaningfulness of different variables or processes to explain economic growth. We are going to cite only those that we believe have enlarged the field of study, though many others may deserve attention as well. A very good example is Grossman and Helpman's model.[25] The engine of growth is knowledge. New knowledge, either through product improvements or new products, guarantees oligopolistic competition rents so individual agents dedicates resources to create it. Knowledge accumulates as a byproduct of manufacturing and can be freely used by other firms. These spillover effects drive growth. In their model of a small open economy, trade policies can further foster growth if they encourage investment in knowledge-based sectors. In addition, if the economy is open enough, firms can take advantage of the stock of knowledge of other countries to increase output.

Another example is the above-cited model of Aghion and Howitt. Romer's model relies on oligopolistic competition in the production of different intermediate goods that increase per capita output. The model of Aghion and Howitt stresses vertical innovation that substitutes intermediate inputs by new and better ones that increase productivity and expel the previous products from the market. The Schumpeterian flavour of this model includes the creative destruction and influences the arrival rate of new innovations. As such, this rate determines growth rate.

The model of Mankiw, Romer and Weil we have discussed in the first section is a kind of amendment to endogenous growth models. It shows that adding human capital to a standard Solow's model with technology per capita growth can be explained. The aggregate level of human capital generates spillover effects that offset the decreasing returns of labour and physical capital. The predictions of this enlarged model of Solow fit the data very well and the model shows a slow convergence rate. Mankiw, Romer and Weil claim that to explain the engine of growth it is not necessary to introduce endogeneity into the model. Thus, they focus on fitting the data as the only criterion to judge whether a model is good or not. In addition, they point out some potential weaknesses of endogenous growth models that may reduce their usefulness.

This point has been addressed in two articles by Charles Jones.[26] In the first article he stresses that endogenous growth models of the type we have explained above imply that permanent changes in some endogenous variables have permanent effects on growth rates. Using data from the US and OECD countries, he shows that many endogenous variables have increased considerably, but their permanent effects on growth rate are absent or they have been offset by other factors. He applies this general framework to test if the key variables that explain growth in several endogenous models, including those we have outlined above, have increased. The answer is positive, but economic growth rate has not increased at the same pace so there is a failure somewhere in these models.

The second article addresses the scale effects of the level of resources devoted to R&D on economic growth. He highlights that the amount of these resources in the US has increased more than four times from 1950 to 1987 while per capita growth rates have not. Jones examines this data and takes it further. He affirms that economic growth models must be based on solid microeconomic foundations but without driving theorists to misleading statements. He outlines an endogenous growth model in which technological advance depends on the total amount of manpower multiplied by a specific rate. Thus, this rate depends on a parameter that represents the previous technological level. This parameter is the unity in the endogenous growth models explained above and is null in Solow's model. He demonstrates that the value implicitly assumed in endogenous growth models is very unlikely.

The discussion of Jones highlights two things: On the one hand, there is wide consensus among growth theorists in establishing the microeconomic foundations of their models. On the other hand, microeconomic foundations must produce numerical outcomes that fit the data. Otherwise, they are incorrectly specified and have to be revised. These two implicit rules have been followed by theorists that have built new economic growth models. The successive theoretical improvements have consisted in showing that additional variables play a key role in explaining economic growth.

Before Grossman and Helpman, models explained economic growth in closed economies. They paved the way for a wide array of models exploring the interplay between economic growth and international mobility of goods, people and capital. One salient issue is the diffusion of technology that can be incorporated in capital goods or in learning by doing processes or in imitation processes. Since technology is a key variable in explaining growth, with or without spillover effects, the possibility of using technology developed in other countries can play a key role in internal economic growth. Barro and Sala-i-Martin's model[27] is a good example of this.

Some models have addressed labour mobility through migration. Closed models rely only on internal population as a factor of production but migration modifies part of the setting and, as a consequence, the outcome of growth models. Migration influences growth in several ways that have been explored by theorists. Some examples are Braun's model[28] and Weil's model.[29] Other models stress the role played by finance in economic growth. The raw version of capital that the first models of economic growth displayed has been improved greatly by models based on a continuum of intermediate inputs and those based on vertical innovation. Finance theorists have shed light on the increasing complexity of financing and the influence it exerts on economic growth. A good survey is Levine's article.[30]

Over the last ten years the role of economic institutions in growth has attracted great interest. In many cases the differences between the economic institutions of different countries, whatever the reasons behind them, matter considerably and influence the economic performance of each country.[31] But to include the role of institutions in mathematical models is not straightforward. On the one hand, due to the lack of appropriate data as it is difficult to measure the institutions. On the other hand, mathematical models can seldom cope with the implicit complexity they exhibit. Nevertheless, the analysis of the weight of economic institutions on economic growth has improved and it is a promising research field in itself. A very good survey has been written by Acemoglu.[32]

Growth theory has not been harmed by the financial crisis, contrary to what happened to RBC theory, as we will explain in the fifth part of this chapter (pp. 94–8). First, growth theory addresses long-run phenomena while the crisis belongs to the medium term. In addition, the crisis has not hit countries worldwide, it has hit mainly developed countries. Second, growth theory is not a single model that can be falsified by a specific set of events. On the contrary, the diversity of models addressing different variables to explain growth ensures that some of them may have proven to be defective but others have performed fairly well. Growth theory keeps on improving and its future is promising because it has been able to improve how it fits the data, as well as its internal structure.

Additionally, the improvements have been driven by a careful analysis of economic facts, not only data. Present-day models are more complex, more reliable and more able to explain economic growth than Solow's because theorists have learned how to take into account more relevant facts. Moreover, they are looking for ways to fully incorporate the effects of the institutional framework in the models, even though modelling it is very difficult. There are many challenges ahead, but the evolution of growth theory over the last fifty years reassures us about the possibilities of facing and overcoming these challenges.

## Critical and Auxiliary Variables in RBC Theory

Fynn Kydland and Edward Prescott stated: 'That wine is not made in a day has long been recognized by economists'.[33] This phrase was the beginning of their seminal article, the first version of the RBC model. They pointed out that a correct characterization of investment in each economy has to take into account the 'time to build'. Once the investment decision is made, it takes time for the investment good to be available. They stressed that this feature had been forgotten in previous investment models. As a consequence, they were unable to accurately explain the medium-term cycles of the economy.

Then, they added: 'A thesis of this essay is that the assumption of multiple-period construction is crucial for explaining aggregate fluctuations'.[34] They explained the advantages of this view over the prevailing approach, the single capital good technology. In addition to this new approach, Kydland and Prescott's RBC theory introduces many novelties. RBC theory proposes a completely new approach to the analysis of the medium-term economic cycles. Even though they state that economists before Keynes had already developed it, such a statement is doubtful. In fact, RBC theory should be considered a disruptive paradigm in this field in the sense of Lakatos, as we have discussed in Chapter 3. As we are going to explain afterwards, RBC theory dismantled and rejected the main tenets of the precedent Keynesian approach to aggregate fluctuations. As Solow's approach to economic growth, RBC theory was a starting point, or a new proposal. The success of RBC theory in explaining the facts of aggregate fluctuations and on fitting the data we are going to stress in the next pages, made it the dominant paradigm. It was generally accepted and many theorists made use of it as a common framework of analysing medium-run economics. Thus, it became an established paradigm very early on and, following Kuhn, the phase of 'normal science' started. Experts did not discuss their foundations anymore but use it as a general framework of analysis.

The departure point of RBC theory is Solow's growth theory, which we have examined in the first two sections of this chapter. The key feature of Solow's model is that each variable has a steady state level to which it approaches. This level will be reached sooner or later because of dynamics generated by the subjacent variables of the economy. In Solow's model, these variables are savings rate, depreciation rate and population growth rate. Thus, each economy displays its own steady state equilibrium which is different across countries. The performance of the economy in terms of output can easily be calculated in the present and predicted into the future if we know the values of the above-mentioned key variables. If these values change, the steady state level changes as well. It can take time for the economy to reach the new steady state, but its trajectory can be easily calculated.

Kydland, Prescott and other RBC theorists borrow this approach from growth theory and apply it to medium-term fluctuations. Before RBC, economic cycles were supposedly a roller coaster. RBC theory has shown that there are highs and lows but they are minor and they do not necessarily follow each other; economic variables, including GDP can grow for some periods without experiencing a decrease. The real picture of business cycles is not a movement of endless ups and downs, but a straight line that shows minor disturbances.

This roller-coaster scenario implies that the economy in the medium term is seldom balanced and that disequilibrium prevails. The approach chosen by RBC theory, whose main features we are going to explain later, implies that the economy is almost always in equilibrium or near to equilibrium. This approach is supported by data but it has strong implications for policymaking as well.

Before Kydland and Prescott, Sargent[35] pointed out that co-movements among variables deserved a more in-depth analysis, while highs and lows did not. He believed that equilibrium was much more frequent, so we had to focus on the evolution of the variables over time and the co-movements among them. These co-movements are the structural features of an economy. Highs and lows are the consequence of external shocks that cannot be forecasted. It is not worthwhile to study them because they are less frequent and do not affect the structure of the economy. RBC theorists share this approach which prioritizes the analysis of the transmission mechanism over the impulse mechanism.

This approach is just the opposite of Keynesianism. On the one hand, a Keynesian economy is nearly always out of equilibrium and theorists focus on the causes of the disequilibrium and how to rebalance the economy. On the other hand, Keynesians stress that disequilibrium arises from endogenous factors that can be corrected by an appropriate set of economic policies.

Kyndland and Prescott explain that fluctuations are deviations from the trend. The trend is defined by the computational procedure used to fit the curve to the data. The standard procedure to calculate it is the Hodrick and Prescott filter which aims at minimizing the sum of the squared deviations from a given series while doing so as smoothly as possible. The final outcome is a trade-off between the value of the series and the smoothness of the trend. Once defined, the trend is used to calculate the deviations of each series, its cycle.

The main features of the model are the following: in any economy there is a representative infinitely lived household that aims at maximizing its utility. The household obtains utility of consumption and leisure in each period and it must decide how to split its time between both to maximize its utility. As usual, future utility is discounted by the intertemporal preference rate. The time to build assumption implies that multiple periods are needed to build new capital goods, and only finished capital goods are included in the capital stock despite the fact that all of them require resources.

The representative household takes into account present and future consumption and leisure. Consequently, household preferences exhibit non-time-separable utility. This crucial feature implies a greater intertemporal substitution of leisure. As such, households react to technological changes by increasing the ratio present leisure/future leisure or vice versa. Its reaction heavily depends on the kind of shock, temporary or permanent. Shocks are unexpected and unanticipated, but the representative household adapts to the new circumstances by choosing to work more or less today or in the future. This hypothesis is necessary to explain the aggregate changes in employment over time in an equilibrium model.

Markets are competitive and prices of goods, services, labour and money change very quickly to adapt to the new demand and supply schedules as a consequence of an external shock. Money does not perform any role.[36] When a shock happens real variables change to adapt to the new situation depending on the representative household preferences. Real balances change to suit the new equilibrium level of output and interest rates. Kydland's and Prescott's refusal to include monetary issues aims at establishing a firewall between its model and the Keynesian approach. They wanted to set a new paradigm and they made it. Thus, monetary issues and financial issues are absent from the model. This feature has proved to be very important in explaining why the model has failed to predict the crisis.

The interplay between agent preferences and technological shocks can explain aggregate fluctuations. As Prescott said: 'Economic theory implies that, given the nature of the shocks to technology and people's willingness and ability to intertemporally and intratemporally substitute, the economy will display fluctuations like those the US economy displays'.[37] This is a key statement. RBC theory is correct if it matches the data. This has been the main criterion to judge the theory from its very beginning. As we are going to explain in the next section, the original model could not correctly explain part of the data and this fact fostered the analyses to improve it. Thus, RBC theory became a theoretical success.

RBC theory also challenged the meaning of economic fluctuations. The Keynesian approach had considered the economic cycle to be a disequilibrium phenomenon, implying that there were malfunctions or weaknesses in the economy that generated the cycle. From this assumption it follows that some kind of economic policy should be adopted to reduce the size and length of fluctuations. RBC theory strongly disagrees with this approach: 'Economic fluctuations are optimal responses to uncertainty in the rate of technological change'.[38]

RBC theorists believe that there are two different but related issues. On the one hand, the impulse mechanism, the shock, that is supposedly external to the economy. In the first stages of the theory shocks are always technological, but we will explain in the next section that other shocks have been added to improve the explanatory power of the theory.

On the other hand, we have to examine the transmission mechanism. After the shock, rational agents react and change their intertemporal and intratemporal consumption/leisure decisions to maximize their utility without changing their preferences. Since shocks cannot be predicted their previous choices are no longer optimal and they have to adjust to the new circumstances. Their new choices become optimal again, because they are very well suited to the new environment.

But if their reactions are optimal, as RBC theorists claim, agents choose the best available option, so economic policy cannot outperform it. On the contrary, economic policy is very likely to hamper agents by preventing them from reacting correctly. So, economic policy should not focus on stabilizing the economy because the stabilization process is automatic. Policymakers must refrain from intervening in the self-correcting process. They must focus on the elements that favour technological advance and how to foster it. Sooner or later the technological advances will generate positive technological shocks that will improve the well-being of society.

The general framework of RBC theory is strictly classical, with solid microeconomic foundations that display the acting of rational agents facing external shocks and adapting to them. In the model, the intertemporal and intratemporal substitution of leisure is critical because it allows agents to adapt to new circumstances. Competitive markets are an important piece of the model but we will show in the next section that RBC theory can run without this hypothesis if we introduce some neo-Keynesian flavour into the model. That money does not play any role in the model is a departure point for Kydland and Prescott in clearly distinguishing its model from a Keynesian one, but some experts have shown that money plays a role as part of the impulse mechanism. We will explain this in the next section. The most critical issue is the supposition that shocks are always unanticipated and exogenous. The former is the element of surprise that obliges rational agents to revise their choices in a new environment. Since they are supposedly rational and well informed, anticipated shocks would be taken into account before they happen. The latter was rooted in a strong rejection of the Keynesian approach when the new paradigm was launched, but as the theory evolved some experts explained that endogenous but unanticipated shocks could perform the same role and have the same consequences. Others kept relying on external shocks as the only source of changes.

From the point of view of our meta-theory, RBC models are easy to understand. The characterization of the agents is a key feature of the model because one of the main tenets of RBC theory is the microeconomic foundations of economic agents' behaviour. The agents apply the principle of economic behaviour by maximizing their utility in the case of consumers, or maximizing profits in the case of firms. There is a representative agent that can be envisaged as a kind of 'average agent' that drives utility from consumption and leisure in many, in some cases infinite, periods of time. This agent is able to take into account the information supplied by the environment, mainly the prices of goods, money and labour, to reach its aim. The same applies for each single firm. Firms do not have market power. Perfect competition prevails so all prices change very quickly to adapt to supply and/or demand changes. The interplay between rational agents that can process every single bit of information and perfectly competitive markets is the key to ensuring that market equilibrium prevails, while disequilibrium does not.

All these features belong to the standard mainstream microeconomic model in which the characterization of the agent and the operational environment are closely interlinked. As we are going to explain in the next section, the improvements of RBC theory did not change this general framework and the main criterion for deciding if the model was good or not was whether it fitted the data. Thus, we are not going to review the characterization of the agents and the operational environment in the next section.

## The Evolution of RBC Theory: Improvements and Biases

The improvement process of RBC started very early. Many theorists adapted it as a very useful tool for the analysis of medium-term fluctuations. They realized there were discrepancies between the theory and the data that had to be addressed because the adequacy of the theory to the data was the criterion in determining if the theory performed well or not. Thus, the theory evolved by facing the challenges that the data posed and following its own internal logic. This is, according Kuhn, 'normal science'. We are first going to study the improvements regarding the transmission mechanism and then we are going to look at the impulse mechanism.

The labour market was the main challenge because the outcome of the model and the data were different and even contradicted each other. The data showed that hours worked fluctuated much more than productivity and that the correlation between hours worked and productivity was nearly zero. Hansen and Wright addressed the first issue.[39] It was difficult to explain how small productivity changes caused fluctuations in the hours worked because there were only technological shocks in the economy depicted by RBC theory. It was necessary to assume that short-run labour supply elasticity was large, but the initial RBC model could not explain this feature.

Hansen and Wright postulate that utility depends not only on present leisure but on past leisure as well and that households exhibit no separable preferences. As a consequence agents change the quantity of hours worked considerably to respond to small productivity changes. They want to take advantage of productivity improvements, whether they are small or large. Agents' behaviour is different depending on the kind of shock. If they believe the shock is temporary, they react by changing the amount of hours worked. But it they believe that the shock is permanent they do not change their hours-worked pattern. So, Hansen and Wright reconcile the short-term evidence with the reduction in hours worked in the long run.

A second improvement is described in Hansen's 1985 paper.[40] He states that changes in labour input come about because of changes in the amount of workers, not due to changes in the hours worked. In his model, workers can choose either working a fixed number of hours per day or not working at all. In equilibrium, a random process allocates individuals to jobs. As a consequence, individual labour supply elasticity is small because leisure is valuable as well. But aggregate labour supply elasticity is large and it can explain the response of labour input to small productivity changes.

A second shortcoming was the large positive correlation between productivity and hours worked that the model showed but the data did not confirm. In this case, the improvement came from two different extensions of the model. Christiano and Eichenbaum[41] added government spending shocks. Agents cannot forecast them, so their effects are similar to supply-side shocks, as we have explained in the previous section. Christiano and Eichenbaum stress that they are unanticipated, even though they are not exogenous. They suppose that private and public consumption are not perfect substitutes, so an increase in government spending reduces individual wealth. Agents react by working more because leisure is a normal good. This change can be viewed as labour supply schedule moving to the right and the model displays a relationship between hours worked and productivity that fits the data.

Benhabib, Rogerson and Wright[42] explain that the utility of agents depends not only on market-produced goods, but on home-produced goods as well.

Thus, leisure adds utility but the time spent at home producing consumer goods generates disutility. As a consequence, on the one hand, agents can increase the number of hours worked in the market by reducing the hours worked at home without reducing their utility. On the other hand, supposing that shocks to household production and shocks to market production exhibit no perfect correlation, agents can easily substitute home activity for market activity and vice versa. For instance, if there is a negative shock to market production, agents shift to household production. As a consequence the model fits the data because it shows a weak correlation between productivity and hours worked.

Another good example of improvement is Cooley's and Hansen's model.[43] Kydland and Prescott have stated that money does not generate the cycle.[44] But Cooley and Hansen remind us that Friedman's work was very influential in RBC theory and they offer a model where money plays a role in generating fluctuations. Money is introduced into the model using a cash-in-advance constraint and it only affects consumption because money cannot buy leisure. Investment is not affected either. According to the monetarist tradition, if money is supplied following a rule that all agents know, it performs a neutral role provided the amount of money supplied meets the requirements of the economy. Conversely, if money is supplied in an irregular manner and without taking into account the evolution of the real side of the economy, cyclical fluctuations arise because agents cannot anticipate this irregular pattern. The cash-in-advance constraint only holds in the second case. Consumption volatility is larger than in the first case and price level is quite volatile as well. Besides, correlations between these variables and GDP are smaller. Therefore, the introduction of an erratic money supply in the model improves the explanation of co-movements.

As a consequence of all these improvements, RBC theory fulfilled its main aim: to suit the data. At the beginning the model could be used to explain the evolution of the US economy. More generally, Kydland and Prescott stated that the model could be used to explain the evolution of other developed economies because its general features were nearly the same. The data of other countries was compared with the theoretical results of the enlarged model, the one that incorporates all the improvements of the transmission mechanism. A very wide research field opened in several countries that proved to be successful. Comparisons among different countries were carried out as well and a set of 'stylized facts' emerged. The conclusion was that the RBC transmission mechanism was working very well. In addition, we have to recall that from the beginning of the 1980s smooth economic growth prevailed in developed countries, if we set aside the dotcom crisis. During this period RBC theory improved and refined its analysis and focused more and more on the transmission mechanism, because there were no large shocks. The improvements made did not change the characterization of agent, they just added several mechanisms to shape the model in a way that fitted the data better.

The impulse mechanism did not deserve the same attention for two reasons. On the one hand, because it was exogenous or at least unexpected as we have explained before. On the other hand, because the trend of growth in many countries was smooth, no matter if it was large or small. This smoothness was proof that the impulse mechanism was not very important. However, some experts were conscious of the fact that the size of actual technological shocks was not enough to explain economic fluctuations.

A cornerstone of RBC theory is what Prescott said in an article: 'The finding that when uncertainty in the rate of technological change is incorporated into the growth model it displays the business cycle phenomena was both dramatic and unanticipated'.[45]

The majority of economists endorsed this idea but some of them did not agree. Besides, as we have explained before, other economists believed that technological shocks were not strong enough to unleash cyclical movements. We survey here the main models that tried to improve the impulse mechanism in both ways.

Jordi Galí,[46] a neo-Keynesian economist, criticizes the role of technological shocks on aggregate fluctuations. He builds a different model containing monopolistic competition and sticky prices and analyses the effects of a monetary shock on this model. Money supply grows smoothly according to the technological growth of the economy. As a consequence every technological shock implies a monetary shock. His main finding is that the monetary shock generates a positive co-movement between hours worked and productivity but technological shocks show a negative co-movement. Overall, there is no correlation between productivity and hours worked, fitting the data.

> whether the technology shocks in *actual* economies are responsible for the pattern of GDP and labour-input fluctuations associated with business cycles remains and open question, and one which should provide a critical test of the relevance of a research program that aims to interpret the bulk of aggregate fluctuations as resulting from those shocks.[47]

Other experts maintain that TFP changes are the origin of fluctuations but that other factors amplify them, so small technological shocks can produce the fluctuations that the data show. Burnside, Eichenbaum and Rebelo[48] analyse the amount of work throughout the cycle. They stress that output depends on workers' effort and not only on hours worked. When there is a positive technological shock, firms encourage their workers to increase their effort by paying them more. As a consequence, work effort is pro-cyclical and can partly explain output growth. Thus, a small technological shock drives an upward change in labour effort and a larger increase in output. Applying the same pattern to capital goods,[49] they switch the focus from the amount of capital to the use of it. As in the case of labour, a positive technological shock increases capital utilization and the effect of a small technological shock is amplified as well. Their estimates show that the effect of productivity shocks on GDP decreases up to 70 per cent, but increasing work effort and capital utilization generate the same output fluctuation.

Another approach was proposed by Bernanke, Gertler and Gilchrist.[50] They explain that market credit frictions increase the effects of shocks on output fluctuations. There are agency costs in the intermediation process between lenders and borrowers, which are based on asymmetric information. 'Rich' borrowers invest part of their own money and borrow the rest. As a consequence their incentives and lender's incentives are aligned. Less affluent borrowers cannot invest their own money and must borrow more money. In this case their incentives and lender's incentives may not be aligned and the increase of agency costs drives down the amount of credit. Generally speaking, agent's net wealth is pro-cyclical so when there is economic growth, agency costs diminish and the credit flow eases. This is a financial accelerator that amplifies the positive effect of shocks. Conversely, when economic growth is meagre, borrower's net wealth decreases and credit access worsens. Thus, a small negative shock is transformed by the financial accelerator into a larger output decrease. As an example, they show that an unexpected reduction of 25 base points of the federal funds interest rate increases output by 0,8 per cent after three quarters.

## The Limits of RBC Theory: The Impulse Mechanism

The improvements made in the impulse mechanism implied an implicit recognition of its weakness, including the fact that negative shocks were harder to explain than positive shocks. However, the smoothness of economic growth since 2001 led some economists to suppose that economic cycles had vanished or at least that their scope had reduced. As a consequence, further improvements of the impulse mechanism were not made. The financial crisis dramatically shifted the attention to the causes of the crisis, the impulse mechanism, and RBC theory was not ready to meet the challenge.

We have explained in the first chapter the 'No one saw it coming' version of the causes of the crisis. If we agree on this version we can say that the crisis was unexpected. In the previous section of this chapter we have outlined one improvement of the transmission mechanism of RBC theory that shows that a sudden change in public spending can generate the stylized facts we observe. But public spending is not an exogenous technological shock, so RBC can encompass non-technological shocks as well. The focus switches from the shock being exogenous or not to being expected or unexpected. Christiano and Eichenbaum stress that an unexpected shock can have the same consequences of an exogenous shock, and they prove it in their article. Consequently, if we accept that the financial crisis was an unexpected shock, the model can still run, because we concentrate on the consequences of this shock on the intertemporal consumption and labour choices.

As we have explained before, RBC theory concentrated on the transmission mechanism for two reasons. One, because the impulse mechanism was considered exogenous and unpredictable, so the efforts devoted to it were unproductive; and two, because the analysis of the transmission mechanism in many countries was very fruitful. This drift led RBC theory to become a theory of how an economy reacts to exogenous and/or unexpected shocks. As such, RBC theory was implicitly narrowing its scope. As a consequence RBC theory is useless in explaining why the crisis happened. The contributions made by RBC theory to the transmission mechanism are enormous and they will be valuable in the future. But the intellectual challenge now is to explain why the crisis came about and RBC theory is poorly suited for this task.

One additional issue has to be raised. We have shown in the first chapter that the 'No one saw it coming' version was not true. Many experts predicted the crisis, but they were not believed. After the crisis it can be stated that it was unexpected for the majority of economic agents because they acted as if they were unaware of its likelihood. Could they have believed otherwise? The answer is doubtful. If we posit that economic agents are fully rational they should have been aware of the coming crisis because there were enough signals and data. If they were not aware of the crisis, it is because they could not correctly interpret the information they had. As an example, more than three-quarters of Spanish home-builder firms in 2002 disappeared within ten years. They had the best available information about the sector and they realized it was very cyclical. However, they were trapped by the crisis as if they were newcomers in the sector. For them, the shock was unexpected as well and they had no contingency plans either. These facts point to a different issue: are economic agents as rational as RBC theory believes?

A second issue at stake is the size of the crisis. The improvements made in the impulse mechanism of RBC theory aimed at reducing the gap between the size of the technological shock and their effects. Experts, like Bernanke, realized that available figures of technological shocks could not explain the observed size of their consequences. There was a large mismatch. Amplifiers like erratic money supply helped to narrow the gap but they could not close it. As a consequence, the impulse mechanism was poorly suited to explain the GDP decrease during the financial crisis. In addition, and more important still, in RBC theory GDP decrease can only be driven by negative technological shocks amplified by other mechanisms. This kind of technological regress is very unlikely to happen and minor disturbances should have been followed by very large amplifier mechanisms, which are very unlikely as well. We have explained that Kydland and Prescott refused to concede any role to monetary issues and they only relied on the real side of the economy. This has been a critical supposition of RBC theory and it has not been refuted by the facts for more than twenty years. We want to stress that it was a supposition. Kydland and Prescott affirmed that the only shocks were technological and exogenous. The crisis has falsified this proposition. Exogenous technological shocks cannot explain what has happened. The impulse mechanism of RBC theory has failed to pass the test of the facts. According to Popper[51] a scientific theory cannot be verified by the facts, but it can be falsified. If it cannot be falsified it is not scientific. We have stressed several times that RBC theory was willing to explain the facts and fit the data. The improvements were aimed at meeting this objective and the theory succeeded in doing so as far as the transmission mechanism is concerned. But the impulse mechanism has not improved enough and it has proven to be unable to explain why the crisis has happened. The impulse mechanism has been falsified and must be discarded. This is a very serious weakness of RBC theory.

Returning to the model itself, in the third section of this chapter (pp. 86–90) we have outlined the main features of RBC theory. As long as it is a model of the real side of the economy, money does not play any role. And the same applies to finance and the financial system. Therefore the theory cannot explain a financial crisis. Financial issues are absent from the theory and they cannot be taken into account in any way. This flaw is common among many models. We will explain in the last chapter that the financial side of the economy has become increasingly important, but models and theories have not evolved to include it. The theoretical debates have focused on the historical dichotomy: classical approaches versus Keynesian approaches. Mainstream economics have incorporated many neo-Keynesian features in a general array of models, but the role of the financial side has been underestimated. From this point of view, RBC theory is disappointing because it cannot cope with financial issues.

From another point of view, financial issues are an important element of the economy that interplay with production and interchange so it cannot be seen as an exogenous part in any way. The financial crisis we have experienced, the consequences of which will be long-lasting, is endogenous, internal to the economic system. The perfect storm that has devastated some countries, impoverished others and hit the majority of developed economies has come about as a consequence of the internal dynamics of economic agents that are not well described by RBC theory in any way. The evidence of endogenous dynamics is cumbersome and we must take it into account in our models.

Last, but not least, there is economic policy. The crisis is a kind of natural experiment that allows us to measure the effects of different approaches to economic policy and different economic policies as well. In Chapter 5 we discuss the challenges faced by policymakers from the onset of the crisis and how they managed in trying to solve them. Here we recall that RBC theory implies that the economy is in equilibrium. External shocks disturb equilibrium but agents quickly reach a new equilibrium by taking into account the new circumstances in their intertemporal leisure and consumption choice. Therefore, public intervention cannot improve the final outcome, and it is very likely to worsen it. This is not a hypothesis of the model, but its logical consequence. The hypotheses are that agents are rational enough and that the economic system is flexible enough to reach the best available outcome given the circumstances. RBC theory displays these hypotheses because they belong to the backbone of every classical model and it cannot function without them.

The debate about the effectiveness of economic policy during the financial crisis is wide and very nuanced but the general picture is quite clear. Setting aside the details which will be examined in Chapter 5, we can state that there have been two opposite approaches to this issue. In the European Union and more precisely in the Eurozone, the recipe for recovery has been austerity and structural reforms. Some structural reforms have been undertaken while others have not and its application has differed among countries. But austerity has been the general rule. As a consequence, active fiscal policy has been absent. Monetary policy is designed and carried out by the European Central Bank, which has launched two rounds of quantitative easing aimed at stabilizing financial markets and at preventing the euro from collapsing. But its aim was not to help economic recovery, just to avoid the worst. In the US, the government and the Federal Reserve put into practice a more proactive economic policy aimed at improving economic growth and cutting down unemployment.[52]

We first address economic policy. Since RBC theory is an equilibrium theory, it is supposed that the adjustment of agents to the new environment is optimal. Thus, either the economic policy is useless or in fact it may worsen the final outcome. The two economic areas that have been affected the most by the turmoil are the US and the Eurozone.

Because of many factors we are not going to explain here, the Eurozone recipe to overcome the crisis has been austerity. The hypothesis is that our indebtedness level was too high and it had to be reduced by any means to rebound from the bottom and to grow again. Austerity is a process of reaching a new equilibrium without any economic policy at work. Thus, it fits the RBC approach to the crisis very well, because it implies that economies can recover without any external, say public, support. But our economies have not recovered. We suffered a deep recession in 2009 and after a slight, weak recovery in some countries in 2010 and 2011 the GDP of the Eurozone stagnated again. Four years after the beginning of the crisis, our economies have not recovered, and they seem to be very far from equilibrium.

Conversely and for many reasons the US has adopted a proactive attitude. From the very beginning the Federal Reserve and the US government have launched recovery programmes. They have used both fiscal and monetary policy to stimulate growth and to avoid the worst consequences of the crisis. Although the US economy plunged into recession in 2009, it has exhibited a continuous growth afterwards. Growth rates have not been brilliant, but the US economy has fared far better than the Eurozone from 2010 on. We may argue to what extent the economic policy of the Federal Reserve and the US government is solely responsible for the performance of the US economy. But the difference between the US and the Eurozone economies is undeniable. Economic policy has succeeded while the absence of it has not. This statement can be made now, when we observe the consequences of economic policy measures taken in different economic areas. But in 2007 and 2008, when the crisis hit the economies, the landscape was very different. The problem, and the urge, was how to act to solve an unexpected and unpredicted financial crisis. Experts and policymakers looked to their standard toolbox of models and theories for help and discovered that they were almost totally useless. And they started to improvise to solve the problems they were facing.

# 5 GOVERNMENTS AND THE FINANCIAL CRISIS: MAKING ECONOMIC POLICY IN THE DARK

What has been said in previous chapters about economic theory and modelling could have been just an idle mental exercise if the 2008 financial crisis had never happened. But it did, and it happened in such a way that we were shocked for months, uncertain about what was actually occurring. In this chapter we are going to review what the policymakers did during that time from the point of view of economic theory and modelling. In previous chapters we have looked at what we really know about economic processes. Now we are going to compare this with what policymakers did during that time, and examine which of these models and theories will survive the 'stress test' of the Great Recession. Of course this will not be a complete account of the entire sequence of events starting in 2007. Rather, it is simply a brief journey through a select number of policymaking decisions which marked a salient departure from the 'rules of the game'. It will not be a thorough historical examination of what was done in that time.

## Economic Policies during the Crisis

During the months before and after the fall of Lehman Brothers, policymakers worldwide had to face the political challenges of the most unexpected of all of the economic and financial crises up to that point. We have shown (see Chapter 1) that no economic theory or model was able to predict the Great Recession, with the exception of some insightful authors. Most of the economic researchers and think tanks – including the IMF and WB – never envisaged such an abrupt and deep recession at the core of the world economy. The financial and economic risks were almost invariantly linked to emergent and less developed countries. There were growing concerns about the huge US current account deficit and a sudden correction of the dollar in currency markets. At the same time, the EU was called 'Euroland' and it was hard to find anybody who foresaw a possible breakdown of the Eurozone. What the Federal Reserve and the ECB faced was an unexpected collapse of international financial markets with little or no information at all about what was happening inside the international banking system. A mix of a poor informative framework, myopic modelling and a blind faith in market wisdom created the 'perfect storm'. In Chapters 2 and 3 we analysed the logical structure of economic theories and modelling, and in Chapter 4 we saw that the mainstream macroeconomic modelling was not looking at those places where the storm was growing. Policymakers, working along the lines designed by economic theories, were installed in a 'benign neglect' policy, beginning with main central banks. According to textbooks, they simply had to focus on stabilizing unemployment and inflation rates, and leave the global and domestic financial issues in markets hands. For instance, global imbalances (e.g. US current account deficit) or debt accumulation were out of the scope of regular practice, as Greenspan stated two years before the crash. So when the financial crisis was unleashed, they (all of us) were first shocked and, later, wondering about how they were going to solve it. There did not seem to be a quick and smart solution to the problem, at least not using standard economic wisdom.

The first answer to the panic was the bailout of the international banking system. Even the soundest financial institutions were 'intoxicated' by sophisticated financial products issued mostly by Wall Street. The old Schumpeter idea of 'too big to fail' triggered apocalyptic images reminding one the worst days of the Great Depression and created fears of a global economic collapse. So the priority was to avoid a global bank rush and, in turn, a sudden and sharp contraction of the monetary aggregates, as happened in the 1930s. That contraction was, in fact, contained by the determined combined actions of the main central banks. What they could not stop were the spillover effects on the macroeconomic activity. As banking activity slowed, the non-financial sector began to struggle to repay and/or rollover debts, which in turn triggered the Great Recession.

The second wave of challenges came from the macroeconomic side. A classic aggregate demand recession was developing and most Western countries answered with the classic toolkit: an expansive fiscal and/or monetary policy mix. The US relied on both, but mainly on the monetary side, and the EU did so timidly on the fiscal side. The old Keynesian handbooks were recovered from dusty shelves and put on the tables of the global political leaders, no matter their political affiliation. But when the worst seemed to have passed, the Eurozone debt crisis erupted and again threatened the global economy with a 'double dip' recession. The problem was that the Keynesian handbook was no longer available: the financial crisis had toppled the fiscal revenues and there was no funding at hand to implement a second round of economic stimulus. So the austerity measures had to be implemented and a second and longer slump began throughout the European periphery, affecting the economic growth of the whole area.

So, why did everything go wrong? Why were we unable to solve the problem without a prohibitive toll on taxes and unemployment? We can blame politicians, nothing new. But we can also recognize that the regular economic modelling was of no help during those days. We can begin with humbly recognizing that key parts of the functioning of the financial system were (and still are) out of the scope of macroeconomic modelling or, simply, are not categorized as a 'macroeconomic problem'. They were not and still are not in the research agenda of mainstream macroeconomic researchers. So, the policymakers' 'toolkit' was incomplete and they did the only thing they are able to do: swamp the financial market with fresh money and the economy with massive fiscal stimulus. And it could be said that they did what they were supposed to do according to the theory. Nevertheless, the data demonstrate that it has not been enough.

All those solutions implemented after the 2007 turmoil broke with the explicit international consensus and rules adopted in the previous years. The massive troubled assets purchases or the banks bailouts all over the world were among the kind of things that the so-called *Washington Consensus* did not recommend as a policy measures. When the Federal Reserve began to monetize debt, both public and private, it *de facto* left the international consensus that the IMF and other institutions implemented during two decades in countries which looked for its financial support. But the point here is not if the Federal Reserve did or did not act according to the consensus standards. The point is that it acted as it did because of the opportunity costs of not doing so. If the Federal Reserve had not purchased that massive amount of toxic assets, the whole world would have faced a financial collapse of unprecedented consequences. This is just an example to illustrate that policymakers have regularly chosen *ad hoc* solutions to avoid the collapse, rather than implement a comprehensive programme to solve the problems caused by the crisis. Of course they can be blamed for that, but we can also wonder if they were endowed with the appropriate tools for implementing such a programme.

As the events unfolded, there was a growing consciousness that there was a huge lack of information and accountability regarding the activities of the financial system. And that has had manifold implications. First, after years of deregulation, the banking industry has concealed risky investments, excessive borrowing and unacceptable leverage levels in off-balance-sheet entities or derivative positions. Second, the evolution of financial markets from 2003 until now seems to challenge the efficient market hypothesis: if we assume that prices convey all the relevant information about financial assets, we can conclude that the 'true relevant information' is scarce and/or masked somewhere in the balances of entities. Third, if the information collected by regulatory agencies and central banks is inaccurate, should they change the data collection process and/or the sort of data themselves? And finally, what should they do with that data? Should they abort financial bubbles or, as they have been doing, 'mop up after'?

From the mid-1980s, the banking industry has suffered a huge transformation mainly due to the deregulatory policies which followed the end of the Bretton

Woods system and the opening up of international capital flows. Focarelli and Pozzolo[1] point towards the *de facto* repeal of the Glass–Steagall Act of 1933, the euro and the unique market banking in Europe and the Basel agreements of 1988 among other key milestones in this process. One of the most important outcomes of this transformation has been the development of shadow banking, at least from the point of view of the 2008 financial crisis. Shadow banks work more or less in the same way as traditional banks, conducting credit and maturity transformation, but they do so without direct, explicit access to the sources of liquidity and tail risk insurance available through the Federal Reserve and the Federal Deposit Insurance Corporation.[2] The lack of such access makes them more fragile than the traditional banks. The problem is that their activity has been intertwined with that of regulated institutions such as bank holding companies and insurance companies, amplifying the systemic risk as a whole.

Developments within the Euro Area follow quite a similar pattern from the point of view of monitoring and surveillance by policymakers. According to the Maastricht Treaty, the only macroeconomic imbalances every government should have had to adjust to were the inflation rate and government deficit and debt. From 1999 to 2011, both the European Commission and the European Central Bank were never seriously worried about the massive external intra-euro deficits and debt. Investors were confident that, in the case of a balance-of-payment crisis, the intervention of those institutions would solve the liquidity problems. But when international capital markets dried up, the financial markets' speculations about a break-up of the currency union led to a capital flight from the countries in trouble. The slow reaction from Eurozone authorities just fostered the fears of the euro vanishing and added more financial pressure to debt-troubled countries. Five years later, the Eurozone is still struggling to attain a second recovery, but it seems that the euro has survived.

## Why do Economic Policy and Economic Theories Differ so Much?

From 2008 onwards we have witnessed a growing decoupling between economic policy and economic modelling and theory. While from the very beginning the policymakers have been using what they labelled 'unconventional' economic policy responses, the mainstream and non-mainstream researchers have been looking at them through the lenses of their respective core hypotheses and modelling, and it is hard to see sizeable changes in their regular *praxis*. Mainstream economics seemed to be overtaken by the fast sequence of events. Heterodox economics seemed to be stuck in their core positions, and there was a déjà vu thrill in most of their works, as they insist on 'we told you' statements and scarcely offer fresh research. Here we are going to focus on mainstream economics as it has been the framework for most economic policy during the whole process, and particularly on RBC and its impulse-mechanism scheme.

Following most of the post-2008 literature, we can identify at least three main factors that triggered the global financial and economic crisis: global imbalances, financial innovation and intra-European imbalances. Although all of them are closely intertwined, they are quite definite and separate processes. Global imbalances, mainly the huge US current account deficit and its surplus counterparts in China, Gulf countries and Japan, have been pointed at as one of the causes of the global recession,[3] although it has been far less known by mass media and policymakers and academics outside those specialized in Economics. The financial innovations that allowed the fast development of the shadow banking system has been blamed worldwide as the main processes but, as we shall see in Chapter 6, it is difficult to understand this development without the first one. And finally, the global economic recession was undoubtedly worsened by the euro crisis, as the global liquidity drought brought about by the financial turmoil hit the Eurozone's weakest countries. We have to deal with these issues a little bit more to understand why economic theory and modelling really missed the mark in the years before the crisis.

Global imbalances have been a key factor in the chain of events that triggered the 2008 financial crisis.[4] The striking issue is that while they are the only factor that was identified as a problem from the very beginning, they have been the least mentioned in the up-to-date accounts of the crisis and it is only seen in the international finance and monetary system literature. The concerns about global imbalances both in theory and policy can be traced back to the IMF/WB meeting held in 2003, and they have been an international policy issue since then. At the same time, research and literature about them started to flourish. During these years, the understanding of the causes and the consequences has varied considerably. Earlier research was focused on the current account positions held by mainly the world's biggest economies and their unwinding. But since then, the focus has shifted to the architecture of the international monetary system,[5] then to imbalances in domestic savings and investment,[6] and later to the links between financial flows and global imbalances.[7] Ricardo Caballero rightly argued that the main concern before the financial crisis burst was that the US would experience a sudden stop of capital flows along with a sharp depreciation of the US dollar.[8] And what happened in 2008 and 2009 was that the US suffered an unexpected inflow of capital and appreciation of the dollar. At the same time, the decline of aggregate demand helped to adjust the US current account deficit, although it never became a surplus, as happened later in similar episodes in Eurozone periphery countries. These different paths also have different readings, as we shall see in Chapter 6.

The link between the global imbalances and the 2008/9 financial turmoil was identified from the very beginning.[9] Current account surpluses in China and Gulf countries fostered unsustainable credit booms in the major developed economies with deficit, mainly the US, which were at the core of the crisis. The capital inflows in advanced economies put significant downward pressure on world interest rates, funding the credit booms. Later literature carefully distinguishes between Bernanke's 'Savings Glut' hypothesis and the 'Liquidity Glut' brought about both by the Federal Reserve and ECB after the dotcom crisis.[10] But what it is clear is that both helped to build an environment of historically low interest rates coupled with an abnormally low risk premia. Caballero and others made a good point linking the global imbalances and the financial innovation process:[11] the global demand for safe assets began to rise above what the US financial system could naturally provide. So financial institutions started to search for ways to generate low-risk, preferably triple-A-rated assets out of riskier products. Sophisticated and highly rated financial instruments were created by the banking industry, which later showed an extreme vulnerability to a systemic shock. Borio and Disyayat also made a good assessment about the theoretical and empirical troubles of that link, warning against a straightforward linking between current account deficit and the financial crisis, as the external *net* financial positions can conceal the true nature of *gross* capital flows.[12] Quiet surprisingly, they rely on the old and non-observable Wicksellian natural interest rate.

Most of this literature pointed to both economic policy practices and structural shortcomings in emergent surplus countries as the main source of the global imbalances.[13] And this explains why the rebalancing of the deficits and surplus has deserved fewer policy efforts during the years of turmoil than the US banking and Eurozone debacle. While most of the quick policy reactions were done on the brink of the financial collapse, the pressure on the US to correct its deficit, and on China to change its exchange-rate policy has scarcely moved beyond soft diplomatic pressure. Here the policymakers were less eager to act:

> Alan Greenspan (Chairman of the US Federal Reserve Board at the time) observed that 'the trade deficit is basically a reflection of the fact that the whole world is basically expanding' ... Henry Paulson (then US Treasury Secretary) captured the short-term dilemma between imbalances and growth in the United States by stating: 'The trade balance is a problem ... but the current situation is better than no deficit and no growth at the same time'. He did not mention, however, the longer-term dilemma between imbalances, financial stability and, ultimately, growth.[14]

The US is at the core of a vast, dense, international financial network, enjoying an enviable position as issuer of the reserve currency of the international monetary system, the 'exorbitant privilege' coined by De Gaulle.[15] It has been able to cope with the Triffin dilemma from the 1960s, proof of which can be found in the unexpected appreciation of the US dollar during the 2009 winter term. So before the 2008 turmoil, the current account deficit was a source of concern for the Bush Administration, but it was not seen as a systemic danger for the US and global economy. During the recession terms, we witnessed a soft correction of it, due to the fall of the aggregate demand and, in turn, a severe downturn in international trade. As the expansionary policy mix began to contain the fall, the correction stopped. Further improvements are expected through substitution of oil and gas imports thanks to new fracking techniques. But it is not one of the top priorities of US policy agenda as the unemployment rate has not approached the Federal Reserve target of 6 per cent.

The same could be said for the Chinese government. It has also felt very comfortable with its current account surpluses year after year and, in turn, has amassed a huge amount of US dollar denominated assets. International pressure has been made recently to change the Chinese growth model, as it has been identified as the 'other half' of the global imbalances problem.

From the very beginning of its economic transition after Mao's death, China has been working on a non-Western – or at least non-mainstream – economic policy scheme. In sharp contrast to the poor outcome of 'shock therapy' applied late in Soviet Union and Eastern Europe Countries, the 'gradualist' strategy adopted by successive Chinese governments has rendered three decades of double-digit growth. Now it is the second largest economy in the world and one of the main holders of US government liabilities.

The model was based – and still is – on a rather pragmatic policy: a rapid capital accumulation pace has been use to restructure the huge surplus of rural population. 'Enhanced labour productivity due to massive flows of employment from agriculture to the more productive manufacturing and services jobs is the main driver of China's economic growth'.[16] The reserve of rural workers has maintained wages at rather moderate levels, which has attracted a steady flow of foreign direct investment and, thus, allowing a rapid access to up-to-date technology. With low wages, gains in productivity and growth were not transformed into domestic consumption and, instead, were redirected towards international trade. This is why Chinese authorities have kept the yuan undervalued for decades. The exchange rate target is explicit for The People's Bank of China: 'Maintaining the Renminbi exchange rate at adaptive and equilibrium level; holding and managing the state foreign exchange and gold reserves'.[17] The management of an undervalued exchange rate has had monetary and financial effects: a repressed private consumption has fuelled a surplus of savings which has been channelled abroad via reserve accumulation. An underdeveloped financial system and a semi-closed capital account have created an environment of financial repression in which public and private savings have few alternatives apart from accumulating US dollars.

This has been one of the engines of the funding of US current account deficit and, in the post-crisis period, of the US government.

The reduction of the current account surplus has not been one on the top priorities of the Chinese government, nor has the correction of global imbalances. But the financial crisis has unravelled an old concern that has always been there: whether US policymakers will still be able to deal with the Triffin dilemma and whether the dollar will continue to work as the reserve currency of the international monetary system. These fears were palpable in the speech of the former Governor of the People's Central Bank of China in 2009:

> The acceptance of credit-based national currencies as major international reserve currencies, as is the case in the current system, is a rare special case in history. The crisis again calls for creative reform of the existing international monetary system towards an international reserve currency with a stable value, rule-based issuance and manageable supply, so as to achieve the objective of safeguarding global economic and financial stability.[18]

These fears about the stability of international monetary systems should be viewed from the perspective of the East Asian countries affected by the 1997 financial crisis. After struggling for a long time to escape from the consequences of balance of payments troubles, sudden stops of capital inflows and domestic currency depreciations, most East Asian countries began to amass reserves in US dollars as a way to build backstops so as to avoid further episodes of financial stress. That deliberate policymaking has been done well above the rules recommended by mainstream economic and policy research, such as the *Greenspan–Guidotti rule* of three months of imports or other model-based rules.[19] The concerns over regional financial stress shifted towards bigger concerns about the disorderly unwinding of the delicate symbiotic equilibrium reached between China and the US as with the 2008 crisis outbreaks. At the same time, a large reserve accumulation is an additional source of risk for the global economy and international financial markets.[20] A massive acquisition of a reserve currency can bring about global risks, such as an artificially low interest rate environment, asset and/or real estate bubbles and misalignments of exchange rates and, above all, a protectionist framework in the form of implicit tariffs and subsidies. All these global risks materialized before and after the 2008 financial crisis.

What is now under discussion is if the Chinese government will be able to restructure its economy, changing from the export-producer model to a domestic demand-led growth. This will be of great help in rebalancing the external relationships with the US and undermining the risks from global imbalances.

But this also implies a slowdown in the economic growth and social costs which the Communist Party will have to deal with.

The problem here was that although both the US and Chinese governments were aware of the problem, both felt comfortable with a situation in which almost *nobody* foresaw anything more than a sudden correction of the US dollar, as mainstream economic modelling said. But there was a missing link in this chain of events: the financial innovation processes that had been taking place on Wall Street and the underestimation of the risks associated with global imbalances.

The second and *now* well-known process that triggered the global financial and economic crisis was the housing bubble in the United States fuelled by securitization of subprime mortgages. Within the RBC framework, the bursting of the bubble was an unexpected negative impulse or shock. The mainstream modelling was unable to predict this shock, so by the time the Federal Reserve and US Treasury were aware of the problem, it was too late. In 2007 a bank run was unleashed, but this time it was not on the deposits, but rather on the securitized subprime mortgages. The novelty in this financial panic is that it was generated and amplified not in the conventional and traditional banking system, but in what is now known as *shadow banking*. The big failure both in modelling and policymaking was the absolute ignorance of the fact that a parallel banking system was growing on Wall Street fuelled by an environment of extraordinary low interest rates and the inflow of external funds coming from all over the world. So the housing bubble, the financial innovations and the panic must be understood through the workings of this shadow system.

'Shadow' is not the most appropriate label for these financial institutions because there is nothing illicit or illegal in their business. In fact, both systems perform the same maturity and liquidity transformations. The main difference lies in that the traditional banking system does so within the same entity whereas shadow banking has 'sliced' them into separate subprocesses, each of them performed by different entities. The traditional banking system uses deposits to fund long-term loans, which are usually guaranteed by some kind of insurance scheme. The liquidity is provided by central bank facilities. Shadow banking performs the same maturity and liquidity transformation but cannot rely directly on these public safety nets: the shadow banking system does not have access to Federal Reserve liquidity facilities nor is there an explicit guarantee of its liabilities. This shadow banking system lies apart from the 'official' system, using instruments and institutions which are in constant evolution due to intense financial innovation processes. The shadow banking system is organized around securitization and wholesale funding: loans, leases and mortgages are securitized and thus become tradable instruments. Funding is also in the form of tradable instruments, such as commercial paper and repos. So instead of deposits with a traditional bank, savers hold money market balances. In a very comprehensive study, Pozsar et al. describe the intermediation process as a

> *vertical slicing* of traditional banks' credit intermediation process and include (1) loan origination, (2) loan warehousing, (3) ABS issuance, (4) ABS warehousing, (5) ABS CDO issuance, (6) ABS intermediation and (7) wholesale funding. It was done in a strict, sequential order with each step performed by a specific type of shadow bank and through a specific funding technique.[21]

The asset-backed securities (ABS) and collateralized debt obligations (CDO) are the best-known new instruments. These instruments fostered the banking model of 'originate-to-distribute': once the mortgage is originated, it could be transferred through a pool of credits to other institutions (official or not) and, with it, the credit risk. These and other techniques[22] were the kind of instruments and financial innovations which the US National Financial Crisis Inquiry Commission (FCIC) report blamed as the main factor in the unleashing of the crisis.

While systematic academic research about shadow banking began after the financial crisis outbreak, the policymakers were also unconscious of the full implications of their evolution. In his book *On the Brink*, Henry Paulson, US Secretary of Treasury during the crisis, describes how both the Federal Reserve and his own office had only scarce knowledge of what was going on, which is unbelievable as he was the former chief executive officer of Goldman Sachs. In Chapter 3 of his book, Paulson recognized that, at the beginning of the crisis, he and his team were more worried by the first signs of financial distress in Europe than the developments coming from the bursting of the US housing bubble. In an environment of extreme uncertainty, the combined operations of the US Treasury and the Federal Reserve had to deal with the worst financial crisis since 1929 with little information and/or *knowledge* of the source of the problem. The management of the crisis suffered from this lack of a comprehensive picture, and many of the decisions made during that time are still under discussion.

When Fannie Mae and Freddie Mac had to be rescued, top policymakers began to notice that something was wrong, but most of them were sure that there was a kind of 'safety net' which would prevent a hard landing. When they realized that there was no net at all, they began to look for strategies to contain the flood. So, in September 2008 both enterprises were put under the conservatorship of the Federal Housing Finance Agency. Previously in July, the national debt ceiling had to be raised as a preventive measure allowing the Treasury to support them. That was a true signal of panic, coming from a Republican administration with a strong commitment to a free market approach. They had to do anything to avoid a complete destabilization, not only of the financial system, but of the political and social order as a whole.

The Lehman Brothers bankruptcy was the next step in the unfolding of the financial crisis. The figures are well-known: bank debt of $613 billion, bond debt of $155 billion and assets worth $639 billion, as Lehman reported in its bankruptcy filing. The US Treasury and the Federal Reserve tried to convince Bank of America and Barclays to buy the firm, but they rejected the deal. Although Barclays and Nomura bought parts of the firm later, that point was the beginning of a large and continuous intervention by policymakers in the global financial institutions: the following weeks witnessed the bailouts of Merril Lynch, Washington Mutual, Wachovia and so on. Markets were also hit, and the Dow Jones registered its biggest fall since the terrorist attacks of 11 September 2001. That was also the beginning of a new kind of massive intervention in the financial system. A group of Wall Street firms and the New York Federal Reserve provided financial assistance for an orderly liquidation of Lehman. The Federal Reserve agreed to buy low-quality assets in exchange for government assistance. That was the starting point of quantitative easing (QE).

But bailouts were not enough to contain the second round of problems. In the aftermath of Lehman's failure, the credit markets froze. None of the big banks wanted to lend to each other, fearing that these borrowers would be the next to fail. But at the same time, in order to raise as much liquidity as possible, they cut credit to homes and industries. So big companies that had nothing to do with banking were not able to get daily funding requirements, as happened with the automobile industry. And the 'financial turmoil' turned into the 'Great Recession'.

Whether the financial and economic collapse following Lehman's fall was due to a failure of policymakers or due to bad financial regulation is still under discussion, as Fitzpatrick and Thomson summarize.[23] There are two main views here. Some argue that it was the result of wrong expectations: the US Government let Lehman fail when the market expected a rescue, as it did with Freddie Mac and Fannie Mae. The reason: everybody thought Lehman 'was too big to fail'. According to the US National Financial Crisis Inquiry Commission Report, 'the decision to rescue Bear Stearns and then to place Fannie Mae and Freddie Mac into conservatorship, followed by its decision not to save Lehman Brothers and then to save AIG – increased uncertainty and panic in the market'.[24] On the other side, there are those who argue that the markets' collapse was an outcome of the disorderly resolution of Lehman's problems. The problem for them was the use of a bankruptcy filing to resolve a systemic institution in an 'orderly' fashion. These lessons concern 'whether the insolvency of large or complex financial companies can be adequately handled through the judicial process of bankruptcy'.[25] The point here is that four years later, there is no widespread consensus about how to deal with another 'Lehman moment'. It is true that the Dodd–Frank Consumer Protection Act of 2010 (DFA) mandates that these systemic firms must elabourate 'living wills' (otherwise called 'funeral plans'), which entails preparing orderly resolution plans in case of bankruptcy. The question is whether it will work under extreme financial stress such as that of September 2008.

From that point, the situation evolved into complete uncertainty for policy-makers, who were overwhelmed by a frenetic chain of events. The top priority of the US Treasury was to avoid a severe slowdown despite the 'free market' slant of the Republican Administration of George Bush. Just after Lehman's fall, the rescue package for AIG followed, then the 'Paulson plan' to clean up problematic mortgages, the Trouble Assets Relief Program (TARP), and so on. All these measures were implemented as the financial markets' shutdown led more and more firms into liquidity problems and, eventually, insolvency. Whether the crash was unleashed by Lehman's bankruptcy filing or not will be debated for years. But what seems to be clear is that the financial crisis was misunderstood from the very beginning by those who supposedly were appointed to prevent these sorts of things. This appears even in the US FCIC report, where it is said that the crisis was due 'to ill-prepared key policy-makers', among several other causes. If true, at the same time, it is recognized that they (policymakers) 'did not have a clear grasp of the financial system they were charged with overseeing ... This was in no small measure due to the lack of transparency in key markets'.[26] We could add that this may well be the case for top policymakers, but not of their supposedly well-trained staff, coming from the world's best business and economics schools and departments. We will turn to the issue of macro-financial modelling in the next chapter.

One additional remark needs to be made on shadow banking. While Bernanke points towards a 'savings glut'[27] coming from emergent and oil producing countries, and Borio and Disyayat to an extremely relaxed monetary policy,[28] the size of the liabilities of these institutions and their role in the monetary system should also be mention. As Adrian and Ashcraft argue, the credit intermediated by bank liabilities has fallen from 75 per cent in the mid-1940s to 15 per cent in 2007 (21 per cent in 2011):

> the reduced importance of bank maturity transformation is being offset partly by shadow maturity transformation. The consequence is that the fraction of the aggregate money supply issued by shadow intermediaries has increased significantly, peaking at 45 percent in the early 2000s before declining to 28 percent in 2011, a level not seen since 1993. While ... the amount of credit funded through shadow intermediation even at the peak is modest (approximately 10 percent), the growing importance of shadow money in the aggregate supply of money was an important factor in amplifying the shocks to the economy more broadly.[29]

This hypothesis, which Adrian and Ashcraft do not fully explore, would eventually lead to a strong case in favour of an *endogenous* money supply, as some post-

Keynesians and Austrians had argued at a much earlier stage. The point is that the mix of financial innovation and deregulation set the basis for the development of an industry of liquidity creation which, just before the crash, amounted to $22 trillion in assets held versus $14 trillion of traditional banking[30] with an estimated contraction of $5 trillion during the crisis. Thus, we can say that the global recession was brought about by a sharp contraction of the US monetary supply.

While the US Treasury and the Federal Reserve were rescuing the US financial system, the effects of the financial collapse began to spread all over the world. And they unravelled the systemic deficiencies of the other great innovation of the 2000s, the euro.

As happened with the global financial crisis of 2007–9, analysts and policymakers failed in their foresight and management of the Eurozone crisis. Although there are common causes in this misunderstanding, the European crisis shows some distinctive issues. To begin with, it was the first financial crisis within a 'free' monetary union, which was built on the agreement of all the member states and was not forced by a dominant power or state, such as the former Soviet Union. It is interesting to distinguish here between a common currency area within a political union and a currency union of politically sovereign member states.[31] The EMU is a monetary union of sovereign states, all of them with their own fiscal and banking systems. And the implications of this fact had not been fully understood until the outbreak of the Greek crisis. Afterwards, although there is no crystal-clear diagnosis of the crisis, there seems to be a general consensus on some issues. An issue on which almost everybody agrees is the contagion effects coming from the 2007–8 global financial crisis, which are the ultimate cause of the intra-European financial stress. The wholesale funding markets dried up for worldwide banking systems. European countries answered with massive bailout packages of systemic entities. But it is worth mentioning the misunderstanding of the problem by key policymakers. In July 2008, when the financial turmoil was evident in the United States and some systemic European entities were reporting increasing difficulties, the ECB raised the interest rate of the main refinancing operation by 25 basis points, from 4 to 4.25 per cent, and that of the marginal lending facility from 5 to 5.25 per cent. Only two months later, it had to lower rates by 100 basis points in the midst of the Lehman bankruptcy market crisis.

But the Eurozone financial and economic crisis has specific elements that make it a separate development from that of the global financial crisis. As happened with the links between global imbalances and shadow banking developments, there are close relationships between the global financial crisis and the euro crisis but it must be considered a separate process. The main reason is that non-Euro European countries have been able to weather the effects of the global financial crisis much better than peripheral countries. The way in which the architecture of the Eurozone was implemented, allowed the accumulation of external imbalances among the member states although the zone as a whole was in equilibrium. Massive current account deficits in peripheral countries along with a huge surplus in Germany were regarded by policymakers with growing concern but without practical consequences, as was the case of the US and Chinese external imbalances. The unwinding of these imbalances was responsible for the intra-European balance-of-payment crisis[32] but, in this case, there was not an issuer of international currency to provide relief and there was no room for a realignment of exchange rates, or at least not within the same currency area. But again, as happens with the global imbalances, there is a financial history behind the Eurozone crisis.

First of all, there is a wide agreement that the launching of the euro in 2002 led to a massive miscalculation of financial risk. Due to the erroneous belief that all government bonds of the euro were, if not warranted, at least under the large umbrella of the German and northern Europe financial solvency, financial markets led the yields on periphery member states bonds to historically low records. This allowed exceptionally cheap funding for these countries, a kind of 'soft budget constraint' which delayed the necessary measures to – at least – maintain their competitiveness in the global economy.

Second, due to these capital inflows, real exchange rates in southern Europe and Ireland began to rise. A stalled productivity combined with inflation rates two basis points above the EU average, brought about growing current account deficits (and the corresponding external debt) at the same time that the core-EU countries accrued surpluses (and external assets). In a free-floating exchange rate regime, this would have eventually led to a more or less abrupt correction of the nominal exchange rate and a more realistic valuation of the risk. Within a fixed exchange rate, a balance-of-payments crisis, such as in 1993, the affected countries would have been forced to a realignment of the rates. At that time, the cost was a 1 per cent GDP decrease in the Spanish economy, for instance. But under a monetary union, the perception of these problems was misunderstood due to the belief that both the ECB and the European Commission guaranteed a smooth functioning of the intra-European payment systems.

Perhaps European policymakers allowed peripheral external imbalances because some member states wrongly believed that they were shielded from the repercussions of lax domestic policies and poor financial market regulation, as Dorrucci and McKay point out.[33] But there was also a more or less implicit consensus on the *Lawson doctrine*: to the extent that current account deficits involve private savings and investment decisions, that there are no distortions, and that expectations are rational, there are no reasons for the government to intervene.[34] This doctrine has been supported by mainstream economics and key institutions such as the IMF, as Blanchard evidenced.[35] As Spain and Portugal amassed current account deficits of 10 per cent GDP in the years previous to the crisis, Camarero et al. rightly argue that the adjustment of that imbalance should be a priority, given that exchange-rate realignments within the Euro Area were no longer available. Following the Lawson doctrine, Blanchard argued that 'For the distortions I have looked at, optimal policy typically did not involve current account deficit reduction'.[36]

Financial markets suffered from the same myopic view of external imbalances within the Euro Area. They were providing cheap funding to these countries and largely ignoring sovereign risk within the Euro Area, and financing both the public and private sectors. But even here there was a biased view of the problem. While the European Commission has been strictly monitoring fiscal deficits, the accumulation of large private liabilities due to the real estate bubble in Spain, for instance, has not deserved much attention, although the housing bubble did get some attention from the IMF long before the euro crisis.[37]

So, broadly speaking, between 2002 and 2008–9, almost everybody took for granted the European support for member states in trouble, as happened in the US with Illinois' or California's fiscal problems. It was assumed that the joint action of the European Commission and the European central bank could avoid intra-European balance-of-payments problems. But that belief was clearly a mistake, as the bailouts in Greece, Ireland, Portugal, Spain and Cyprus have shown. Since 2009, financial markets have been speculating for almost five years about the break-up of the currency union, due to the fragility of the fiscal and/or banking systems of these countries. The fear of a default has fed massive capital outflows, growing interest rates and economic recession in these countries, which, in turn, deepened their fiscal and financial troubles in a classical self-fulfilling balance-of-payments crisis. A slow and awkward response by part of the European Commission first, and by the European Council later, did the rest of the work. The European central bank took four years to say it would do 'whatever it takes' to keep the euro alive, in the words of its president, Mario Draghi. And from then, the fears of a break-up have almost disappeared, although the economic problems seem far from being solved.

After five bailout programmes (two for Greece), it seems to be clear that the option to keep the EMU together has succeeded. What is now being discussed is the 'independency' of the national fiscal and banking system, paving the way for a closer monetary and political union. The analytical framework which supports this choice is, nevertheless, less clear. Again, there seems to be a kind of opportunity cost calculation about the social and political consequences of the dissolution of the currency union. During these years much has been said about the costs and benefits for the member states of an orderly exit of the troubled countries, mainly Greece. Broadly speaking, that means new and depreciated currencies which – supposedly – could foster economic growth in the short term. More specifically, on the benefits side, the most important of them could be to avoid a harsh economic adjustment – mainly in social spending and wage cuts – and massive unemployment. The second one could be the economic stability of the EMU, especially that of the creditor countries. On the costs side, it has been argued that the implementation of a new currency is so complex that the process could threaten the economic performance even more than if the country stayed within the EMU. And, of course, the likely haircuts for lenders, as the exiting country cannot afford to pay their debts in euros because the new currency will depreciate more than 20 per cent. So, the resolution has been far less than 'orthodox': a high-level, European political agreement has seemed to be reached by means of which the troubled countries will stay within the Eurozone, but subjected to a comprehensive 'macroeconomic imbalance procedure' that conditioned further financial support.

Returning to the main topic, we have seen that the decoupling of economic policy and economic modelling and theory affect all the factors that triggered the global financial and economic recession. And the decoupling seems to be more evident when we look at the 'unconventional' economic policy responses which had to be implemented in real-time processes as the global financial system was on the edge of collapse. We will examine this issue further by analysing the evolution of monetary policy during these years.

## A Salient Example: The Quantitative Easing. May it Reshape Economic Theory?

Monetary policy has been at the forefront in the worldwide reaction to the financial crisis and the subsequent economic downturn. The massive intervention in financial markets and the long-lasting zero or near zero interest rates policies have been the key instrument in avoiding a global deflationary recession. Nevertheless, the way in which monetary policy is conducted has changed dramatically during these years. New targets and new instruments have transformed the pre-crisis scheme of policymaking. While these new measures have been implemented as traditional tools proved to be useless, economic modelling and researching has situated itself behind the lines, focusing on the effects of the new measures rather than providing new insights to cope with the financial stress. The fact that RBC and mainstream macroeconomic modelling lack a comprehensive picture of the role of the financial system in economic performance has a lot to do with this.

The monetary policy framework prior to the 2008–9 turmoil was based worldwide on an inflation targeting scheme. As a rule, 2 per cent CPI inflation rate was adopted by central banks as a good measure of price stability. Most of them rely upon short-term interest rates to modify aggregate demand and, through it, to reach the target. Conventional wisdom was embodied in a more or less sophisticated version of a Taylor rule, which established an econometric relationship among the central bank main financing operation rate, the differential between effective and targeting inflation rates and the differential between effective and potential GDP growth rates or effective and natural unemployment rate. The historical role of central banks as lenders of last resort was never eschewed, but it remains as a sort of relic from the past. Central banks did not refuse to deal with the effects of asset bubbles but they did it *only* as they affected the price stability measured by CPI or in case of a severe downturn, as happened with the dotcom crisis. The strategy never included deliberate actions to prevent asset or real estate bubbles, rather just a mop-up after.

From the very beginning of the crisis, first the Federal Reserve and later the rest of the world's central banks launched programmes to provide liquidity to financial markets. That was not the first time, but it had never been done on such a scale. All these programmes were labelled later as 'unconventional monetary policy' measures. The change was taking shape during 2008 Q4 and 2009 Q1. Initially, the strategy was 'conventional': it was just the traditional function of lender of last resort as banking credit and wholesale funding markets froze. Interest rates were cut until the feared zero lower bound and special relief programmes were launched. But from the very beginning, the Federal Reserve and the Bank of England (BoE) programmes differed from those of the Bank of Japan (BoJ), and the ECB. The Federal Reserve and BoE focused on direct assets purchases rather than lending directly to banks, because their financial systems rely more on markets rather than on banking. Conversely, BoJ and ECB provided liquidity mainly through banks, as their systems rely more on banking intermediation. As early as 19 September 2008, the Federal Reserve created the *Asset-Backed Commercial Paper (ABCP) Money Market Mutual Fund Liquidity Facility*, which lent money to banks for the purpose of purchasing high-quality ABCP. Shortly after, on 7 October, the Federal Reserve launched the *Commercial Paper Funding Facility (CPFF)* to directly purchase high-quality commercial paper. On 29 September 2008, the ECB launched a one-month 'special term refinancing operation ... to improve the overall liquidity position of the euro area banking system'. As there were concerns about the systemic and global character of the crisis, the Federal Reserve quickly reacted as *issuer of the international currency*. On 18 September, the Federal Reserve expanded its foreign exchange swap lines with foreign central banks, and on 13 October it announced that its swap lines with the BoE, ECB and the Swiss National Bank would accommodate any quantity of funds requested.

After these emergency measures were launched, the central banks were increasingly aware that they were facing not only a severe financial collapse, but a deep economic downturn. That was when they embarked on the 'unconventional monetary policy'.

The most important 'unconventional' measure adopted was the so-called quantitative easing (QE), consisting of large-scale asset purchases financed by issuing central bank money. At the time of writing it is four years later, and QE is still working and is now considered the 'conventional' unconventional monetary policy to distinguish it from further steps taken by central banks that are even less conventional.[38] The aim was to hit the long-term interest rates, rather than the shorter-term ones, because they had reached the zero lower bound and central banks needed additional tools as the threat of a deflationary recession loomed. But in so doing, they created a rupture with the traditional monetary policy scheme which was established as the regular practice in the 1990s. There are several issues here that must be taken into account as they are important departures from the previous mainstream orthodoxy.

The first effect of massive asset purchases by central banks is that their balance sheets expand. The assets figure on their balance now, as well as the liabilities of the central bank, because the purchases are funded by new base money (commercial bank reserves) or by bank deposits. There is nothing new here, as they are the traditional 'open market operations', although they have been operating in a completely different situation and magnitude. The Federal Reserve and BoE have purchased not only short-term debt, which would be the regular open market operation, but also longer-date bonds as well as private sector assets, including mortgage-backed securities. To figure out the magnitude of the intervention, the Federal Reserve reports that

> since the beginning of the financial market turmoil in August 2007, the Federal Reserve's balance sheet has grown in size and has changed in composition. Total assets of the Federal Reserve have increased significantly from $869 billion on August 8, 2007, to well over $2 trillion.[39]

The data available on the web page for 26 March 2014 show that asset amounts at $4,226,971 million. The evolution can be seen in Figure 5.1.

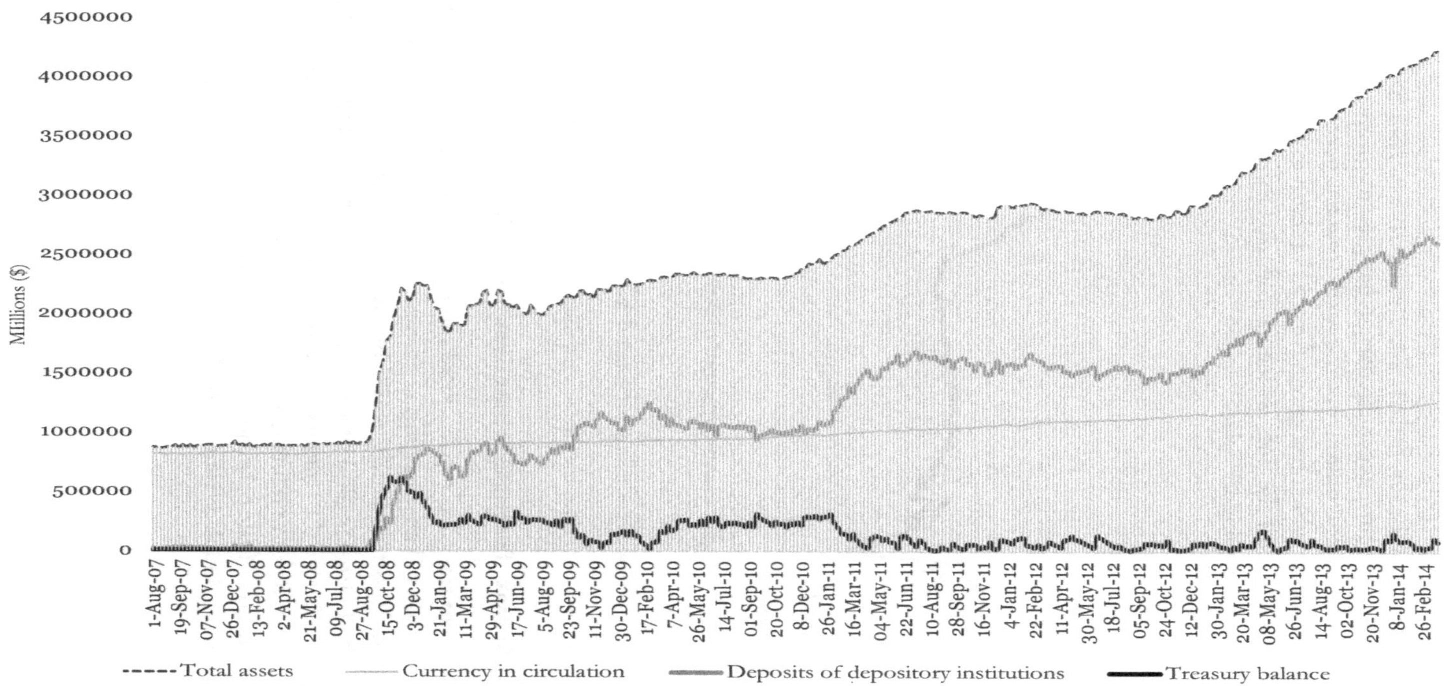


**Figure 5.1: US Federal Reserve balance sheet. Source: http://www.federalreserve.gov/monetarypolicy/bst_recenttrends.htm [accessed 14 August 2014].**

As a consequence of QE, the Federal Reserve has quadrupled its balance. On the liabilities side, the currency in circulation has grown considerably, from nearly $814 billion to $1,268 billion, but the main issue has been the deposits of depositary institutions, which has grown from $17 billion to $2,611 billion. The same has happened with the BoE, which has followed a similar pace to that of the Federal Reserve (see Figure 5.2).

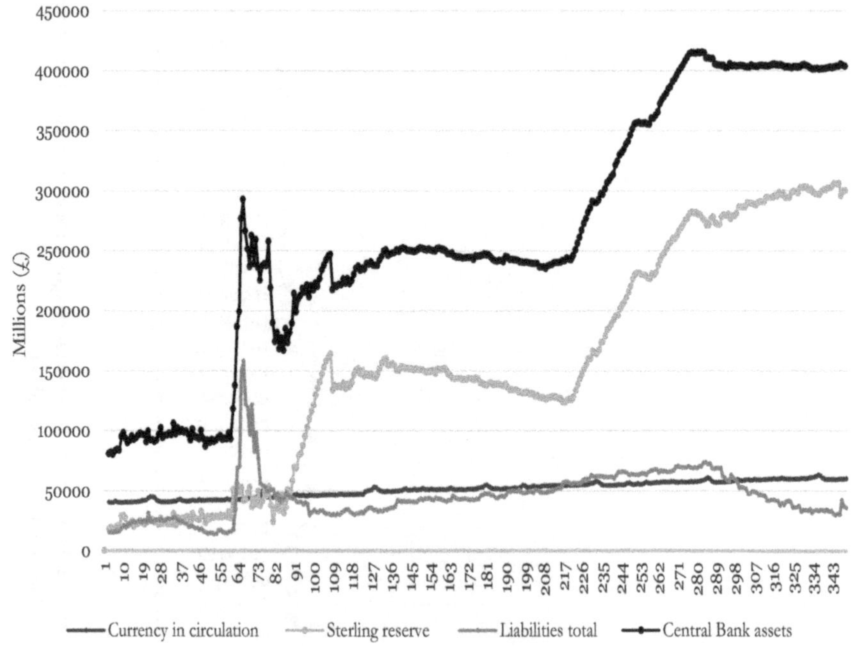


**Figure 5.2: Bank of England's balance sheet. Source: Bank of England.**

The ECB, on the contrary, has concentrated more on providing funding to the banking system, rather than engaging in massive purchases of assets. In fact, as it refused to buy short-term debt issued by member states, the transmission mechanism in the Eurozone did not work, as the interest rate spreads peaked to 600 basis points before the bailouts. Instead, it launched another unconventional measure, the long-term refinancing operation (LTRO), intended to boost lending. The evolution of the base money aggregate is quite similar to the other central banks, having doubled from the outbreak of the crisis (see Figure 5.3).

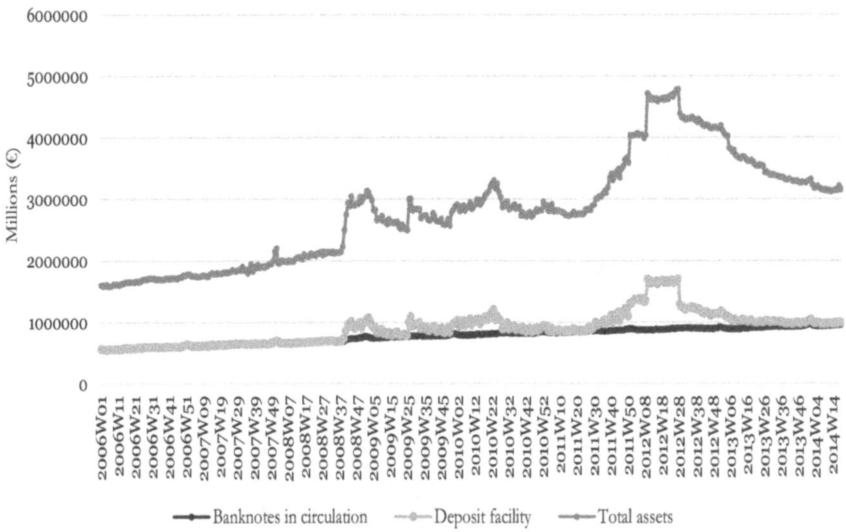


**Figure 5.3: European Central Bank monetary base. Source: European Central Bank.**

There is another salient feature that breaks with past consensus: the BoE has bought UK government bonds from the non-banking private sector and the Federal Reserve has bought US Treasuries at the reported amount of $2,311 trillion by March 2014. Nevertheless, it is hard to find some mention in the literature of the fact that both the Federal Reserve and BoE are monetizing debt. As the issue has deserved some attention in the media, the Federal Reserve of Saint Louis denied the fact.[40] One of the main agreements of the pre-crisis economic policy consensus (the so-called *Washington Consensus*)[41] was that of fiscal discipline as a way to avoid a balance-of-payments crisis and high inflation rates through debt monetization as happened in Latin America and other developing countries in the 1980s and 1990s. Nevertheless, the US has been running federal budget deficits from the burst of the dotcom bubble and the national debt has reached about 100 per cent of GDP in 2013 Q4, which amounts to $17.226 trillion. By January 2014, China owed $1.273 trillion and Japan, $1.201 trillion.[42] As the Federal Reserve owed $2.137 trillion in the same period,[43] it is the main creditor of the Federal Government, with roughly 12 per cent of the total debt. Bernanke has repeatedly explained that the Federal Reserve is not monetizing debt because:

> The securities that the Fed purchases in the conduct of monetary policy are held in our portfolio and earn interest. The great bulk of these interest earnings is sent to the Treasury, thereby helping reduce the government deficit. In the past three years, the Fed remitted $200 billion to the federal government. Ultimately, the securities held by the Fed will mature or will be sold back into the market. So the odds are high that the purchase programs that the Fed has undertaken in support of the recovery will

> end up reducing, not increasing, the federal debt, both through the interest earnings we send the Treasury and because a stronger economy tends to lead to higher tax revenues and reduced government spending (on unemployment benefits, for example).[44]

So the Federal Reserve buys debts, holds them, earns an interest and finally the debt matures. What happens when the treasuries mature? The US Treasury will have to repay the principal to the holder (the Federal Reserve) and that generates a charge on the Treasury account of the Federal Reserve. Supposedly, the Federal Reserve has to sterilize the amount. But, during that time, the Federal Reserve is *subsidizing* the burden of the debt that the Treasury has to repay, because interests are put in its account again. In the same speech, Bernanke announced that the Federal Reserve would buy

> mortgage-backed securities guaranteed by the government-sponsored enterprises at a rate of $40 billion per month. Those purchases, along with the continuation of a previous program involving Treasury securities, mean we are buying $85 billion of longer-term securities per month through the end of the year.

If we consider that the government-sponsored enterprises are Freddie Mac and Fannie Mae, all the debt they are buying *is* Federal debt. Nevertheless, the scenario is quite different from others, where monetizing debt episodes systematically produced double-digit inflation rates, which is certainly not the case in the US economy right now. In any event, as 'unconventional' policymaking it is a very significant departure from the previous mainstream 'orthodoxy'.

Finally, during these years, a new target for monetary policy seems to have arisen, namely financial stability. In fact, what we have seen until now is that the diverse QE and unconventional programmes seem to focus on the macroeconomic effects of the financial collapse. Not only central banks, but also the IMF, BIS and others reinforced or launched similar programmes or working groups to deal with a more or less explicit broad concept of financial stability. Before the crisis these activities were devoted to the surveillance of financial markets and institutions. Then, the focus turned to preventing the macroeconomic effects of financial activities, a *praxis* now labelled as *macroprudential* or *macro financial environment*. The definition is rather elusive. In ECB words: 'a condition in which the financial system – intermediaries, markets and market infrastructures – can withstand shocks without major disruption in financial intermediation and in the effective allocation of savings to productive investment'.[45] But the obscure slant of central bankers cannot conceal a very simple and important departure from mainstream economic modelling: they are not going to wait for the next financial and 'unpredictable' shock and then 'mop up' after, as they have been doing until now. The macroprudential programme aims to avoid this kind of systemic downturns, and is a widely accepted mission for central banks. But the problem now is how to match some kind of reliable financial early warning system with DGSE modelling. We will deal with this issue in Chapter 6.

In addition to the several QE programmes – the conventional 'unconventional' monetary policy – central banks have been developing additional measures and instruments now broadly labelled as true unconventional 'unconventional'. As the QE measures have not achieved a fully fledged recovery in four years, central banks have been trying to affect the macroeconomic activity through alternative ways. Bowdler and Radia consider at least three initiatives: policies of forward guidance, broad liquidity and credit easing.[46] The 'true' unconventional character seems to be less 'unconventional', as they rely more or less on existing knowledge. Forward guidance aims to assure a long perspective of low interest rate policy so as to foster inflationary expectations. That was tried before in Japan with little success. But the communication policy of the Federal Reserve and others seems to follow this path. Broad liquidity measures aims to supply additional funding to financial institutions, as is the case with the ECB's programme of LTROs. In two LTRO programmes in December 2011 and February 2012, the ECB provided a gross lending of over €1 trillion for 3-year terms for banks from across Europe. To be sure, the ECB has made scarce use of the kind of massive asset purchases carried out by the BoE and the Federal Reserve because of the controversy over whether 'buying public debt from member states' is under its functions. In any case, the launching of the LTROs was aimed at reducing the huge interest rates spreads that plagued the Eurozone and endangered the whole monetary transmission mechanism. Finally, credit easing could be understood as an extension of LTROs to commercial banks, as they suffered the same interest rate spreads as peripheral member states of the Eurozone and thus they were unable to conduct lending.

What seems to be clear after four years of unconventional monetary policy is that the inflation targeting framework that predominated in the 1990s and early 2000s must be reviewed in depth.

## Improving Economic Theory: Main Issues

If we connect the new measures implemented by central banks during the global recession with the global imbalances, shadow banking and the surveillance of monetary unions, we quickly realize that there are several paths opened for further improvement in economic modelling and theory.

We have seen that monetary policy should have as its target financial stability, in the broad sense of the term. Developing an early warning system will be of a great help in the steering of future policymaking but it will be not enough. Global imbalances have proven to be a source of economic and financial instability on both sides of the equation, both in deficit and surplus countries.

Understanding the role of the gross and net financial flows is critical in the assessment of unsustainable balance-of-payments developments. As Chinese officials have pointed out, an excessive elasticity of the international monetary system in providing reserve currency must be accompanied by enhanced programmes of monitoring and surveillance of external imbalances. Nevertheless, China is not a good example as we have seen by reviewing its policymaking over the last thirty years. Alternatives to the Lawson doctrine should be developed, providing policy schemes that prevent the development of large current account imbalances while maintaining the benefits of the international capital flows.

The same is true of financial innovation and shadow banking. The ability of the financial industry to develop new and better instruments to match the savers' preferences should not be done outside the safety nets provided by central banks and other liquidity facilities. But it is true that the emergence of $22 trillion in shadow banking liabilities versus the $14 trillion in traditional banking cannot be explained only by the development of financial innovations. It seems to be that the new instruments were developed in a very special environment, linked both to the gross international capital flow as well as to a very loose monetary policy which first lowered interest rates and later relaxed credit standards. There are striking coincidences in data: the growing of asset growth in the Federal Reserve's balance sheet (near $4 trillion) is almost the same as the reduction in the liabilities of shadow banking ($5 trillion). The Federal Reserve has avoided the bank runs that unleashed the Great Depression in the 1930s by putting in the system the liquidity destroyed by the shadow banking runs in 2007 and 2008. Some lessons must be learned here about the 'pro-cyclical' character of liquidity production, both public (base money) and private (shadow banking).

A broader and more in-depth analysis of these issues will occur in Chapter 6. There, we will answer some of the questions raised by the policymakers during these years. We have seen in this chapter that problems such as global imbalances have been correctly foreseen by economic theory and modelling, but policymakers did not have the appropriate incentives to solve these. Economic theory must not only give advice to policymakers but must also provide reliable solutions to political problems. The problem with global imbalances is that the international monetary system does not provide the appropriate political incentives to prevent and/or solve them. As there were no other choices, the US boosted the economy by means of an expansive policy mix while China repressed its financial system so as to accumulate a huge amount of US currency reserves and assets and kept lowering the exchange rate. Large financial flows underpinned this situation as long as was possible, that is, until the financial crisis. Nevertheless, as the US is the issuer of the international reserve currency, it does not suffer the harsh adjustment that other countries in similar situations are suffering, mostly from the European periphery. So the imbalance still exists and the problem is not yet solved.

The development of shadow banking and financial innovations was the other problem the policymakers had to face. Here the situation is the opposite of the global imbalances situation: as we have seen, neither the US Treasury nor the Federal Reserve foresaw that a global financial collapse was coming, or at least not in its full scale. They can rightly argue that there was no theory and/or data at hand reliable enough to warn them about the collapse. Here we can identify two kinds of shortcomings: the first one is truly theoretical, as the macroeconomic modelling had never fully grasped the scale on which the financial system affects the economic performance. Mainstream and non-mainstream authors have identified this as one of the main pitfall of economic theory during that period. We will see this in the next chapter in full detail. The other one is the quality of financial data available. If financial intermediaries work on over-the-counter operations, it is very difficult for both central banks and statistic bureaus to estimate the total amount of the funds transferred. When we look at gross international flows, the problems grow exponentially as tax havens play a crucial role here. This adds more troubles to economic modelling, as we lack reliable benchmarks to assess its reliability.

Finally, the much debated 'austerity' measures implemented as a way of solving the Eurozone crisis are still posing critical challenges to economic theory and modelling. The crisis in Europe was equally not foreseen as the financial crisis. Nevertheless, as the interest rates spreads began to soar, the European policymakers' answer was a combination of public spending cuts and a not-so-expansive monetary policy. Fiscal consolidation can help to reduce the financial stress within a monetary union, but a second economic recession slashed tax revenues and, finally, raised the public debt. It is true that contraction of aggregate demand and high unemployment have improved the competitiveness of the stressed economies and almost all of them have corrected their current account imbalances. Nevertheless, there are important financial imbalances *within* the euro system, as the national central banks positions in TARGET2 reveals.[47] At the time of writing, in April 2014, as deflation looms all over Europe, strong pressure has been put on the ECB to launch a true QE, as the Federal Reserve and the BoE did. Additionally, the Macroeconomic Imbalances Procedure (MIP) launched by the European Commission is acting as a truly 'international' mechanism of surveillance and monitoring. The enforcement is assured by sound financial state members denying additional financial help to borrowing members. Here we find that the checklist does not include new and sophisticated indicators. Rather, it is just a long extension of the Maastricht criteria. But as the interest rate spread has returned in April 2014 to a pre-crisis level, the prospect of additional spending cuts has seemed to evaporate as the pressure on over-indebted countries is relaxing. Could a fully fledged QE avoid the euro crisis? Or would it just roll over the debts of borrowing countries, not solving the competitiveness problem? Will a

QE finally be implemented to avoid a deflationary recession? There are still many questions open for European policymakers, and economic modelling is not providing reliable answers for them. We will address some of them in next chapter, as the shortcomings in all cases have common grounds.

# 6 EXPLAINING MORE COMPLEX PHENOMENA: THE FINANCIAL SYSTEM

## The Evolution of the Financial System: Quantitative and Qualitative Issues

In the previous chapters we have moved from a broad sketch of the developments of the 2008 global economic and financial crisis to the policymaking responses to that challenge. But we have done so through its theoretical scaffolding, starting with the anthropological structure of the competing economic schools of thought, passing through the common logical structure of economic theories, and the framework of modern contemporary mainstream macroeconomic modelling. Rather than making a case against both conventional and unconventional economic wisdom, we have been looking for solutions by broadening the scope of the regular praxis. Most of these reflections could have been made with no reference at all to the 2008 developments. Nevertheless, the social costs assumed by people almost everywhere in the world, forces a serious self-examination about the reliability of our present-day macroeconomic research. From the very beginning, our view has been critical but quite inclusive as well. Rather than eschewing all previous work as useless, we take it as a valuable starting point. As we saw in Chapter 3, the logical structure of economic theory, the meta-theory, can provide us with a general framework for improving our modelling as well as a benchmark to test the successes and failures of a specific research programme. The analysis of RBC theory carried out in Chapter 4 shows that its theoretical structure did not allow a proper understating of the financial processes that brought about the crisis. As these theories were the workhorse for economic policy recommendations and analysis, when the crisis broke out the policymakers were rather lost about what they had to do, as we have seen in Chapter 5. Massive liquidity injections are the classical recipe for a financial panic. But the problem is that five years later there are no new instruments available to fight against massive unemployment and financial instability. Central banks balances are still growing at a wild rate, but there are no signals of the feared hyperinflation. Rather, in the spring of 2014 we are still speaking about deflation in Europe, in spite of the billions of euros injected by the ECB in conventional and unconventional operations.

So now we must focus on what should be done from today onwards. We need to take into account as much as possible of what was missed before 2008. Once we have a detailed account of what we missed, maybe we will be able to solve some of the current problems and, much more important, to prevent similar systemic crises in the future. Here we are going to focus on the shortcomings of the macroeconomic modelling in regarding the financial aspects of economic performance, as we believe this is the most critical issue right now. Yet, while focusing on this, we will see that financial issues are closely related to other processes which have not received enough attention.

Financial crises are not new in economic history and many experts have studied them.[1] All of them share common features, while other features are clearly different. The most outstanding feature of the present financial crisis, and the one that differentiates it from others, is the size and complexity of the financial system. The relationship between credit to private sector and the GDP increased in all countries from 1980 to 2005. In Germany, the first figure was 76.03 per cent and the second 112.59 per cent. In the UK it increased from 27.33 per cent to 158.54 per cent, from 20.19 per cent to 39.4 per cent in India, from 97.4 per cent to 195.76 per cent in the US and in Japan from 129.36 per cent to 192.87 per cent.[2] The small sample we have chosen includes the largest world economies except China because its data is not available for the same period. The indicator is different among countries but the increasing trend is the same. Figures have increased by 50 per cent at least, and by much more in India, the UK and the US. The indicator is very meaningful. Though external credit is also important, its share in overall credit to the private sector is reduced. Firms and households borrow much more easily from internal financial institutions than from international ones. Thus, its increase over these twenty-five years implies that households and firms have become increasingly dependent on the financial system. As a consequence, the financial crisis hit them hard.

There are several sources of data that point in the same direction. According to a report from the London School of Economics in 1970 the financial intermediation was the 5 per cent of Gross Value Added of the UK economy.[3] In 2007 it was 8 per cent. In the US in 1950 financial intermediation was a meagre 2 per cent of its Gross Value Added and it reached 8 per cent in 2010. There is some controversy as to how to measure the Gross Value Added of the financial intermediation sector, but since the methodology is the same over time comparisons are meaningful. This increase in both economies is relevant because they are the world's largest financial markets. As long as the financial sector grows other sectors shrink so its weight in overall GDP increases. The UK average GDP growth between 1971 and 2008 has been 2.4 per cent while financial intermediation has grown by an average of 3.8 per cent.[4] This process has changed the operational environment of the economies. The financial sector is far more important than thirty or fifty years ago. Fifty years ago the dominant macroeconomic models were the neoclassical synthesis made by Hicks and Hansen departing from Keynesian ideas. When they built their models the financial system was far less important. As we are going to explain in the second section of this chapter, the financial system was absent from these models. It is not relevant if this absence was purposeful or not, but the sizeable increase of the financial system damages its ability to explain economic processes and the financial crisis. The operational environment has changed considerably, while the models have not. The same applies to RBC theory and, more generally, to DGSE models. Thirty years ago, when the first version of these models was created by Kydland and Prescott, the financial system was much more reduced than it was just before the crisis. At that time, the authors could dispense with including the financial system in their models, but the changes in the operational environment have not been followed by changes in the models, and, as we have explained in Chapter 4, RBC theory failed to forecast the crisis because its impulse mechanism was obsolete. Modelling has to face difficult choices, as we have explained in Chapter 3. Sometimes the realism of hypotheses has to be sacrificed for the explanatory power of the model. Unrealistic hypotheses regarding activities that account for 3 per cent of Gross Value Added can be acceptable. No hypothesis at all is a difficult pill to swallow, but the model can survive without them anyway. When the sector accounts for 8 per cent of Gross Value Added and models do not take it into account, they are assuming an operational environment that does not exist anymore. As a consequence, models become completely unable to explain the financial crisis.

The perils in describing the operation environment in a manner that is obsolete increase when qualitative changes add up to quantitative ones. Since the mid-1980s, many countries whose financial system was developed decided to deregulate and open it up to international competition. For instance, UK banks were allowed to enter the securities business in 1986 as a way to foster competition. In 1989 the introduction of a single banking license in Europe aimed at the same thing and the largest European banks took advantage of this fact to expanding to other banking markets. In 1999 the Glass–Steagall Act that separated commercial banks from investment banking in the US was substituted by the Gramm–Leach–Bliley Act. As a consequence, both types of banks crossed the border between these two types of businesses and consolidated, giving room to very large banking corporations. The deregulation process was fuelled by strongly held beliefs about the good functioning of markets and their capacity for self-regulation. At the same time public intervention, for instance the Glass–Steagall Act, was envisaged as useless or even inconvenient because it hampered economic growth. These facts boosted a process of financial innovation where commercial branches of large banks relied upon their investment branches to finance their daily running. Larger banks internationalized and became key players of a complex process of mergers, leveraged buyouts, etc. Thus, the operational environment of the financial system switched from individual countries to the world and links among financial institutions and among the financial systems of each country tightened.

This process was interlinked with the technological advances in telecommunications, data processing and computation. The banking business is based on a great amount of reliable data and the ability to use it in the decision-making process. Data processing and computation have substituted many handwritten processes with mechanical ones in the financial sector. Costs have been significantly reduced and the amount of operations has increased exponentially. This is crucial for the financial sector because it raises productivity. This is one of the reasons why the financial sector size has increased, as we have explained. Telecommunications has helped to exponentially increase the size of available information worldwide, and world-class banks have taken advantage of it. Together, the technological advances of telecommunications, deregulation and the opening up of national financial sectors gave birth to very large financial institutions that operate in nearly all markets and negotiate nearly all financial products. As a consequence, the degree of complexity of the financial system has scaled up as well.

In addition, improvements in data processing and computation have spurred financial innovation by creating new products and new markets. New products, for instance futures, options and swaps, are difficult to handle if a single employee has to oversee it. But he can easily manage them with the help of the latest generation of computers. As better technological tools have become available, the financial system has launched new and more sophisticated financial products. This has been a continuous process since 1980. But we have to recall that a new financial product is not similar to a new model of car. Cars can be as complex as customers are willing to pay for but drivers do not care about all these innovations, they just feel more comfortable, safer and more satisfied. They do not need to learn more to drive their better cars. But the same does not apply to financial services customers. Dealing with and investing in very complex financial products requires a high level of analytical skills and a very good understanding of the processes. Experts can advise customers, but as we have explained in the previous chapter: to what extent did experts actually master the issues they were dealing with? In addition, investors are the ones that bear the risk, but they are unable to rate it. They strongly depend on rating agencies or individual advisors. If they fail to perform their task, risk spreads over the entire economy. This is not just a minor consequence of financial innovation, but a crucial change that affects the behaviour of agents and the aggregate outcome of their interactions.

Financial innovation includes new devices such as automated teller machines, debit cards and automated clearinghouse mechanisms that create a wide array of new possibilities for exchanging goods and services and for easing payments. Some of them are placed just on the border of liquidity creation mechanisms that are difficult to control by monetary authorities. This is one of the most outstanding features of financial innovation: by whatever means, individual agents increase their rank of choices and opportunities while monetary authorities face increasing difficulties to fulfil their duties. In addition, deregulation reduces the weapons they can use to control financial processes.

Securitization is another important part of financial innovation. Banks, but not only banks, realized that they can earn money from commissions by releasing new financial products that are tradable in secondary markets based on assets which in essence are non-tradable. Banks generated financial products in this way to distribute them among investors, whose financial expertise was very different. Investors bear the risk while banks do not. As a consequence, banks expand their balance and grow. Part of the increase of the financial system size over the last thirty years is due to securitization, as we have explained in the preceding chapter. Again, this expansion relies on investor's willingness to bear new risks. And, again, we should not take for granted that investors are able to properly manage the complexity of these new products.

Securitization has had consequences that are long-lasting and large in size, as we have explained in the previous chapter. When financial institutions, mainly but not only banks, decide to engage in these types of processes they are outsourcing part of the tasks they usually perform. The difference is that before securitization, banking operations were controlled, to a certain extent, by monetary authorities that provide in exchange a safety net to the institutions that can rely on it. The actual strength of the safety net was unknown and there were perverse incentives to the 'too big to fail' financial institutions to use their size to oblige monetary authorities to help them. But there was a safety net. Securitization implies that a large part of the financial operations are out of the reach of the monetary authorities because they lack the information they need to control them. These operations are carried out in the shadow and labelled shadow banking. We have outlined their main features in the previous chapter. Here we want to point out that shadow banking increases the difficulty of managing the financial system because, in addition to its quantitative and qualitative growth, some parts of it remain hidden. In Chapter 5 we explained the lack of information that the US monetary authorities have concerning operations conducted through shadow banking.

These developments make the operational environment of economies much more difficult to describe and to include in economic models. The financial system's increase in size makes it more demanding to model, because it is not a negligible part of the economy any more. But complexity is far more difficult to manage. Our models used to be simple for tractability reasons, as we explained with reference to growth theory. But simplicity is just the opposite of complexity. A simple model can explain many simple issues if it is well specified, but it is poorly suited to encompass complexity.

Financial innovation also raises many doubts about the characterization of the agents. New financial markets and new financial products are very demanding regarding the ability of agents to understand and use high-level technical information. The computational and informational requirements are large as well. We have shown in Chapter 1 how the efficient market hypothesis failed before the crisis. The hypothesis is a device to insure that each agent in the market can be as smart as the other because all the relevant information of an asset is included in its price. For years, the hypothesis has hidden the actual complexity of financial markets and financial products and it has exempted theorists from a more in-depth analysis. Its failure proved that we did not understand how financial markets were running.

## The Financial System in Microeconomic and Macroeconomic Models

The financial system has three elements: markets, products and institutions. Basic textbooks on finance describe and classify them accurately. We have explained that the number of markets, products and institutions has increased considerably over the last thirty years and their complexity has augmented as well. Financial innovation has had a very large impact that led theorists to focus on the technical details of every single part.

Microeconomics has addressed mainly two issues in dealing with the financial system: on the one hand, how to explain financial products and how to sort out which are the most adequate for investing. On the other hand, macroeconomics has addressed the analyses of financial institutions and, more precisely, the banking sector. Financial markets have not been addressed as such, but we are going to explain that the study of financial products includes hypotheses about how financial markets work.

Models on financial products are aimed at explaining how a rational agent can choose the right portfolio under uncertainty by balancing expected returns and risk.[5] An explicit hypothesis of this approach is that markets are efficient and convey all relevant information.[6] The hypothesis exempts theorists from a more in-depth analysis of how markets actually work. Many detailed models that address the explication of several financial products make use of it. Thus, this hypothesis is critical as we have explained in Chapter 3. If we remove it from models, we have to rebuild them wholly. As a consequence, as we have explained in Chapter 1 in a general way and in Chapter 4 regarding RBC theory, if the hypothesis is falsified the models become useless, at least partly.

This theory is labelled 'modern portfolio theory'.[7] From this departure point two main models have focused on asset pricing. The capital asset pricing model shows how markets in equilibrium are able to set an asset's price, taking into account their risk. The more risk, the higher the price, and vice-versa. The Black–Scholes–Merton theory is a mathematical model that is coherent with and depends on the capital asset pricing model. The theory is based on a partial differential equation that describes the price of the option over time. It includes derivative instruments in such a way that allows agents to eliminate the risk. The underlying asset can be bought and sold in the right way to hedge the option. Assuming that there is only one correct price, investors may derive the Black–Scholes option price from the equation. Both models aim at helping investors to decide and make sound calculations and they have been very useful. But both critically rely on the efficiency of markets. If, for whatever reasons, markets are not efficient, investors may systematically make wrong choices. We have to recall that these models have been used not only by individuals, but by institutional investors that decide where and how to invest a sizeable amount of money. They do not rely exclusively on the models and they enter into the fine details in their decision-making processes, but models constitute their departure point. As a consequence, models' weaknesses and deficiencies harm their analyses considerably. The postmodern portfolio theory created in 1991 by Brian M. Rom and Kathleen Ferguson differs from the previous ones because it focuses on the internal rate of return and measures risks and reward, taking these factors into account. But the critical hypotheses outlined above do not change, so the preceding remarks apply.

The analysis of the role of banking, the microeconomics of banking, starts from the shortcomings of the Arrow–Debreu generalized model in which there is no role for financial intermediation and the institutions that perform this role. Descriptive literature had studied the functioning of these institutions and their daily routine, but there were no links between this literature and microeconomic theory. From a more general point of view, the analysis of economic institutions had been ruled out because the general competitive framework had no room for them. One of the underlying hypotheses of this framework was that the information was symmetric. Many examples and cases have shown that this assumption was untrue in many cases, so a new research field opened up to explore the effects of asymmetric information in the financial system. This feature is the rationale for institutions, for instance banking, to exist.

The microeconomic approach to banking can be extended in some cases to other financial institutions that are not directly addressed by it, but it is noteworthy that only banking has been incorporated into economic theory. Other financial institutions, for instance pension funds, investment funds or hedge funds, have not deserved the same attention. Further research on these issues has to be carried out to get a complete picture because some of these institutions play a key role in the financial system.

The microeconomics of banking addresses several different but related issues. The first is to explain why financial intermediation exists. If the activity could be carried out in a frictionless manner financial intermediation would not be necessary. Friction gives rise to the existence of institutions that can cope with it, such as banks, among others. In addition, banks deal with assets than cannot be easily sold, as other financial intermediaries would do with other types of assets. If there is a meaningful lapse of time between the buying and the selling of an asset a specialized institution, a bank, is required. Moreover, banks are intermediaries because the contracts that lenders are willing to sign are different than those desired by borrowers. Banks transform titles with a set of features into titles with a different set. This operation is very specialized and cannot be carried out by every financial intermediary.

From another point of view, if we can assume, as the Arrow–Debreu model does, that perfect competition prevails in financial intermediation, market mechanisms would be enough. Since this has proven to be untrue, theorists have had to engage in detailed analyses of how firms act in a non-competitive environment. It follows that banking can be examined as any other productive sector using approaches and tools from industrial organization. Thus, several models address the interplay between banks of different sizes and capabilities, monopoly, oligopolistic competition, etc. As a corollary, issues concerning non-competitive sectors' regulations are also important and there is much literature on it.

Banking services, and intermediation more generally, deal with contracts of many types. Almost all of them are dynamic in nature, because the initial period and the final period are far apart. As a consequence, the set of possible contingences over this lapse of time is too large and contracts seldom take all of them into account. The study of this type of contract has developed another branch of models in the microeconomics of banking. The Arrow–Debreu model took for granted that contracts were always complete. Since they are not complete, further theoretical research is needed. We want to stress at this point that the Arrow–Debreu general framework suits the frictionless macroeconomic models that we are going to explain in the next section very well. The microeconomics of banking stresses that Arrow–Debreu's model is good for benchmarking, but it describes the financial system's main features very poorly.

Bank runs and systemic risk is another important field of research in the microeconomics of banking. Setting aside the few cases of narrow banking, the fractional reserve banks system is a continuous source of concern. The mismatch between long-term investments made by banks and their short-term liabilities is unavoidable. The financial intermediation and the financial margin are based on this mismatch, and so are the risks of the activity. As a consequence, there is a wide array of models to explain how to manage it.

The microeconomics of banking is an increasingly important branch in studying financial institutions and the financial system. Financial innovation has fostered its development because both institutions and markets have increased and became more complex. Have macroeconomic models incorporated it?

With respect to macroeconomics we should take a quick look at the main macroeconomic models that were used during the last thirty years before the crisis to compare them with microeconomic models we have explained. In fact, we are going to explain the aggregate demand/aggregate supply Keynesian model, and DGSE modelling. The first one was dominant from the end of World War II to the beginning of the 1980s. We analyse it because Keynesianism, or more precisely post-Keynesianism, is one competing paradigm as we have explained in Chapter 2, though few macroeconomists rely on it. DGSE modelling is not a model in itself, but a workhorse that has been adopted by theorists due to its simplicity and workability. Before the crisis it is important to point out that DGSE was synonymous with macroeconomic modelling. To what extent the crisis is threatening the dominance of DGSE is a matter for discussion.

It is very well known that the Keynesian model includes a market for money in which the supply side – the central bank – and the demand side – agents, generally speaking – determine the interest rate. In turn the interest rate influences aggregate demand in several ways, and through the interrelation with aggregate supply the economy reaches equilibrium. It is noteworthy that the financial system is absent from this picture. It is assumed that savings and investment are equal, so savings flows are channelled into investment without further analysis. In the model there are just three markets: goods and services, money and labour. Theorists assume that financial issues are included in some unexplained way in the money market. In addition, the market of goods and the market of labour exhibit rigidities and prices adjust slowly. But the market for money adjusts quickly and easily. As a consequence, in the Keynesian model, aggregate fluctuations and crises are produced by stickiness in labour markets and markets for goods or services. Keynesian modelling aims at explaining why labour markets and goods and services markets are seldom in equilibrium. Involuntary unemployment and output gap are the symptoms of a more general disease that has to be addressed using the appropriate economic policies. As a consequence, there is no room for crises unleashed by financial factors because they do not play any role.

DGSE modelling's starting point is Kydland's and Prescott's 1982 article.[8] We have explained in Chapter 4 how this line of research developed and evolved over time, so we are not going to repeat it, we will simply focus on the role of the financial system in this modelling. But prior to that, we want to stress that DGSE modelling is classical, but the same workhorse has been used by neo-Keynesians introducing price and wage stickiness.[9] Since the other parts of the modelling are the same we are going to focus on DGSE modelling in general.

Remember that Kydland and Prescott explicitly wanted to discard any role for money as a source of aggregate fluctuations. As a consequence they built a general model in which money was a variable that adjusted quickly and easily to respond to changes in income and interest rates. The role of money in its model was null, and this feature has influenced considerably the development of DGSE modelling. The transmission mechanism does not take it into account. Regarding the impulse mechanism, things are slightly different. As we have explained in Chapter 4, Kydland and Prescott relied only on exogenous technological shocks as impulse mechanism. As the model improved, theorists realized that these shocks were not enough to explain the size of economic fluctuations and added some other pieces to the model, for instance the financial accelerator.[10] This device is related to the microeconomics of banking because it assumes that if there is a positive shock banks lend more money because there are more trustworthy borrowers, while if the shock is negative bank's credit decreases because they only lend to their best customers. It can be said that there is an endogenous feature that generates the financial accelerator mechanism. But financial issues cannot unleash an economic crisis, because they only amplify the effects of a previous technological shock. So, DGSE modelling does not include the financial system either.

## Mismatches between the Role of the Financial System in Modern Economics and Economic Models

Textbooks on finance and the financial system include money and money markets among other issues, for instance banking, stock markets and currency exchange markets. We have shown in the previous epigraphs that our textbook, the financial system, has increased considerably in size and complexity. If we use it as a metaphor, the textbook becomes continuously larger and the share of money and money markets shrinks.

What happens to economic theory? To a certain extent we have answered this question in the preceding sections, because we have explained the scope of microeconomic theory and macroeconomic theory on this issue. But we want here to summarize and organize the main ideas. The first issue is that microeconomic theory deals, to a certain extent, with the financial system, while macroeconomics does not. Macroeconomics takes into account only money and money markets.[11] As a consequence, the main macroeconomic models, the ones that policymakers, international organisms and advising firms use, display a serious weakness. When the financial system was a small part of the whole economic system, this weakness was negligible and theorists could fare well without modelling the financial system. This is not true anymore. Macroeconomic models, no matter their aggregation level, must be fixed by incorporating the financial system into them. The financial crisis has proven that financial phenomena exert a very large influence on the normal running of economies, far more than it was supposed to do. Many theorists have compared our crisis with the Great Depression. There are some similarities but in our opinion the largest difference is the role played by the financial system in our Great Recession. The interconnectedness of the worldwide financial system has created a strong negative feedback loop that has harmed many countries for many years. Still more meaningful is the fact that financial troubles have driven the crisis. It is difficult to find just one feature of the crisis unrelated to financial issues. If finance is the blood flow of the economy we have learnt how much poison this flow can carry and how harmful it can be.

Returning to microeconomics, the theoretical advances in studying finance have been large, but they are not enough. As we have explained in the second section of this chapter there is a lot of work ahead. Asset pricing models have improved considerably, but they are technical devices to help investors in their decision-making processes and they rely on assumptions about economic agents that have been seriously challenged by the crisis. The microeconomics of banking is much more promising because it encompasses more realistic features, but other institutions such as pension or investment funds deserve the same attention from theorists. The theoretical analysis of derivatives of any kind and their effects on the economy remain a no-man's land that calls out for explorers.

Macroeconomics should take advantage of the theoretical advances of microeconomics in the above-mentioned fields in order to reduce the existing mismatch between both in dealing with finance. At the same time microeconomics should continue working in other fields of study on finance in order to chart new territories. The quest for microeconomic foundations of macroeconomics has been the most important feature of scientific research in economics over the last thirty years. The same applies to future research in finance. This future research should aim for a better understanding of the operational environment of the economies. Our models have failed to properly taking this into account and it is urgent to overcome this failure. But this process will certainly entail a complete revision of the characterization of the agents as well. In the last part of this chapter we will address this topic.

The crisis has shaken economic theory and has exposed the weakness of our modelling and the urgency for improving it. As a salient example, in his statement on the House Committee on Science and Technology, Robert Solow said:

> Here we are, still at the bottom of a deep and prolonged recession, with the immediate future uncertain, desperately short of jobs, and the approach to macroeconomics that dominates serious thinking, certainly in our elite universities and in many central banks and other influential political circles, seems to have nothing to say about the problem. Not only does it offer no guidance or insight, it really seems to have nothing useful to say.[12]

On 7–8 March 2011, a conference was held at the IMF's headquarters in Washington, the topic of which was 'Macro and Growth Policies in the Wake of the Crisis'. Many first-level theorists joined the conference to analyse, among other issues, how well economic theory had fared during the crisis. Joseph E. Stiglitz[13] wrote and presented one paper dealing, among other issues, with the responsibility of economic theory in the unleashing of the crisis. Relying on the report of the US Financial Crisis Inquiry Commission, he stated that the crisis was not inevitable and that policies of the US monetary and regulatory authorities should be blamed for it. And, talking about the responsibilities for the crisis he wrote:

> But economists (and their models) also bear responsibility for the crisis. Flawed monetary and regulatory policies were guided by economists' models, and the dominant models failed to predict the crisis and said that such a crisis could not or would not happen.[14]

More technically, an occasional paper from the European Central Bank deals with the same issue.[15] Geoff Kenny and Julian Morgan devote a chapter to evaluating how economic analysis fared during the crisis, analysing the near-term outlook for macroeconomic models. Their statements about models' performance are very similar to what we have explained in the preceding parts of this chapter.[16]

> the financial crisis also pointed to weaknesses in the macroeconomic models which support our projections. In particular, criticism has been directed to state-of-art dynamics stochastic general equilibrium (DGSE) models, although much of this is actually just as relevant to the other, more traditional, 'workhorse' models used for forecasting in central banks, including those implemented within the Euro-system.[17]

All these concerns about the role of economic theories in explaining and predicting the financial crisis are, to a certain extent, widely shared. As Stiglitz points out, many regulatory and explanatory failures can be explained because policymakers and regulatory authorities acted following the economic theory they trusted. As we have explained in the previous chapter, in many cases the problem was not that the theory was weak, but that the theory did not exist. If economic theory assumes that, for instance, endogenous shocks do not happen, it will be unable to explain anything if an endogenous shock hits the economy. If economic theory does not take the financial system into account, the problems generated inside it cannot be managed in any way. There is a growing awareness that some part of the economic theory has failed or that it is too simple to cope with actual economic problems. To recognize the flaws is the first step to improving our theories.

## How to Improve Financial Issues in Macroeconomic Models

As we have seen throughout these chapters, there are two fundamental factors in the unleashing of the current global financial and economic crisis: the financial innovation and global imbalances. Several authors agree on this and on the close relationship between them. As this link has been overlooked by macroeconomic theory and modelling during the years prior to the crisis, financial issues do not play a significant role within them, as we have seen in previous sections. This has been changing in the last few years, although there is still not a clear consensus about how to include it. Mainstream economics has been developing valuable insight about how to deal with a comprehensive explanation of the present global financial and economic crisis, some of them coming up with more heterodox positions. For instance, Minsky's financial fragility concept has been considered a suitable hypothesis by some mainstream economists, as well as the idea of a full reserve banking system offered by Fisher, Allais and Friedman, but also Mises and Hayek. Fruitful collaboration among the different traditions and schools can bring about better explanations but also useful policymaking and reforms to avoid another global financial collapse.

Here we are going to present a general framework which takes into account the factors signalled by current literature as the producer of the crisis, by establishing the links among them and the way they are intertwined with the evolutions of the global economy. While all of us would agree on the political and financial factors – short- and medium-term factors – that determined the onset of global imbalances, nevertheless less attention has been paid to the more fundamental, long-term factors behind them. Once the 'big picture' is depicted, we will see which parts of it have been identified by the mainstream and/or heterodox economists.

### *Taking into Account the Main Findings of Models Explaining the Financial System*

We have realized that financial issues must play a much more important role in macroeconomic modelling and theory. But what we have seen recently is that financial issues are far more than a domestic or regional concern. The financial system is a vast network covering almost every single country which amplifies the impulses issued by the core. From the Bretton Woods system collapse, we have witnessed financial, balance-of-payments and exchange crises all over the world. From Mexico to Russia, they usually hit less developed and emerging countries due to the mismanagement of exchange rates, monetary and/or fiscal policy, among other factors. When Maurice Obstfeld says that the kind of phenomena we have seen during 2008–9 crisis are 'familiar' to international economists, he omitted one key difference: this time, advanced economies were the epicentre of the earthquake, instead of financially 'unstable', less developed countries. In fact, the epicentre was at the core of the international financial and monetary systems, the US economy. This time some blame the mismanagement of monetary, fiscal and/or regulatory issues on the US policymakers. This, however, is not the whole story.

We must turn towards long-term fundamentals. And the most important development is labelled by Richard Freeman[18] as *the Great Doubling* of the global labour force. In 1985, the global economic world (America, Western Europe, Japan, Asian Tigers and Africa) consisted of 2.5 billion people. In 2000, as a result of the collapse of communism, India's turn away from autarchy and China's shift to market capitalism, the global economy encompassed 6 billion people. Thus, in less than ten years, the global labour force more than doubled, adding 3 billon people to the labour market. That massive process has unleashed downward wage pressure and job losses in developed and old developing countries. During the 2000s, outsourcing has been a regular practice for multinational firms, and one of their most preferred destinies has been first China and then India, as the two main sources of a cheap labour force. The pressure for low-skilled workers in developed countries has led first to unemployment and then to lower wages. Not surprisingly, developed countries where unit labour costs have decreased from 2000, such as Germany, accumulate current account surpluses, against those like Spain or Greece, where in the same period of time unit labour costs rose more than 20 per cent without a similar development in the quality ladders of the output produced (see Figure 6.1). A similar development happened in the US and UK economies, both suffering heavy current account deficits. Surprisingly, this long-term trend has scarcely been considered in the global financial and economic crisis, although it has been mentioned by an influential paper of Claudio Borio[19] as one of the main factors:

> Finally, the globalization of the real economy, representing a sequence of pervasive favorable 'supply side' shocks – an outward shift in the production possibility frontier for the global economy – could raise world growth potential and help keep inflation down while at the same time encouraging asset price booms on the back of easier funding conditions.

Borio first mentioned this factor on p. 9 of his work, but did not elaborate on it. The same is true of the valuable work of Dorrucci and McKay about the international monetary system, but they did not elaborate further. But we are certain this can help us to understand both the developments which brought about the financial and economic imbalances as well as those which have happened since.

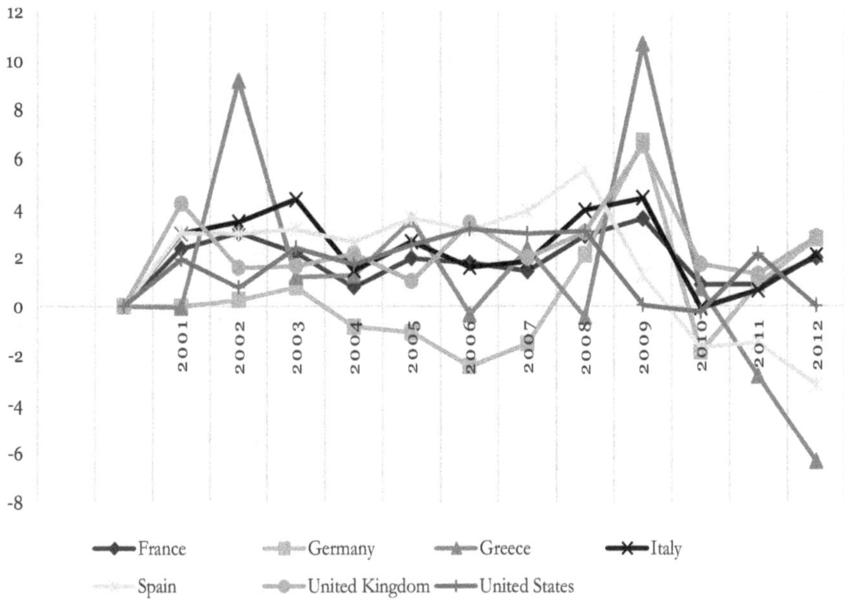


**Figure 6.1: Unit labour costs.**

Clearly, the winners in this process have been – and still are – the low-skilled/low-wage workers coming mostly from Asian countries, mainly China, where heavy current account deficits have been accumulating during the last years. High-skilled/low-wage workers have also benefited from this process, as they can rely on emigration and offshoring as a regular source of better paid jobs.

The trends unleashed by the Great Doubling are still with us, although there are signs of unsustainable wages in China – weighted by quality ladders. It has been reported that European firms have moved their outsourced low-skilled/low-wager production lines back to France or Europe as massive unemployment has pushed down wages in traditional manufacturing regions or areas. The peripheral European countries with massive unemployment have gained competitiveness through deflationary policies in prices and wages, and they have been increasingly entering into current account surplus. Spain is the most important example, having corrected a 10 per cent GDP current account deficit. Once the adjustment in wages and prices was carried out, the economic activity started to grow (estimated growth of 1.5 per cent GDP by 2014). That should not give comfort to mainstream economics, as most of the massive unemployment (peaked at 26 per cent in 2013) could have been avoided if policymakers had stopped the real estate bubble at its onset.

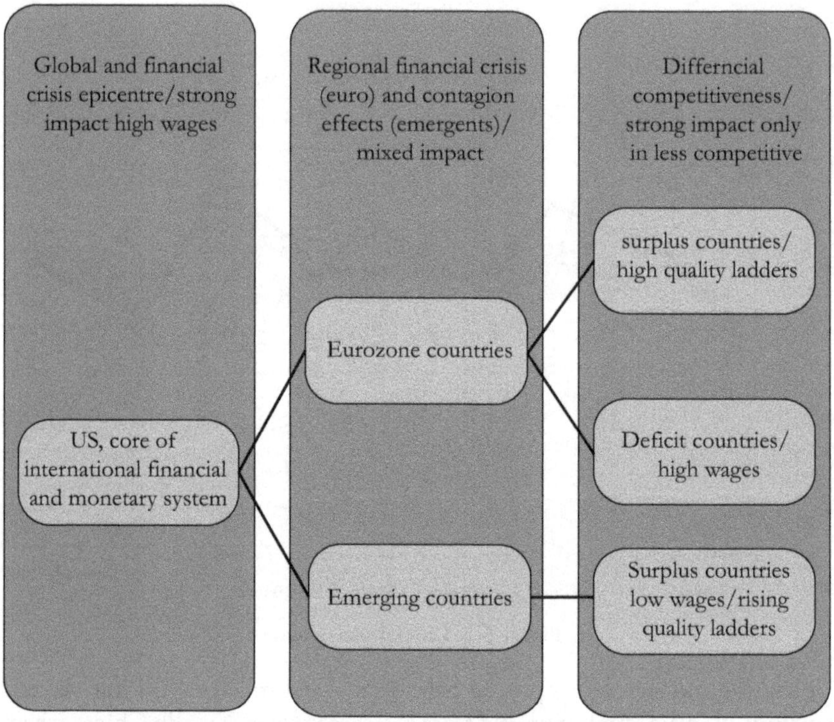


**Figure 6.2: The effects of regional and global imbalances.**

The US and other developed economies have not been forced to make such an adjustment in wages and prices. As the US is the issuer of international currency and the core of the international financial system, it can benefit from seigniorage income and the spread of interest rates. As the 2009 events have shown, it is very unlikely that the US will suffer a sudden stop or an exchange rate crisis. As it enjoys a worldwide demand for its currency and it is the ablest issuer of financial instruments, it can avoid the sort of harsh adjustment that other countries have suffered. In the UK, the flexible exchange rate regime assures a smooth adjustment though depreciation. As it is a first-class international financial centre, it has been able to avoid harsh adjustment through international brokerage. Nevertheless, the same uneven financial globalization that gave them a comparative advantage in international finance could have been the source of the housing bubbles that both suffered before the crisis. The mix of savings and liquidity gluts which flooded the international financial system was channelled to mortgage-backed securities as they seemed to be the best option offered by the financial industry at that time. This process prevented the kind of painful adjustment that Germany implemented in the early 2000s to adjust the sky-rocketing wages to the new global labour situation brought about by the Great Doubling. European peripheral countries did not make the adjustments and, additionally, were flooded by financial inflows due to the lower risk perceived thanks to the euro launching. The US and the UK were nevertheless hit by the bursting of their real estate bubbles, although they adjusted their economies in a very different manner.

What does all of this have to do with the financial crisis and the shortcomings of macroeconomic modelling? This development would have taken place with or without the 2008 financial mess, so why is it so important? The problem again is the manner with which the lack of appropriate financial modelling inside macroeconomic thinking interacted with the conducting of monetary policy in the previous years. Borio and others point first towards the *disinflationary* character of the global labour market: the Great Doubling allowed credit booms in developed countries *without* inflationary pressures. The tradable goods prices did not show inflationary pressures as the upward wage pressures in these countries were counterbalanced by deflationary pressures coming from massive low-wage labour supply from emergent countries. As nobody worried about the current account deficits because they were tolerated as 'equilibrium responses' of the markets, nothing was done to correct the imbalances and, most important, the credit booms. In the same fashion, these booms unleashed strong inflationary pressures on non-tradable goods, i.e, real estate bubbles in the US, the UK, Ireland and Spain. And here lies the problem and the link between the financial and labour trends: central banks targeted the consumer price index (CPI) and not asset or real estate price indexes. If central banks were not worried about the evolution of these bubbles, they were issuing a strong signal to markets: cheap money for a long time but, more important, they did not see *systemic risks* as a whole. The financial system, relying on the same theoretical framework, also did not see the risks. If the CPI is below the target value, nobody expects central banks to raise interest rates. So a loose monetary policy fuelled the credit booms unleashed by the savings glut and uneven financial globalization.

Central bankers did not realize the problem because they were certain they were doing the right thing. Supposedly, they did not have to worry about current account deficits, financial stability or financial innovation developments. They just had to focus on the long and well-established relationship between short-term interest rates and CPI evolution. They were sure that expectations were solidly anchored to their inflation targeting, so wages grew but they were supposedly under control, at least from the *domestic* point of view. The same occurs with asset prices and financial innovation: they were seen as pure free market developments, reflecting the growing liquidity and soundness of the financial system. As shadow banking escaped their control (especially in the US), there was nothing to be worried about, until the first foreclosures in 2006. Everybody in the financial and monetary system underestimated not only the domestic risks but the critical, systemic, risks. And the reason for this underestimation was not due to a lack of experts; the reason is that they were using models and tools which did not warn them at all about those risks, as we have seen in previous sections. This is the link between global labour trends, monetary policy conducting and financial recklessness: nobody had a complete picture of what was happening because the *goggles*, economic models and theories, were unfocused.

So, for developed countries, there were two impulses: first a positive shock in the form of a credit boom, and a negative one later on in the form of a financial crisis. In both cases, the origin was the international financial and monetary system. Obstfeld has correctly argued that we need to take a 'systemic view of global financial stability, a view that analyses the global economy much as one would analyse an integrated domestic economy'.[20] This is true, but should this systemic view consider 'unpredictable' systemic crises? Or rather, should we be able to predict this kind of 'systemic' crises? If we consider the analysis of the global economy in the same way as domestic economies, we are mainly addressing the issue of the unwinding of global imbalances. But we will not solve the issue of financial instability that arises from both global financial innovation and the uneven globalization of financial markets. As we have seen before, macroeconomic modelling does not gather all the complex issues that power the international financial system. Thus, the impulses issued by international finance have not been fully understood, as Obstfeld argues.

**The Neoclassical 'Theoretical Goggles'**

Nevertheless, the landscape of the economic system is too wide to see all of it from one observation post. Different 'theoretical goggles' offer different interpretations of the same phenomena and also direct the focus towards certain elements and relationships that emerge naturally from the corresponding theoretical structures. Economic theories are proactive in the suggestion of how the economic system operates and which symptoms should be monitored by the analysts and policymakers. Of course, this implies an intentional oblivion of many other aspects of the problem under scrutiny but, also, the discovery of hidden aspects of it. As this occurs with all the economic traditions we have dealt with in this book, at this point we would like to underline their main findings.

Neoclassical and mainstream economics have focused on the predictive success of their models, at least since Milton Friedman's 1953 essay.[21] So they have been the more authoritative and reliable source of economic forecasting for global policymakers. The DGSE models have been used to prepare the indicators upon which the monetary and fiscal policies have been conducted. Focusing on monetary policy, the basic toolkit is CPI targeting through short-term interest rates. The theoretical framework is based on Taylor's rule, whose independent variables are real CPI and real GDP growth rates. Setting aside the problems with CPI that we have seen before, the DGSE models are used to prepare real GDP estimates to compare them with the supposed long-run GDP growth. In 2008 the main failure was that using this macromodelling, not only central banks' staff, but the IMF and the BIS, were unable to foresee the Great Recession. The rise in interest rates in July 2008 by the ECB in the midst of a severe financial stress shows this: the target was 2 per cent GDP growth and there were no signs of a severe economic downturn *according to the models*. Relying on conventional wisdom, the ECB proceeded to raise interest rates. The key point here is that DGSE models were looking to other places rather than to the development of the international financial system, so it was absolutely impossible for them to predict a financial crisis. The question is why they were looking at some places instead of looking at the financial turmoil. The problem lies in their internal logical structure.

As in many other economic models, the objective is to obtain economic laws, that is, logical relations inferred from the model itself. In this case, the first version of DGSE models, the RBC theory, is characterized by a representative agent for households represented by a utility function (often logarithmic or exponential) with two arguments, consumption and leisure. The agent allocates resources between investment and consumption but also time between leisure and work. The model also includes a production function with capital and work as inputs that generates the only good of the economy that is so versatile as to serve as consumption and capital good. The equilibria obtained are competitive and Pareto optimal, and the model excludes explicitly all sectors of the economy except the real one (there is no definition of the monetary and financial systems). Other characteristics of the model include the hypothesis of rational expectations instead of mechanisms for generating expectations and the dichotomy between real and monetary sectors.

In this basic version, the economic laws are the first order conditions of the optimization problem under the intertemporal budget constraint defined, the so-called the intertemporal Euler equation. The Euler equation is the result of applying the principle of optimizing behaviour to the definitions of the representative agent and the operational environment and it explains not only the decision the agent makes, but how this decision can change if any of the exogenous variables of the Euler equation changes.

But there is another source of variation that influences the process of decision making in a dynamic fashion. The operational environment changes due to different kinds of shocks, permanent or temporary. For instance, in the budget constraint the production function plays an important role in determining the resources of the agent. If we assume that the dynamics of this production function is ruled by a stochastic process of technological shocks this fact permit us to study the evolution of the agent's decision making and how he/she substitutes consumption or labour effort over time. RBC literature explores the evolution of the budget constraint changes in many different ways, not only attributing it to real shocks but also to monetary or fiscal shocks.

In any case, the basic RBC model eventually arrives at the Euler equations that specify the equality between the marginal rate of substitution of intertemporal consumption and leisure with the marginal product of labour or the marginal rate of substitution of intertemporal consumption (the consumption and investment decision) and the rate of interest. These economic laws are the empirically testable expression of the model and, as such, they are in direct contact with reality. Thanks to the Euler equations it is possible to understand how the substitution effects between present and future consumption, or between consumption and leisure, produce oscillations in economic activity. Mainstream economics has fostered the practical apparatus for gathering and interpreting the economic reality in order to study the real behaviour of those logical relations. It would be ideal if the trajectory of relations and variables produced by the models would replicate those observed in the data. But this is one of the problems RBC has found in the present financial crisis; they are not able to generate them. This is what Ohanian argues when he studies the Great Recession of 2007–9 and the Crash of 1929. The evolution of the predicted and the observed variables are different. Values of marginal rate of substitution between consumption and leisure and marginal productivity of labour diverge.

> Standard business cycle models with financial market imperfections have no mechanism for generating this deviation from standard theory, and thus do not mechanism for generating this deviation from standard theory, and thus do not shed light on the key factor underlying the recession of 2007–2009. This does not imply that the financial crisis is unimportant in understanding the recession, but it does indicate that we do not understand the channels through which financial it does indicate that we do not understand the channels through which financial distress reduced labour input.[22]

Usually, deviations between the observed evolution of magnitudes and those predicted by the models is not taken as a falsifying instance but as evidence of some missing factor in the analysis, but 'provide a diagnostic tool for looking at the underlying causes of recession'.[23] Ricardo J. Caballero warns of two perils concerning this strict adherence to the internal logic of a theory, because it is possible to lose sight of reality itself and, also, to forget about the limits of theories.[24] Caballero reminds us how rich and varied is the research in the mainstream and how the core of the School, with its rigidities, can be complemented with a periphery of different models, also neoclassical, but more flexible. There are specific analyses of different phenomena related to the financial crisis, for example liquidity runs, leverage cycles and bubbles. Probably the most immediate challenge for mainstream economics is the integration of this periphery of hypotheses into the core, a truly complex matter. But there still remains the positivistic prejudice against the non-mathematized theories that are described as mere 'narratives'.

But Caballero himself has advanced rather intuitive insights to explain this global downturn, using new concepts such as financial fragility and uneven financial globalization. He specifically recognized that the crisis was the result of the negative feedback loop in the financial industry. Essentially, the financial sector was able to create 'safe' assets from the securitization of lower quality ones, as the demand for them grew in emerging economies.

> A key structural factor behind this crisis is the large demand for riskless assets from the rest of the world ... While in emerging markets the concern with capital flows is in their speculative nature, in the U.S. the risk in capital inflows derives from the opposite concern: capital flows into the U.S. are mostly non-speculative and in search of safety. As a result, the U.S. sells riskless assets to foreigners, and in so doing, it raises the effective leverage of its financial institutions. In other words, as global imbalances rise, the U.S. increasingly specializes in holding its *toxic waste*.[25]

Caballero has labelled this conceptual framework the *macroeconomics of asset shortage*, a term he first coined in 2006. The hypothesis seems to be counterfactual: the international financial system has a shortage of safe assets. The problem is not that savings and liquidity gluts have flooded the domestic financial systems with new and short-term assets. Rather, the problem is that the system as a whole is unable to provide enough safe assets for a growing worldwide demand. This hypothesis needs to be framed: the shortage comes from the countries with accelerating economic growth and savings – mostly emerging. But these countries are unable to channel these surpluses into domestic investments because they lack the kind of financial system (not only markets, but also banks) needed to do that with guarantees. Savers look for safe assets and the only place where there is a financial industry big enough to provide these assets on such a scale is the US. These flows, according to Caballero in 2006, unleash asset price bubbles worldwide. The 'equilibrium response' would have macroeconomic implications: global imbalances, recurrent speculative 'bubbles', low levels of long-term real interest rate, low inflation and deflation. From an economic modelling perspective, the important issue is in Caballero's equilibrium response. Because, as he said later: 'The policy prescriptions that follow from this asset-shortage view include: Recognize that high valuations (bubbles) are part of the equilibrium (reflect scarcity of store of value instruments).' This is the kind of narrative that predominates in the mainstream before the financial crisis: we may wonder if Caballero still endorses it. Nevertheless, there are elements in his hypothesis that may still be valid: the labour force that entered into global markets in 2000, as living without welfare safety nets, has a saving behaviour far more marked than the other half of the world population. But their domestic financial and monetary systems have not yet developed into the the kind of financial and banking industry needed to channel the savings into sufficient domestic investment.

In the end, their financial and monetary intermediaries buy assets and liquidity from the only industry able to do so on such a scale: the US financial and monetary system. The problem is that developed economies have a high ratio of capital to labour, so it is difficult to find assets in these countries with an attractive yield. On the contrary, the emergent countries have a low capital-to-labour ratio. They could offer better yields if capital could be appropriately transferred into safe assets, and here is where the international and monetary system failed. Again, mainstream economics has been able to grasp an essential feature of this: the so-called 'Lucas puzzle'.[26] Lucas highlighted in 1990 that standard neoclassical growth models fail to explain the 'uphill' behaviour of international capital flows, going from low-income countries to high-income countries. He explained this behaviour by arguing that institutional shortcomings lowered the returns adjusted by risk. Later research, nevertheless, pointed out that foreign direct investment (FDI) follows the downhill pattern described by the model. This uneven financial globalization will still be the source of more impulses using the RBC terminology. Downhill FDI will raise the capital-to-labour ratio in emerging economies. Further economic growth and savings could unleash new bubbles all over the world until the emerging financial system is able to do the job. So, the demand of safe assets to developed systems stops and the perspective of economic cycles sustained by real estate credit booms cease. In any case, what it is doubtful is that mainstream economics labels 'equilibrium response' episodes like the subprime housing bubble.

### The Post-Keynesian 'Theoretical Goggles'

There have been interesting theoretical developments in the heterodox camp too, but we are going to focus on post-Keynesians and Austrians, as they have developed a systematic critique about the way the financial and monetary systems are organized. In fact, for different reasons, both point to financial issues as the source of macroeconomic instability. In the Keynesian camp, there has also been a remarkable attempt to explain the current global crisis using the Japanese experience as a benchmark – the Koo theory of the 'balance sheet recession' – which we are going to see later in more detail.

The post-Keynesian school acts as a gravitational force for its myriad of different interpretations preventing the rupture of the School that is inherently diverse and creative. In the *General Theory* (*GT*), Keynes explained how the economic crisis is produced by the exhaustion of the marginal efficiency of capital (due to decreasing returns) and the relatively high rate of interest (due to the liquidity premium) that together produces a reversion of the economic agents' expectations. Once this happens, conventional behaviour takes command of decision making and the raised uncertainty precipitates the crisis violently. In this process, Keynes did not attach an important role to the financial system. His theory of liquidity was, rather, oriented to explaining how the depression should be avoided with the aid of a central bank.

After the publication of the *GT*, Keynes was involved in an academic controversy with Bertil Ohlin concerning the distinction between the demand for money and the demand for credit. For Keynes, the equality of demand and supply for money determined the interest rate but Ohlin, in line with the Stockholm School, argued that interest rates depended on the demand and supply for credit. In the subsequent exchange of ideas, Keynes extended his theory of money demand, adding a new motive to the traditional three. The finance motive for the demand of money stated that 'an investment decision may sometimes involve a temporary demand for money before it is carried out, quite distinct from the demand for active balances which will arise as a result of the investment activity whilst it is going on'.[27]

This finance motive was related to the investment decision and, hence, to the accumulation of capital in the economic system. The role of the financial system in this liquidity theory would be to provide the amounts of money needed to satisfy the demand for money (including the finance motive too), even creating credit. In this line of thought, Minsky complemented the theory of liquidity introducing the effects of the liabilities structures of enterprises and banks. Minsky's attention is focused on 'capital assets, financing arrangements that center around banks and money creation, constraints imposed by liabilities, and the problems associated with knowledge about uncertain futures',[28] problems the neoclassical synthesis usually assumes away. Keynes devoted little attention to the liabilities structure of the economic agent or the attributes of an asset in this perspective. In Chapter 17 of the *GT*, Keynes is more centred on describing the importance of the liquidity premium than in how the balance sheet can produce a situation of illiquidity or insolvency.

These aspects were studied by Minsky in depth. The financial instability hypothesis tries to explain the probable evolution of liabilities structures in different economic agents throughout the business cycle. He started by recognizing the behavioural asymmetry of agents in different moments of the cycle. When financial cycles begin, behaviour tends to be conservative and prudent because of the fresh memory of recent bad times. Investment has a sound basis and the liabilities structure of the agents is liquid in the sense that actives and passives are equilibrated in the short and long terms. The elevated risk premium acts as a guarantee of success for entrepreneurs which, with the passage of time, will slowly change agent's aversion to risk.

Optimism eventually would catch the imagination of the agents who would be more inclined to buy speculative assets and to invest in increasingly risky businesses. One consequence of this 'euphoric economy'[29] is the growing necessity of new sources for financing. Banks are fundamental in providing the external funds for the expansion of economic activity. The transition from more liquid liabilities structures to more illiquid ones is explained by the changing concerns about risk. The capability to honour debts will become more and more degraded as the boom of the economy unfolds. Then, financial innovation flourishes with two consequences. First, 'the market price of existing assets will rise' and, second, 'by lowering the cost of financing, financial innovations lower the supply price of investment output'.[30]

Under these circumstances of economic growth, optimism, financial innovation and increasing illiquidity of the balance sheets, 'much investment activity depends on financing relations in which total short-term debt outstanding increases because the interest that is due on earlier borrowing exceeds the income earned by assets. I called this *Ponzi financing*.'[31] The investments that were promising at the beginning of the cycle become speculative with the high interest rates and the illiquidity of balance sheets. The rise of the liquidity premium would mark the moment of inflection for the cycle and the proximity of economic depression.

In the wake of post-Keynesian and Minskian thought, Richard Koo, a Nomura Institute researcher, has advanced a remarkable hypothesis about the balance sheet character of the current crisis, which has also attracted attention from mainstream economists. The idea is based on Japan's lost decade recession and Koo generalized it to the US and European countries, as they are all caught in a 'recession driven by deleveraging'. But the aim of the work is to look for tools to escape to the long-lasting effects of deleveraging on economic activity, as Japan has been unable to do that since 1990. Koo rightly argues that traditional policy mix cannot do the job, as Japan shows. Massive public spending mixed with zero interest rates during decades has not brought about the desired effect of a sizeable GDP growth rate. His analysis aims to explain why the massive policy stimulus has been mostly ineffective in Japan, rather than explaining the source of the impulse and the mechanism of propagation of the current crisis. But the starting point is seriously flawed: there is a key difference in the 1990 Japanese financial crisis and that of 2008. The Japanese crisis was a classical credit boom financed through the domestic financial sector. There were no sizeable inflows of foreign capital as there were high savings levels and a competitive tradable sector. The 2008 financial collapse and its spillovers have been largely unleashed by international capital flows and originated in one country, the US, with low savings levels. Nevertheless, the hypothesis about how the private sector reacts to a burst bubble is workable and may be of help in the explanation of the subsequent economic stagnation and the supposed ineffectiveness of massive fiscal and monetary stimulus.

Private sector behaviour after an asset prices collapse can lead to a 'recession driven by deleveraging' as households and firms try to recover the financial soundness of their balance sheets:

> When the bubble bursts, asset prices collapse while liabilities remain, leaving millions of private sector balance sheets underwater. This leaves the private sector with no choice but to minimize debt in order to climb out of negative equity territory and regain its credit ratings.[32]

In order to purge their balance sheets and recover their financial health and credit ratings, households and businesses are forced to increase their savings levels and pay down debts. The key process is financial deleveraging, which reduces aggregate demand and unleashes a 'balance sheet recession'. Koo's approach is pure Keynesianism in two ways: first, he rejects the traditional anthropological core assumptions of neoclassical mainstreams and, second, predicts a sort of 'liquidity trap' in which monetary policy reaches zero lower bound interests rates and remains ineffective in restoring economic activity for a long time.

Koo departs from the neoclassical usual hypothesis about economic agent behaviour in two ways. First, as we have said, he poses the main factor of the crisis not in the structure of international financial and monetary systems but in the purely financial, non-rational, idiosyncratic and recurrent tendency of the private sector to 'lose its mind and discipline in a bubble' once every few decades. This is a 'true' Keynesian hypothesis, a kind of 'animal spirits' living both in households and business financial behaviour. Once this non-rational behaviour starts, the private sector get caught up 'believing that they are going to make tons of money, leverage themselves up to the hilt as they borrow and invest in all sorts of assets'. The bubble unfolds not as 'rational, equilibrium response' as some neoclassicals like Caballero will argue. Rather, it evolves in an irrational way as it is fed by financial and non-financial private sectors by leveraging. The over-optimistic expectations of huge and quick windfalls get both sectors caught up in a deadly debt trap. When the bubble bursts and the asset prices collapse, the households' and firms' balance sheets go 'underwater'. The second departure from the neoclassical hypotheses core is made when Koo goes on to explain the behaviour of non-financial private sectors when their balances are underwater. From the observed and well-documented behaviour of Japanese, the US, the UK and European countries, he assumes that firms and household change their previous conduct and engage in a minimizing debt dynamic rather than maximizing profits or utility. After asset prices collapse, private savings soar even in the landscape of zero interest rates. The same feedback, idiosyncratic behaviour that unleashed the bubble, brings about a deleveraging process which continuously reduces aggregate demand 'until either private sector financial health is restored or the private sector as a whole has become too poor to save any money'. This amount of savings, at near-zero interest rates, remains in the financial sector balances and becomes a 'leakage to the income stream and a deflationary gap in the economy'.

When the debt minimization behaviour spreads throughout the whole economy, monetary policy has no room for additional margin in fighting against recession. Why? The operational environment of monetary policy is the financial system and its role is to match borrowers and lenders. People with 'underwater' balance sheets will not be interested in increasing borrowing at any interest rate. Nor will there be many willing lenders for those with impaired balance sheets, especially when the lenders themselves have balance sheet problems. Koo also describes the process as a contraction of the money supply, as agents use the bank deposits to repay debts. The massive liquidity injections will be ineffective because they are simply used to minimize debt, rather than foster credit growth. Of course, following Keynesian orthodoxy, the solution is fiscal stimulus.

**The Austrian 'Theoretical Goggles'**

Finally, it is time to revise what the Austrian School sees with its 'theoretical goggles'. The Austrian business cycle theory is rooted in the notion of subjective knowledge and the temporal dimension of decision making. Both explain two important elements of Austrian theory, the time preference and the concept of capital goods. Time preference is a hypothesis on the behaviour of agents and states that, *ceteris paribus*, agents wish to satisfy their needs as soon as possible. That is, the same good is more valuable today than tomorrow. The concept of capital is referred to as the stages of a plan of action: 'all intermediate stages which an actor subjectively views as such, and which embody any production process he employs, are capital goods'.[33] These 'high-order economic goods' need to set aside inputs from consumption and re-elaborate them in time to be accumulated. Because the production processes of different first-order goods, i.e. consumer goods, require different accumulations of capital and different periods of time to be produced, in capitalistic economies there is a complex structure of capital goods that evolves over time. This productive structure involves all the stages or capital goods of all the production processes of the economy: 'These goods consist of machines, tools, computers, software, buildings, semi-manufactured goods, etc., and they exist due to prior saving by the nation's citizens'.[34]

The concept of capital goods distinguishes itself from the concept of 'capital' as the market price of capital goods that is dependent on the expected profits of the consumer goods. Throughout the business cycle, the composition of the productive structure changes in two dimensions: first, the variety and number of consumer goods can be greater or lesser and, second, the complexity of stages of production can be longer or shorter. This 'widening' and 'lengthening' of the productive structure is mainly affected by the relation between future earnings expectations and the rate of interest. In the absence of any external intervention, Austrians defend that the economic system tends to spontaneously order the capital structure to the expected earnings, the interest rate and the time preference of the agents. The structure is sustainable because, first, entrepreneurs are efficient in localizing and exploiting profit opportunities (this human trait, especially present in entrepreneurs, is what the Austrians called the 'entrepreneurial function'); second, because interest rates coordinate the intertemporal plans of action of agents (demanders and suppliers of loanable funds or savings) whenever it is determined by a time preference agreement.

But unfortunately for Austrians, interest rates can be artificially changed in modern economies thanks to the corruption of two social institutions: money and the deposit contracts. Money is a typical human institution, that is, a spontaneously discovered pattern of behaviour aimed at solving a human need: facilitating trade and, hence, the satisfaction of human needs. When the State monopolizes the emission of money through fiduciary media, it is introducing the possibility of altering its value (and the level of interest rates) and relative prices through money creation. Relative prices and interest rates are fundamental guiding signals in economic calculation for entrepreneurial activity.

In Mises's approach, the existence of a sole money issuer combined with the capacity of money creation of commercial banks, can artificially alter the interest rates, completely changing the guiding signals for productive investment. An artificial reduction of interest rates is misguiding because it creates the promise of an economic profit that will be impossible in the medium and long terms. When interest rates are low, entrepreneurs are correct in thinking that savers are willing to wait for a longer period of time. This can be understood as the possibility for entrepreneurs to engage in longer investment processes because, in the future, savers will increase their purchasing power and will buy their products. But, according to forced savings doctrine, the promising future will disappear when investors discover that the expected future purchasing power does not exist. This will revert the expectations, precipitate a credit crunch and drive the economy into depression. Although the debate about forced savings happened more than seventy years ago and the Austrian insights were discarded by both neoclassicals and Keynesians, the argument is quite similar to that of Koo's balance sheet recessions. If we simply take asset or real estate prices instead of CPI, the outcome is quite similar: a recession brought about by a credit boom.

To avoid the kind of problems posed by 'artificial' credit led Austrians to propose a reform in the banking system consisting of 100 per cent reserve on deposits, which means that the commercial banking business would be limited to the safekeeping and payment management, and their earnings would derive from fees only. Lending activity would be carried out by 'investment' or 'lending' banks which cannot collect bank deposits and their funding sources would come from equity, securities and all forms of financial instruments other than bank deposits. That reform was thought for the banking system in the first third of the twentieth century and, in fact, it was not only an Austrian proposal. Many other neoclassical economists such as Irving Fisher, Henry C. Simons, Milton Friedman, James Tobin and Maurice Allais were also strong supporters.[35] But while the issue has almost disappeared from mainstream literature, it has been claimed by Austrians as the main source of cyclical fluctuations. Austrians clearly warned about the inherent instability of a fractional reserve banking system and its role as a main source of financial crisis and highly volatile business cycles. A fractional reserve system gives the financial system huge elasticity in the creation of means of payment when economic activity is booming. In fact, the greater the debt capacity of the banking sector, the greater this elasticity will be and the higher its capacity to fuel the supply of liquid short terms assets – quasi money.

Nevertheless, the proposal of a reform of the banking system with a 100 per cent of reserve coefficient was designed to be applied to financial institutions that can be labelled as 'traditional banking'. We have seen that the evolution of the banking system in the last fifteen years has brought about a parallel banking system which does not rely on banking deposits as a main source of funding. This shadow banking, whose liabilities almost double those of traditional banking, has alternative short-term funding, mostly backed by longer-term collateral assets, and again is used to fund other long-term assets. So, one might argue that a 100 per cent reserve banking system is not a solution for the financial problems of the twenty-first century. And it is true that, as far as we know, Austrians have not worked on a reform of the current financial system.

Nevertheless, from a financial point of view the management of the 'traditional' and 'shadow' systems is quite similar. They both share the same temporal structure and they both transform *maturities* and *risk*. The difference between current account deposits and repos is that the deposits are insured by specific and 'official' trustee institutions and the issuer is backed by the lender of last resort. The repo agreements are insured in some cases by 'private' insurance institutions and they lack the support of central banks facilities. But they *both* are short-term liabilities used to fund long-term liabilities. If we ban the use of current account deposits to fund longer-term operations and limit the commercial banking to the safekeeping and payment managements, the problem will simply be transferred to the shadow banking system. And of course though it will prevent traditional bank runs it won't prevent the kind of financial and pro-cyclical instability that lies at the heart of the current economic downturns. Further research about the macroeconomic issues of the maturity mismatch is needed, far beyond the valuable but out-of-date reform of 100 per cent reserve coefficient.

## *Methodological Issues*

In Chapter 3 we have seen how the realism of assumptions and hypotheses has been considered less and less by mainstream economists, whether for theoretical reasons (Friedman's and Lucas's arguments) or for practical reasons (the success of the neoclassical paradigm), and, to such extent, methodological issues are nowadays of almost negligible importance to them. Unfortunately, methodology always accompanies the work of the scientist and its difficulties do not disappear simply by ignoring them. For neoclassicals, positivism is a double-edged sword. On the one hand, it inclines theory towards empiricism and prediction but, on the other hand, it pushes research to mathematical formalism and the use of simplistic and unreal assumptions. This is reflected in the characterization of economic agents and, for instance, in how mainstream economics has refused to explain the generation of expectations thanks to the hypothesis of rational expectations. Human action is clearly an intentional behaviour and, in this sense, we rightly assume the existence of rationality behind every decision that is made. The hypothesis of rational expectations makes an especially strong interpretation of that assumption and equals individual agent expectations with the probability of the occurrence of events predicted by a formal economic model. The hypothesis, then, supposes as correct two different things: first, that in an economy the aggregate of individuals tends to distribute their expectations around the correct prediction of what will happen and, second, that that model is basically correct. The same can be said about how the operational environment is defined without a financial system or how EMH is attributed to markets with no hesitations. This unrealism can only be supported by the 'as if' clause and the logical constraints for certain mathematical problems. Often scientists ought to restrict their research to a limited number of functions and boundary conditions in order to obtain a meaningful solution (that is, meaningful equilibria). As a consequence of all these problems, methodological issues must be pushed to the forefront again.

The financial crisis has shed light on the fact that these unrealistic characterizations of the agents and/or the operational environment made it impossible for mainstream economics to explain and forecast the crisis. The Friedman/Lucas approach was an attempt: non-realistic models can be useful if they explain data and facts. With the recent experience at hand, this approach does seem to be successful. And this opens again the unending controversy between prediction and explanation in science that, in economics, presents characteristics of its own. Economics is an applied science by nature because it is not only made by the action of the members of the economy but it also affects their lives and welfare to a great extent. Governments as well as enterprises or citizens need guidelines for sound decision making. But, what seems to be paradoxical is that the way in which economics has chosen to make accurate predictions tends to obscure the comprehension of what is happening in the economic system.

One of many direct attacks against logical positivism was centred on the so-called 'thesis of symmetry', according to which explanation and prediction are structurally symmetrical. The only difference between them would be temporary: explanation is *ex post* and prediction *ex ante*. But prediction can be done without explanation (as in an extrapolation) and explanation without prediction (as in unique events). But explanation and prediction can also be understood as qualities of the models, as different dimensions of the scientific task. In economics we certainly need both of them.

The puzzlement of professional economists and politicians throughout the financial crisis, as we have explained in Chapter 1 and Chapter 5, is symptomatic because, for those who are in charge and have responsibilities in managing and governing economic institutions, to comprehend the economic phenomena and their evolution in a timely manner is essential. Otherwise, they do not understand what is happening and will be unable to predict what the future could bring. In this sense, we dissent from Hempel's 'thesis of symmetry' when he argues that a good explanation is already a good prediction and that a good prediction is already a good explanation. Better explanations provide the foundations for better predictions but better predictions can be absolutely useless in explaining a phenomenon. We have to go deeper in the understanding of agent's behaviour and of the markets but comprehension also requires realism in its assumptions.

We probably have ventured too far into mathematical modelling and it may help to step back to gain perspective. We need explanations of the events to reduce the surprise that crises produce but also to understand the events in themselves. The problem, of course, is the unavoidable trade-off between explanation and accurate prediction, which is a long road to go for economists. But at the very least, those involved in dealing with economic models, explanations, recommendations and predictions must be aware that all of these professional activities have very defined limits. 'Even if prediction is not the goal, the predictive qualities of a model should be reported alongside its explanatory power so that it can be fairly evaluated in terms of its capabilities and compared to other models.'[36]

The economic profession has to recover the sense of proportion when dealing with economic models. The critical hypotheses of the theories are extremely sensitive elements for this goal. For instance, the philosophical foundations of the models that we dealt with in Chapter 2 give sensitive clues about the nature of the theory and the predictions we can expect from them. The same can be said about the field of definition of the models that is already contained in the critical hypotheses. As we have explained in Chapter 3 the critical hypotheses can destroy a model or theory if they do not perform well because they make the model or theory unable to explain the facts. The example in Chapter 4, namely RBC, is straightforward. As a consequence we must carefully distinguish in each model which hypotheses are critical and we should not take for granted that they hold. We must check it out. We should rely on less demanding hypotheses to ensure that we are focusing on the right things.

We recognize that the trade-off between the workability and realism of the hypotheses is difficult to deal with. Narrow, but mathematically workable hypotheses would not be adequate in a first approach towards the kind of processes we have described in the previous section. As we face a largely unexplored territory, we should not discard any plausible explanation although it cannot be fitted into a mathematical or econometric model.

Another interesting point refers to some methodological instruments of the modern economic theory such as the concept of equilibrium. As a mental category, the concept of equilibrium in economics serves to make 'mental experiments' and, in this sense, it is a useful way to understand certain events. But the methodological assumption does not correspond with the historical reality of the equilibrium. For instance, the price of copper on 10 July 2006 implies an equilibrium between demanders and suppliers. We are aware of the constant tendency of markets to reach the equilibrium as well as the constant disruption of that tendency for different reasons. In mainstream economics the concept of 'long-term equilibrium' is popular, as well as its dynamic counterparts, the natural rates of interest, growth, inflation and so on. The problem with this approach is also one of realism. Markets are very efficient in bringing the economy back to equilibrium but, as Keynes observed, there may exist institutional restrictions that force a rest situation out of a neoclassical equilibrium (as in labour markets or under a 'liquidity trap' condition). Equilibrium is not a permanent condition of the operation of economies. Moreover, the dynamic concept of 'long-term equilibrium' has never been completely explained by mainstream economics, as is evident in the use of the Hodrick–Prescott filter in RBC when it is used to characterize business cycles and to establish stylized facts among macro magnitudes. As in other filters with the same purpose, there is no definition of the trend of the economy as a dynamic 'long-term equilibrium' which would justify the conclusion that the difference between that trend and the observed time series is really the cyclical component of the economy, the pathological part of its performance.

A new disequilibrium approach, or at least a new concept of economic equilibrium and its usefulness, would be necessary. Austrian market process theory, as developed by Kirzner (1992) and Lachmann (1977), is a good starting point. A more refined version is the concept of *restless capitalism* developed by Metcalfe, working on the evolutionary theory of economic change by Nelson and Winter. In both cases, the economy is in a state of disequilibrium all of the time. Equilibrium is merely a mere conceptual state. Following this reasoning, we could envisage equilibrium not as the regular state of the economy but a mere benchmark or sorting device of diverse disequilibrium states. What we see in the real life economy is that it does not show either equilibrating or explosive trajectories. A conceptual framework of the most usual kinds of disequilibria should be devised as a first step in designing a reliable early warning system.

## *The Role of the Economic Agent*

Throughout the history of economic thought, the characterization of the economic agent has not been, strictly speaking, a scientific endeavour. We have devoted attention in Chapter 2 to showing how philosophy has played a fundamental role in the determination of the image of the human being that can be found within every contemporary economic model. This evidence, no matter how odd it is or how much it differs from our preconceptions, is also a natural implication of the object of study: the human being. The weight of personal philosophical convictions has been, and still is today, of radical importance in the definition of the economic agent. So, it is not difficult to understand the inflexibility with which economists from all bands stand beside their models and oppose alternative paradigms of equal strength.

At the same time, scientific knowledge and theories about human beings have accumulated and developed in the last decades – research that we can use for the benefit of our future characterizations of the economic agent. In Chapter 3 we presented an illustration of this possibility through an example taken from the psychological theory of personality. Many more fruitful opportunities for cooperation between economics and other sciences of the human being can be found and used in the future.

At present, it is possible, operative and recommendable to profit from the clear complementarities of the diverse characterizations of the economic agent that we have at our disposal. For instance, in the path followed by the business cycle, the agent's behaviour changes endogenously depending on the moment of slump, recession, recovery or boom. This behaviour can be modelled as a phase change. In the normal phases of the cycle, when the operational environment is stable, the behaviour of agents seems to be well described by the Austrian type of economic agent. Agents respond rationally to the signals that markets are sending and the observed feasibility of almost all investing decisions. But the moments of turmoil, when the recovery is transforming itself into a boom, or when the slump pushes the economy into recession, seem to be better described by the Keynesian type of economic agent. Uncertainty transforms individual action into collective 'conventional-guide' decision making and, suddenly, the economic system 'becomes a by-product of the activities of a casino' as Keynes said in the *GT*. These different and endogenous behaviours are very common in financial issues (stock markets, the bears and the bulls, bubbles occurring and bubbles bursting, etc.). This observation has not been obviated by the neoclassical theorists and there is an incipient body of literature which is trying to fit agents' risk perception as an endogenous variable within DSGE models.[37]

Another lesson we learned from our study of the financial crisis is that the size and complexity of the financial system forces us to include the financial system in every macroeconomic model, not only as a key part, but as an economic agent. We are not talking about monetary issues, but about financial issues, as we have outlined in Chapter 5. The financial system should be considered on level terms with public sector, or private consumption. Investment should be addressed as one aspect of the financial system, not isolated in any way. We can avoid modelling the financial system in long-term models, mainly economic growth, because the effects of the financial system are uncertain (models showing that deep and sound financial systems help the economy to grow, or at least there is a correlation between the degree of financial deepness and economic growth, and models showing that beyond a point the financial system can harm the economy by consuming valuable resources). But the crisis has proved that medium-term models (dynamic in all cases) do not perform well without it.

Envisaging the financial system as an economic agent paves the way for a careful rethinking of its role in modern economics. We have explained in Chapter 4 and Chapter 5 that one important reason in explaining why traditional economic theories underscored this role is because they implicitly assumed that the monetary system, and the financial system more broadly, were only the counterpart of the real side of the economy. This argument can be right or wrong but it deserves a more in-depth analysis, though as a first attempt it may work. But traditional economic theories have deducted from this assumption a questionable assertion: that the monetary and financial systems are logically dependent on the real side of the economy. So, they took for granted that the real side of the economy was the starting point of all economic processes. The financial crisis has proven that this assumption is incorrect. In Chapter 5 we saw how economic processes that were originated in the financial side of the economy had large effects on the real side. For instance, the cheap financing of peripheral Eurozone countries by financial markets that believed they were bearing the same risk as in financing Germany. This process has had large consequences on GDP and unemployment in these countries as we have explained previously. The lesson that must be learnt is that the logical precedence of the real side of the economy over the financial side takes place sometimes, but sometimes the process runs in the opposite direction. As a consequence, we have to eliminate this 'a priori' hypothesis from our theories and models and study what occurs in every single case. This approach is not entirely new. These ideas can be found in a very primitive way in the 'endogenous money supply' concept. They assume that the banking system has a pro-cyclical behaviour that creates a surplus of banking deposits through credit booms. Our proposal has to bear in mind, in every case, that an economic process can depart from the real side of the economy or from the financial system. Moreover, the financial system, as an agent of the economy, has its own objectives that must be taken into account. Since it is not an ancillary system anymore it deserves an analysis of its aims and restrictions, as the public sector does. The securitization process we have mentioned in Chapter 5 is a good example. The financial system engaged in the securitization process because the 'generate to distribute' model was very profitable for financial institutions. The crisis stopped or slowed down the process, but incentives have not disappeared, so we should bear in mind that the financial institutions will develop it again. We believe that this process has been harmful, and that it should be overseen very carefully as we will explain in the last part of this chapter.

One of the key features of the banking system is the maturity transformation. This transformation is carried out by the traditional banking system as well as the shadow banking system. The long-term investment funding by shorter term assets is a primary source of financial instability. Any reform of the international monetary and financial system must rely on an accurate representation of the macroeconomic implication of this process, and not only from the monetary policy angle. The way the banking industry carries out the maturity transformation determines the level of consumption and investment of the economy, as leveraging or deleveraging processes have shaped the GDP rates of several developed and systemic economies, as in the case of the US, the UK, Spain and others.

### *Improving the Operational Environment*

The success in fighting against the crisis has been uneven, better in the US than in the EU. It has also been partial, as the figures of unemployment and GDP growth in Europe show and, as we have explained in Chapter 1, it has been very costly. In addition, this uneven performance has relied on economic policy measures whose theoretical grounds are not based on mainstream economics. In the second part of this chapter we have shown that these theories did not encompass many influential phenomena because their operational environment did not take them into account. So, what is needed is a widening of the operational environment of economic theory. The financial system has increased in size and complexity to an extent that virtually influences every economic process. Macroeconomic theories and models must include it as a relevant part of the overall picture. One important controversy between different paradigms up to now has been about the relative importance of the real side versus the monetary side of the economy. The financial crisis has shown once and for all that the monetary side of the economy must be included in the operational environment of each model. In addition, we have learnt that the monetary side has to be enlarged to include the whole financial system. This is a very important change and very difficult as well, but it is unavoidable. The financial system should be included at the same level as the public sector or private consumption, because it does not respond automatically to changes in the real side of the economy, but displays a high degree of autonomy. There is an active interaction between, for instance, the public sector and the financial system as we have witnessed during the crisis. The behaviour of the public sector is influenced by the dynamics of the financial system, and vice versa. For instance, before the crisis, the international financial system fostered the private indebtedness of peripheral European countries such as Spain, Greece and Ireland. The drying up of international financial markets in 2008 led to drastic processes of fiscal consolidation in many countries. The amount of private debt, which in some cases turned into public debt, became unserviceable once the crisis started and forced the EU to put into practice financial rescues whose consequences will last for years, affecting their GDPs and unemployment rates. Models and theories that deal with medium-term economic phenomena have to enlarge their operational environment to include the financial system. We have explained in detail in Chapter 4 how and why the absence of the financial system in RBC theory has harmed it considerably.

The private indebtedness of peripheral European countries sheds light on two different and wider issues and the extent of the influence of the financial system as part of the operational environment. Economic theory did not pay much attention to private debt before the crisis. Public debt focused on the analyses of theorists that warned about their dangers and their potential unsustainability in the long run. These concerns led to the design and implementation of economic policy rules that were applied to those countries that wanted to join the Eurozone. The rules pointed to the risks for a monetary union of countries exhibiting large public debt figures. Private indebtedness did not provoke the same concerns. Public debt was important because the public sector was a key part of economic theories and their financing was an issue that had to be addressed. Conversely, private indebtedness was simply the counterpart and the consequence of the economic activity of private markets for goods and services and its evolution would change as soon as the fundamentals changed. The crisis has shown that private indebtedness is one of the worst imbalances that an economy can suffer and that it can drive a country to the brink, as we have explained in Chapter 5. Again, the operational environment of economic models and theories missed this part.

Moreover, the effects of the action of the financial system have influenced the GDP of some countries. The flow of cheap financing in economies like Spain is one of the main factors that underlie the unprecedented period of high economic growth. Spain grew on average around 3.5 per cent from 2001 to 2007, far more than any other European country except Ireland. Meanwhile, the current account deficit grew at the same pace, reaching 10 per cent of Spanish GDP. Without this cheap financing, private consumption would have increased less, and the same applies to investment. Spanish economic agents, mainly private agents, were led to increase their consumption and to invest much more because they could do so at very low interest rates. Private agents engaged in an accelerated process of leveraging because financing was cheap and economic prospects were brilliant. In that way, the international financial system fostered growth in Spain. When the crisis arrived, cheap financing turned into a drying up of financial markets, and things became ugly. The same financial impulse that had led the Spanish economic growth plunged the country into recession.

There is an additional difficulty in describing the financial system as a part of the operational environment. For years, it was thought that the main operation of the financial system, the maturity transformation, was carried out by banks and other financial institutions that were controlled to a certain extent by monetary authorities. Moreover, it was generally assumed that their main role was not to control this transformation, but to take care of interest rates as an instrument of monetary policy. The financial crisis has shown that monetary authorities should pay much more attention to the maturity transformation and should oversee it, so we need to include it in the operational environment of the models. But this is not enough because the financial innovation we have explained in the first part of this chapter has led to an unstoppable process of securitization and the emergence of shadow banking. Shadow banking performs the same operations as traditional financial institutions but out of the reach of monetary authorities. The first step in controlling this is to include it in the operational environment of our models. The way in which 'standard' financial institutions and shadow banking carry out maturity transformation exerts a strong influence on the real side of the economy. Economic policy measures to cope with that require a reliable economic theory which encompasses all the factors that are relevant. The challenge is very complicated.

In Chapter 1 we have explained that the Austrian business cycle theory (ABCT) is very good in explaining a financial crisis because it stresses that throughout the cycle there is a mismatch between producers that want to invest in production goods and consumers that prefer consumer goods. This mismatch remains unobservable because of the effects of monetary policy on interest rates, but sooner or later it unleashes a crisis. So, we believe that a very good departure point for enlarging and improving the operational environment of economic models regarding the financial system is to use the ABCT approach. Theorists did not credit it before the crisis for many reasons, but the facts have shown that it was worthwhile. The theory is useful because it offers a better description of the running of the financial system, and economic theory can utilize it without being obliged to adhere to the Austrian economics paradigm in full. In Chapter 3 we have pointed out that economic theories can be complementary because one of them addresses a specific issue far better than the others. This is the case of the financial crisis and ABCT. But ABCT is not the last word either. To be more workable it needs more data. Fitting the data must continue to be the aim of economic theory. Theories are built up bearing this objective in mind. But at the same time, theories shape the type of data they need to analyse and to provisionally confirm or reject them. Dominant theories, such as mainstream economics, have fostered research on those data they needed, as in the case of growth theory as we have explained in Chapter 4, and data sets have increased. But ABCT has not been able to generate this process, so the required data to analyse the evolution of the financial system throughout the cycle is lacking. A research agenda on this issue is required.

The same applies to Minsky's approach to the financial system, the 'financial fragility hypothesis'. It describes financial crises much better than any mainstream economics model, but it was belittled, partly because it was unable to establish the timing of the processes. The reason was, again, the lack of data. We can use Minsky's hypothesis to improve the understanding of the functioning of the financial system, but we need more reliable and comprehensive data sets. We realize that this is easier said than done because data in financial issues are scattered and perverse incentives have led agents to hide the data, even at small offshore financial locations. But the effort is worthwhile.

From a broader point of view, the financial crisis has challenged one of the main assumptions of the macroeconomic models of mainstream economics:[38] in the operational environment equilibrium prevails and disequilibrium is nearly always temporary and is corrected by market forces. We have explained in Chapter 1 how the EMH guided the behaviour of agents in financial markets before the crisis and how it misled many of them in their decision-making processes. The main tenant of the EMH is that any additional piece of information affecting assets will change their price in the correct way so economic agents need not search for additional information to value the assets they want to buy or sell. This fact assures the agent that he is always acting in equilibrium or very close to it. As a consequence, uncertainty is small and decision-making processes are easy. The financial crisis showed that EMH failed to explain what was going on. Beyond this failure, if EMH is not trustworthy, we should not state that asset prices are usually in equilibrium or very near to equilibrium, but to assume that they seldom are in equilibrium.

The same applies to other issues like global imbalances, whose effects we have explained in Chapter 5. In a previous section we have shown that before the crisis, many experts believed global imbalances were an equilibrium response of international financial flows to the fundamentals of the world's largest economies. As such, they would diminish as long as the fundamentals changed. Again, this equilibrium approach was very reassuring because we could expect they would correct themselves. After the crisis, global imbalances have been envisaged as a disequilibrium phenomenon whose dangers can be large. The switch in the way we envisage EMH and global imbalances before and after the crisis is very meaningful. Although we are more comfortable believing that economic phenomena are quite always near equilibrium, we should get rid of this assumption. Instead, we should focus on analysing how out-of-equilibrium phenomena evolve and the likelihood of every type of possible evolution. In this new theoretical scenario, equilibrium simply becomes a benchmark or sorting device of diverse disequilibrium states.

## *What is Wrong with Theory and Policymaking*

In Chapters 1, 5 and 6 we have been dealing with the causes and factors that together brought about the current financial crisis and the economic recession. And we have seen in Chapter 6 that macroeconomic modelling has been unable to understand and, of course, predict, the global economic downturn. The consequences of this failure for policymaking and, above all, for societies have been devastating. And the toll is not only the monetary cost of the successive bailouts, foreclosures and tax burdens. Unemployment, poverty, political disaffection and social alienation are, above all, the true toll of the crisis. So policymaking has to rely on more sound, complete and comprehensive maps or models of economic processes than those which we have relied on until now. We have seen in previous sections the kind of research that has to be done to improve macroeconomic modelling and economic theory in general. But we have also seen that there have been interesting developments in diagnosing and understanding the current financial crisis. From this point of view, we do not have a full, articulate and definitive theoretical account. But we can create a very general and tentative framework of some of the main issues involved in *this* crisis, the issues that are still missing, and the measures that can be adopted in order to prevent another crisis *similar* to this one. Of course we cannot expect to be fully prepared to prevent whatever economic crisis arises in the future, because technological and financial innovations will change the general landscape in ways we are unable to foresee at present. But we can be prepared to avoid the same kind of mistakes or omissions in policymaking that took place in the years before the 2008 turmoil.

What have we learnt from this crisis for the future of policymaking? Returning to the causes that we have analysed in this book, we can generally group them in four broad categories: long-term, global trends in labour supply; global imbalances; the global banking industry; and international and national monetary systems. Policymaking and regulation can act directly only on the last three because the labour supply, formal or informal, is a demographic and geopolitical factor that is out of the scope of macroeconomic modelling, though its consequences, the global imbalances, are not.

As to global imbalances, here the ultimate problem has been a lack of understanding of what is and what is not a 'disequilibrium' from a theoretical point of view. If, as Nigel Lawson, Allan Greenspan and others have contented, we regard a current account deficit of 10 per cent of GDP as an 'equilibrium' phenomenon, then we should not be concerned about this. But, as we have seen, if we consider that an uneven financial globalization, a *Great Doubling* in labour supply and the gross financial flows unleashed by the net international financial position of surplus and deficit countries are the kind of disequilibrium phenomena we must worry about, then specific policy targeting and measures should be considered to tackle them. Current account deficits, and their counterpart, the net international investment position, were a concern in other international monetary systems, such as Bretton Woods or Gold Standard. Then, although the target was the fixed exchange rate, the focus was on preventing the accumulation of large external imbalances through domestic policymaking and/or capital controls. Currently, with an international monetary system based on a flexible exchange rate regime, it is assumed that the tendency will be toward a correction of these imbalances through currency depreciation. But we have seen that this has not been the case, on the contrary, the global financial industry has fuelled and allowed the accumulation of large external imbalances which brought about unsustainable levels of external debt in some developed countries. It is true that China's exchange rate policy has been of no help in this process, but the *Great Doubling* and the supposed convergence of wages weighted by quality ladders did not take place *due to the credit boom* and its effect on nominal wages. While Germany has been able to cope with this, the rest of the developed world is still struggling with a general loss of competitiveness, with unsustainable rates of unemployment and a fragile economic recovery. When we look back, we realize that much of the social wreck could have been avoided if current account deficit countries targeted their unsustainable levels of external debt, instead of considering them as an 'equilibrium response'.

The second factor was the financial innovation and regulation of the global banking industry. Here the lack of an early warning system has been the main failure from the policymakers' perspective because they were absolutely unaware of what was going on in the financial system they oversaw. But the problem is deeper and has more implications for both policymaking and economic theory. While the global imbalances were well understood and well identified (although not targeted as a policy issue), the implications of financial innovation and the development of shadow banking largely escaped the scrutiny of researchers, regulation agencies and policymakers. One may well argue that there was an ideological, neoconservative bias, in that non-attendance, as Phillip Mirowski does.[39] But throughout Chapter 5 and in previous sections of Chapter 6, we have seen that there is a deeper fault line and a much more defective understanding of the size, scope and working of the global financial system. As the size of the shadow banking system is several times that of the sum of governments, it does not make sense to consider it a mere intermediary or as a mere 'friction' in the matching of domestic savings and investment. Rather, the global banking industry should be considered as an 'additional' agent, along with firms, households and governments. From the very beginning the EU has focused exclusively on fiscal deficits, disregarding 'private' deficits and balance sheets disequilibria unleashed by capital inflows and outflows. The international financial system can provoke domestic fiscal consolidations by simply widening the interest rates spreads, as the euro crisis has shown. Macroeconomic modelling should consider this 'new' agent in the same way it considers government: an agent with its own objectives and budget constraints. But an early warning system built around this kind of new macroeconomic modelling is not going to be available *before* the next financial crisis. New financial innovations will appear and, *under some circumstances*, may trigger new and deeper financial crises. So, as happened with global imbalances, policymakers should focus on surveillance and monitoring of the balance sheet of private agents, and targeting unsustainable developments such as excessive leverage or long-term borrowing. A fiscal policy can do the job more quickly than regulatory changes, through a tax increase on the activities that originate the leveraging or borrowing.

The *circumstances* that can fuel the financial innovation and subsequent bubbles are deeply rooted in the nature of the monetary system. Here we must distinguish between the domestic conduct of monetary policy and the architecture of the international monetary system. Central banks worldwide, through their signalling policy about interest rates, can modify not only long-term interest rates, but also the perception of financial risk, as we have seen in the years previous to the 2008 crisis. The widely accepted use of Taylor's rules and specific targeting of CPI inflation rates only, have set aside the financial stability problems that central bankers had to solve after the 2008 meltdown. We must also recall that research on the links between global imbalances and the financial crisis has pointed towards the liquidity glut brought about by central banks after the dotcom crisis as one of the main sources of troubles. But while the macro-prudential policymaking scheme is in its first stages, central bankers should make decisions about interest rates and sound monetary policy so as to guarantee financial stability or, at least, avoid the kind of financial instability we have suffered during the last decade. Working on alternative, more restrictive Taylor's rules could be a solution. As has been argued, if negative *real* interest rates have always been present in real estate bubbles, central banks can begin by targeting *non-negative* real interest rates, rather than a specific inflation rate figure, as a way to deal with consumer goods and assets prices at the same time. The sort of troubles that the maturity mismatch within the banking industry creates will still be there, but not with the blessing of a too elastic, pro-cyclical and risk-misleading monetary policy. And from an international perspective, there is little room for additional manoeuvring as far as the Chinese government would not allow the full convertibility of the renminbi, and the US dollar would stand as the international currency. Despite the research about the benefits of a multipolar international monetary system, or whether the dollar will steadily decline as a reserve currency, domestic governments of developed and emerging countries have no incentives to act in a coordinated manner. Only after brief episodes where the global financial collapse has loomed, have we seen a true cooperation among the main international players. But if the current international monetary system allows some countries to bear continued current account deficits, the targeting of domestic economic policy on unsustainable private and public debt will limit the size of those deficits. Riskier investors would turn to FDI or asset purchases in the big emerging markets as a way to obtain better yields in capital shortage economies than in mature economies. But that will be a *political* process, and it is difficult to see global markets doing the job.

When we connect these three factors and look back to past international monetary orders, it is easy to be worried about the kind of liquidity shortages and the corresponding deflationary pressures that the Gold Standard suffered, the collapse of international finance and trade after the Great Depression or the prohibition of international capital flows during Bretton Woods. Economic history shows that none of them were effective measures in attaining any degree of stability. The free movement of trade and capital that currently shapes the global economy is a historical process fostered by technological advances that are here to stay. But this should not allow policymakers to leave the balance sheets of both their public and private sectors to accumulate massive volumes of debt which, in turn, will collapse not only their domestic economies but the global economy as a whole.

# FINAL REMARKS

Science is a self-correcting endeavour. Our hypotheses and results are tentative statements that have to be checked and revised as new evidence arises. Once we notice a sizeable gap between theory and reality, we must assume that some changes have to be made in the structure of the theory. In some cases the changes affect only auxiliary, non-critical assumptions, and we can still rely on that theory as a source of knowledge. Sometimes, core, critical assumptions have to be changed or even removed from the logical structure of the theory and, and such, the whole research programme has to be reshaped. Researchers can adopt a true progressive attitude toward change or can be reluctant until new, stronger evidence arises.

Nevertheless, this ideal picture of scientific progress has hardly anything to do with reality, at least in economics. Researchers support long established competing programmes which stand simply because there are ideological and/or political biases that sustain them. We have seen in Chapters 2 and 3 that neoclassicals, Keynesians and Austrians have long been struggling for the survival of their research programmes in spite of the growing empirical evidence that neglects some of their critical hypotheses as well as their main results. New and alternative research programmes have arisen in the last decades, although there is very little contact between these programmes, and also between them and the mainstream programmes. Thomas Kuhn was absolutely right when he spoke about the sociological, idiosyncratic character of the scientific enterprise. Revolutions are rare and they only occur when massive, historical evidence arises. Setting aside the ideological *milieu* of that time, the general theory would not have unleashed a scientific revolution without the Great Depression. The neoliberal revolution would have had little support if the Berlin Wall was still standing and the command economy had not collapsed.

The Great Recession and the first true global financial and economic crisis is the sort of historical event that provides massive evidence of the failure of conventional wisdom in triggering a scientific revolution. We have seen that economics, as a science, has been unable to foresee, prevent and solve a massive collapse of the world economy which has led to unemployment, poverty and social breakdown for millions of people worldwide. Although politicians and financiers have been blamed as the main culprits, they both relied on macroeconomic models and theories which have proven to be useless in their self-proclaimed claims. If, as Popper, Kuhn or Lakatos do, we support the ideal of a self-correcting science, a research that is committed to double-checking its results and outcomes, we ought to devote some time and effort to guessing what was wrong from 2000 on. Or, at least, we must report back why we were not able to prevent the collapse and/or if we will be able to predict the next one.

Revolutions begin with eschewing all the old systems, customs and beliefs in order to proceed to some brilliant, new future. We have learnt from history that this ends with a social and economic mess that usually worsens the previous situation. Throughout this book we have carefully tried to avoid this kind of mistake. Rather, we assume that there is a lot of true, reliable knowledge inside neoclassical, Keynesian and Austrian research programmes that should not be discarded. Economics has succeeded for years by narrowing its scope and building up models as simple and tractable as possible. As we have shown, the models were not bad, but they were too narrow and short-sighted. Economic theory has assumed that models that focus on several key variables and critical assumptions exhibit strong internal coherence that could explain more complex reality where these critical assumptions do not hold. Or more precisely, they have assumed that critical assumptions were a good description of reality. The problem is that they claimed to explain many more issues than they really did. This flaw was dramatically revealed when policymakers were forced to improvise new measures as they realized there was not a sound and comprehensive analytical framework to cope with the crisis. Nevertheless, we are witnessing a revisionist approach to some of the central pieces of the main research programmes that have brought about quite interesting developments aiming to explain the current crisis, such us the macroeconomics of asset shortage or the balance sheet macroeconomics.

Instead of focusing on partisan disputes such as whether Keynesian economics is better than Austrians economics, or if mainstream is much more 'scientific' than the heterodox 'narratives', we have been working under two central hypotheses: first, we only know a small part of the economic processes and, second, a collaborative attitude among research programmes will render greater benefits. We have incurred in the *fatal conceit* that Hayek pointed out twenty years ago when he criticized some views of economics as a research programme aiming to build a social engineering which would solve all the economic and social problems of the world by central planning. If we set aside the central planning issue, economics has behaved as if it had all the wisdom to cope with all of the issues. The 2008 global financial crisis has reminded us that we know only a little bit about how the economy works. But, at the same time, the financial market efficient hypothesis and the market clearing approach has put us in a situation that Keynes criticized more than seventy years ago, namely the mistaken belief that markets are institutions that smoothly self-correct themselves and that there is no room for large and persistent disequilibria. At the same time, the 2008 crisis has taught us that the social engineering through policymaking lacks a theoretical foundation so as to understand the whole picture of the working of the global economy.

But once we have realized that we know just a little piece of what can be understood as a largely unchartered territory, the issue of 'competing' research programmes makes little sense. All of them can improve our knowledge by means of collaborative efforts, aiming to complete the whole chart. Once this cartography is finished, we can use it to give insights and advices for sound policymaking. For years it has been obvious that the relation between economic theory and economic policy was loose and it was taken for granted that this was the unavoidable price to be paid for the sake of simplicity in economic theory. We realize now that this distance allows for the increasing inability of economic theory to describe facts as they are. We have seen that there are developments in all programmes which can be complementary in bridging the gap between theory and policy. If we still insist on following separate lines, in most cases based on ideological rather than in scientific roots, we will incur the same errors that we did the last few years: we will again be paying attention to incorrect and minor issues instead of focusing on the important ones.

This book was born out of discontent about the performance of economic theory before, during and after the crisis. The effects in terms of GDP losses and unemployment are too large and the discontent with the economic profession plagued both developed as well as emerging countries. We cannot afford to see it repeated again. It is true that, in spite of some promising developments, we are far from obtaining a better economic theory after the crisis. We have some valuable pieces of economic theory that would have been useful before the crisis but their performance was underestimated. Besides, we have shown that economic theory can be improved by a careful re-examination of their main building blocks and their adequacy in terms of the changes in the operational environment that have taken place over the last thirty years. We must critically re-examine economic theories and update them if we really believe in science as a true and sincere self-correcting process.

# NOTES

## Introduction

1. For instance, Spanish citizens suddenly realized that foreign financial markets had dried up, so they could not afford their 10 per cent over GDP current account deficit and were obliged to rebalance it very painfully.
2. We analyse all these reports in the first chapter.
3. Ireland, Spain, the US and, to an extent, the UK.
4. A good example is real business cycle (RBC) theory. We explain our ideas on this issue in Chapter 4.
5. We will enter into the finer details of Keynesianism in Chapter 2.

## 1 The Financial Crisis and Modern Economics: From Surprise to Puzzlement

1. Paul De Grauwe has led this field of research. See, for instance, P. De Grauwe, *Economics of Monetary Union*, 9th edn (Oxford: Oxford University Press, 2012).
2. International Monetary Fund, *Fiscal Implications of the Global Economic and Financial Crisis. Staff Position Paper* (Washington, DC: IMF, June 2009), pp. 6–12.
3. It is noteworthy that experts' forecasts were wrong from the onset of the crisis to 2011. We will explain in the third part of this chapter that their predictions in 2007 and 2008 were strongly refuted by the data. Their forecasts for 2010 and 2011, made some months before the beginning of each year, were positives, while real figures were negative. By the end of 2011 they decided to switch from an optimistic approach to a pessimistic one to avoid performing so badly again. They have changed their mindset to adjust it to the new environment, but it took them three years. What can we expect from non-experts?
4. International Monetary Fund, *World Economic Outlook, Global Prospects and Policies. Spring 2009* (Washington, DC: IMF, June 2009).
5. B. Keeley and P. Love, *From Crisis to Recovery: The Causes, Course and Consequences of the Great Recession* (Paris: Organization for Economic Cooperation and Development, 2010), p. 19.
6. European Commission, *Economic Crisis in Europe: Causes, Consequences and Responses* (Luxembourg: European Commission, 2009).
7. The experts are urged to furnish a quick answer to the events, not to engage in an in-depth analysis. They examine the crisis and realize that financial issues are by far the most important factor. Thus they explain why and how the financial side of the economy has

deteriorated so much. A second-level analysis, the underlining weaknesses of the financial system, is out of their scope.

8. S. Grossman and J. Stiglitz, 'Information and Competitive Price Systems', *American Economic Review*, 66:2 (1976), pp. 246–53.
9. D. Kahneman and A. Tversky, *Choices, Values and Frames* (Cambridge: Cambridge University Press, 2000).
10. R. Thaler and C. Sunstein, 'Human Frailty Causes this Crisis', *Financial Times*, 12 November 2008.
11. F. Kydland and E. Prescott, 'Time to Build and Aggregate Fluctuations', *Econometrica*, 50:6 (November 1982), pp. 1345–70.
12. J. Galí, *Monetary Policy, Inflation and the Business Cycle* (Princeton, NJ: Princeton University Press, 2008).
13. J. Rotemberg and S. Woodford, 'An Optimization-Based Econometric Framework for the Evaluation of Monetary Policy', in B. Bernanke and J. Rotemberg, *NBER Macroeconomics Annual 1997, Volume 12* (Cambridge, MA: MIT Press, 1997), pp. 297–361.
14. R. Solow, 'The State of Macroeconomics', *Journal of Economic Perspectives*, 22:1 (Winter 2008), pp. 243–9.
15. H. P. Minsky, *Stabilizing an Unstable Economy* (New Haven, CT: Yale University Press, 1986).
16. For a critical appraisal of the differences and similarities between Minsky's theory and the Austrians' theory, see D. L. Prychitko, 'Competing Explanations of the Minsky Moment: The Financial Instability Hypothesis in Light of Austrian Theory', *Review of Austrian Economics*, 23 (2010), pp. 199–221.
17. Mises, Hayek, Rothbard and Garrison.
18. International Monetary Fund, *World Outlook* (Washington, DC: IMF, October 2007), p. 1.
19. International Monetary Fund, *World Outlook* (Washington, DC: IMF, October 2008), p. 1.
20. *New York Times*, 17 November 2008.
21. British Academy, 'The Global Financial Crisis – Why Didn't Anybody Notice?', July 2009.
22. D. Bezemer, '"No One Saw this Coming": Understanding Financial Crisis through Accounting Models', *Munich Personal RePec Archive*, 15892 (2009), pp. 1–50.
23. D. Baker, B. DeLong and P. Krugman, 'Assets Returns and Economic Growth', *Brooking Papers on Economic Activity*, 1 (2005), pp. 289–330.
24. S. Keen, 'Why did I See the Financial Crisis Coming and "They" Didn't?', *Analysis*, 2008, at http://www.compareshares.com.au/keen04.php [accessed 11 June 2014].
25. M. Hudson, 'Saving, Asset-Price Inflation, and Debt-Induced Deflation', in L. Randall Wray and M. Fostater (eds), *Money, Financial Instability and Stabilization Policy* (Cheltenham: Edward Elgar, 2006), pp. 104–24.
26. M. Hudson, 'The Road to Serfdom: An Illustrated Guide to the Coming Real Estate Collapse', *Harper's Magazine* (2006), pp. 39–46.
27. K. Richebächer, *The Richebächer Letter: Monthly Analysis of Currencies and Credit Markets*, July 2006.
28. Ibid.
29. R. Rajan, 'Has Financial Development Made the World Riskier?', *National Bureau of Economic Research, Working Papers 11728* (Cambridge, MA: NBER, 2006), pp. 313–69.

30. W. White, 'Is Price Stability Enough?', *Bank International of Settlements Papers* (Basel: BIS Papers, 2006), p. 9.
31. Ibid., p. 12.
32. R. Shiller, *Irrational Exuberance*, 2nd edn (Princeton, NJ: Princeton University Press, 2001).
33. R. J. Caballero, 'On the Macroeconomics of Asset Shortage', *National Bureau of Economic Research, Working Papers 12753* (Cambridge, MA: NBER, 2006).
34. He prepared a statement for the House Committee on Science and Technology on the causes of the crisis.

## 2 A Different Look at Economic Theory: The Anthropological Approach

1. L. Robbins, *An Essay on the Nature and Significance of Economic Science* (London: Macmillan, 1935), p. 16.
2. Economists have not been unfamiliar with philosophical thinking, as Karl Pribram showed in his *History of Economic Reasoning*.
3. R. Rubio de Urquía, 'Ética y Procesos de Asignación de Recursos', *Información Comercial Española*, 691 (1991), pp. 7–16.
4. L. Kolakowski, *The Positivist Philosophy* (London: Penguin, 1972).
5. L. Walras, *Éléments d'Économie Politique Pure au Théorie de la Richesse Sociale* (Paris: R. Pichot et R. Durand Auzias, 1874), third lesson, § 30.
6. F. Y. Edgeworth, *Mathematical Psychics: An Essay on the Application of Mathematics to the Moral Sciences* (London: Macmillan and Co., 1881), pp. 6–17; W. S. Jevons, *The Theory of Political Economy* (London: Macmillan and Co., 1871), p. 44.
7. I. Fisher, *Mathematical Investigations in the Theory of Value and Prices* (New York: August M. Kelley, 1892), pp. 85–6.
8. V. Pareto, *Cours d'Économie Politique II* (Geneva: Droz, 1897), p. 12.
9. L. Amoroso, *Lezioni di Economia Matematica* (Padua: CEDAM Casa Editriche Dottore Antonio Milani, 1921), pp. 370–3.
10. K. J. Arrow and G. Debreu, 'Existence of an Equilibrium for a Competitive Economy', *Econometrica*, 22:3 (1954), pp. 265–90; and G. Debreu, *Theory of Value: An Axiomatic Analysis of Economic Equilibrium* (New Haven, CT, and London: Yale University Press, 1959).
11. Debreu, *Theory of Value*, p. 91.
12. C. McCann, *Probability Foundations of Economics* (New York: Routledge, 1994), p. 109.
13. Debreu, *Theory of Value*, p. 98.
14. 'To ask why the monetary theorists of the 1940s did not make use of the contingent-claim view of equilibrium is, it seems to me, like asking why Hannibal did not use tanks against the Romans instead of elephants. There is no reason to view our ability to think as being any less limited by available technology than is our ability to act (if, indeed, this distinction can be defended) ... That a powerful model-building apparatus specifically designed to help us deal with problems involving choice under uncertainty should simply be passed over in favor of an older apparatus which is (for the most part) incapable of taking these problems into account, would, should it occur, certainly refute rather decisively the point of view toward the development of economic thought that I have

advanced in this paper'. R. E. Lucas, 'Methods and Problems in Business Cycle Theory', *Journal of Money, Credit and Banking*, 12:4 (1980), pp. 696–715.

15. See A. Mas-Colell, M. D. Whinston and J. R. Green, *Microeconomic Theory* (New York: Oxford University Press, 1995), ch. 20.
16. G. W. Stadler, 'Real Business Cycles', *Journal of Economic Literature*, 32:4 (1994), pp. 1750–83.
17. J. E. King, *A History of Post Keynesian Economics since 1936* (Cheltenham: Edward Elgar, 1993).
18. R. Rotheim, 'New Keynesian Macroeconomics and Markets', in R. Rotheim (ed.), *New Keynesian Economics/Post Keynesian Alternatives* (London: Routledge, 1998), pp. 51–70; P. Davidson, *International Money and the Real World* (New York: St. Martin's Press, 1992); J. A. Kregel, 'Aspects of a Post Keynesian Theory of Finance', *Journal of Post Keynesian Economics*, 21:1 (October 1988), pp. 111–33; A. Lindbeck, 'New Keynesianism and Aggregate Economic Activity', *Economic Journal*, 108:446 (1998), pp. 167–80.
19. Bertrand Russell and George Edward Moore had a great influence on Keynes's early philosophical thought. See J. B. Davis, 'Keynes's Later Philosophy', *History of Political Economy*, 27:2 (1995), pp. 237–60, on p. 240 and J. Passmore, *A Hundred Years of Philosophy* (London: Penguin, 1968), p. 204.
20. J. M. Keynes, *A Treatise on Probability* (London: Macmillan, 1921), p. 13.
21. Ibid., p. 14; T. Lawson, 'Probability and Uncertainty in Economic Analysis', *Journal of Post Keynesian Economics*, 11:1 (1988), pp. 38–65, on p. 43.
22. Keynes, *A Treatise on Probability*, p. 345.
23. Conventions 'lull our disquietude' (J. M. Keynes, *The General Theory of Employment, Interest and Money* (London: Macmillan, 1936), p. 116), letting us 'hide from ourselves how little we foresee' (ibid., p. 124). Winslow saw a relation between Keynes's theory of conventions and Freudian psychoanalysis. See E. G. Winslow, 'Keynes and Freud: Psychoanalysis and Keynes's Account of the "Animal Spirits" of Capitalism', *Social Research*, 53:4 (Winter 1986), pp. 549–78.
24. In Chapter 12 of *The General Theory*, Keynes extensively develops the reasons for the fragility of conventions when he analyses the stock market. See Keynes, *The General Theory*, pp. 149–58.
25. J. M. Keynes, *The General Theory and After: A Supplement, Collected Writings, Vol. XXIX* (London: Macmillan, 1972), p. 124 and, also, J. M. Keynes, 'The General Theory of Employment', in J. M. Keynes, *The Collected Writings of John Maynard Keynes, Vol. XIV* (London: Macmillan, 1972), pp. 109–123, on p. 114. This was originally published in the *Quarterly Journal of Economics*, February 1937.
26. Keynes, *The General Theory*, p. 161. See R. Marchionatti, 'On Keynes' Animal Spirits', *Kyklos*, 52:3 (2001), pp. 415–39. Fitzgibbons affirms that the term 'animal spirits' was first used by Plato in the Republic: 'They were so called because action without reward reminded Plato of a dog, which does not distinguish between who feeds him or not, but only does his duty'. A. Fitzgibbons, *Keynes's Vision: A New Political Economy* (Oxford: Clarendon Press, 1988), p. 85. He related this interpretation of Plato's text with this quote of *A Treatise on Probability*: 'Herodotus puts the point quite plainly. "There is nothing more profitable for a man", he says, "than to take good counsel with himself; for even if the event turns out contrary to one's hope, still one's decision was right, even though fortune has made it of no effect: whereas if a man acts contrary to good counsel, although by luck he gets what he had no right to expect, his decision was not any the less foolish"'. J. M. Keynes, *The Collected Writings of John Maynard Keynes: Vol. VIII. A*

*Treatise on Probability* (London: Palgrave MacMillan, 1972), on pp. 339–40, quoted in Fitzgibbons, *Keynes's Vision*, p. 85.

27. Keynes, *The General Theory*, p. 240.
28. Keynes, *Collected Writings, Volume XXIX*, pp. 293–4.
29. See J. Crotty, 'Are Keynesian Uncertainy and Macrotheory Compatible? Conventional Decision Making, Institutional Structures, and Conditional Stability in Keynesian Macromodels', in G. Dimsky and R. Pollin (eds), *New Perspectives in Monetary Macroeconomics* (Ann Arbor, MI: University of Michigan Press, 1994), pp. 105–39. See also D. Dequech, 'On Some Arguments for the Rationality of Conventional Behaviour under Uncertainty', in P. Kriesler and C. Sardoni (eds), *Keynes, Post Keynesianism and Political Economy: Essays in Honour of Geoff. Harcourt, Volume Three* (London: Routledge, 1999), pp. 179–98.
30. Keynes, *The General Theory*, p. 216.
31. See ibid., ch. 17.
32. Relatively high interest rates imply relatively high marginal efficiencies of capital if investment has to offer a prospect of positive yield. But only scarcity assures a positive yield, so capital needs to be scarce (Keynes, *The General Theory*, p. 213). The consequence of a low investment in capital goods is a low effective demand.
33. King, *A History of Post Keynesian Economics since 1936*, p. 111.
34. J. Huerta de Soto, *The Austrian School of Economics* (Aldershot: Edward Elgar, 2008), p. 52.
35. L. von Mises, *Epistemological Problems of Economics*, trans. G. Reisman (Indianapolis, IN: Liberty Fund, 2013), p. 24.
36. Huerta de Soto, *The Austrian School of Economics*, p. 103.
37. L. von Mises, *The Ultimate Foundation of Economic Science* (Princeton, NJ: D. Van Nostrand Company, Inc, 1962), p. 12.
38. Ibid., pp. 12, 14.
39. L. von Mises, *Human Action* (Auburn, AL: Ludwig von Mises Institute, 1998), p. 48 and Mises, *The Ultimate Foundation*, p. 64.
40. Mises, *The Ultimate Foundation*, p. 20.
41. 'Both our authors [Mises and Shackle] emphasize that the mathematical notion of time as a continuum, a dimension in which events take place, does not fit the requirements of a science of human action'. L. M. Lachmann, 'From Mises to Shackle: An Essay in Austrian Economics and Kaleidic Society', *Journal of Economic Literature*, 14:1 (1976), pp. 54–62, on p. 57. See also Mises, *Human Action*, pp. 578–9.
42. Huerta de Soto, *The Austrian School of Economics*, p. 5.
43. Mises, *The Ultimate Foundation*, p. 16.
44. Mises, *Human Action*, pp. 13–4.
45. I. Kirzner, 'Ludwig von Mises and Friedrich von Hayek: The Modern Extension of Austrian Subjectivism', in S. Littlechild (ed.), *Austrian Economics I*. (Aldershot: Edward Elgar, 1990), pp. 342–65.

## 3 The 'Building Blocks' of Modern Economics: We Do Really Need a Meta-Theory

1. R. Rubio de Urquía, 'A Short Note on the Anthropological Foundations of Economic Science', in J. P. Pham (ed.), *Centessimus Annus: Assessment and Perspectives for the Future of Catholic Social Doctrine* (Vatican: Libreria Editrice Vaticana, 1998), pp. 165–73; R. Rubio de Urquía, 'La Naturaleza y Estructura Fundamental de la Teoría Económica y las Relaciones entre Enunciados Teórico-Económicos y Enunciados Antropológicos', in R. Rubio de Urquía, E. M. Ureña and F. F. Muñoz (eds), *Estudios de Teoría Económica y Antropología* (Madrid: IIES de Vitoria-AEDOS-Unión Editorial, 2005), pp. 23–198; A. Rodríguez, 'Austrian Economics as a Progressive Paradigm: Explaining More Complex Economic Phenomena', *Review of Austrian Economics*, 15:4 (2002), pp. 335–57; F. Muñoz, M. Encinar and C. Cañibano, 'On the Role of Intentionality in Evolutionary Economic Change', *Structural Change and Economic Dynamics*, 22 (2011), pp. 193–203; F. Muñoz and M. Encinar, 'Intentionality and the Emergence of Complexity: An Analytical Approach', *Journal of Evolutionary Economics* (2014), forthcoming.
2. R. Rubio de Urquía, 'Acerca del Lugar de las Concepciones Antropológicas en la Constitución y Progreso de la Teoría Económica', *Boletín de la Real Sociedad Bascongada de Amigos del País*, L-2 (1994), pp. 457–81, translated from the original Spanish.
3. That means that long-lasting debates on non-mainstream economics about the selfishness of *homo-oeconomicus* are debates not about the working of the 'economic principle' but of the classification of ends set. The moral and ethical issues which these debates inevitably raise must be viewed from the point of view of the ends pursued and the means used. Most of the criticism about the supposedly selfishness of economic behaviour should be addressed towards the ends and/or means structures, and not towards a 'malfunction' of the principle of economic behaviour. A specific plan could be ethically blameworthy on the basis of the ends pursued, the means used, or both, but not as a choice in itself. Agents always try to make their best option *once* they have decided what they want to do. Economic behaviour works equally for altruistic goals as well as for egoistic goals. What makes a plan or an action ethically acceptable is the nature of those goals and means, not if agents always choose the best option.
4. J. Castañeda, *Lecciones de Teoría Económica* (Madrid: Aguilar, 1968), p. 417.
5. R. F. Harrod, 'An Essay in Dynamic Theory', *Economic Journal*, 49:193 (1939), pp. 14–33; E. Domar, 'Capital Expansion, Rate of Growth, and Employment', *Econometrica*, 14:2 (1946), pp. 137–47.
6. R. Solow, 'A Contribution to the Theory of Economic Growth', *Quarterly Journal of Economics*, 70:1 (1956), pp. 65–94; T. Swan, 'Economic Growth and Capital Accumulation', *Economic Record*, 32:2 (1956), pp. 334–61.
7. T. Hutchison, *The Significance and Basic Postulates of Economic Theory* (New York: Augustus M. Kelley, 1938 reprint), pp. 9–10.
8. V. V. Chari, 'Nobel Laureate Robert E. Lucas, Jr.: Architect of Modern Macroeconomics', *Federal Reserve Bank of Minneapolis Quarterly Review*, 23:2 (1999), pp. 2–12, on p. 2.
9. C. Menger, *Untersuchungen über die Methode der Socialwissenschaften und der Politischen Oekonomie insbesondere*. Translated into English as *Investigations into the Method of the Social Sciences* (Grove City, PA: Libertarian Press, 1996).
10. See S. Moss, 'The History of the Theory of the Firm from Marshall to Robinson and Chamberlin: The Source of Positivism in Economics', *Economica, New Series*, 51:203 (1984), pp. 307–18, on pp. 314–5.

11. See J. D. Hammond, 'Early Drafts of Friedman's Methodology Essay', in U. Maki (ed.), *The Methodology of Positive Economics: Reflections on the Milton Friedman Legacy* (Cambridge: Cambridge University Press, 2009), pp. 68–89.
12. M. Friedman, 'The Methodology of Positive Economics', in M. Friedman, *Essays in Positive Economics* (Chicago, IL: University of Chicago Press, 1953), pp. 3–43, on p. 14.
13. See T. Mayer, 'The Influence of Friedman's Methodological Essay', in Maki (ed.), *The Methodology of Positive Economics*, pp. 119–42.
14. See T. D. Stanley, 'The Cambridge Circus and Other Influences upon Keynes: A Review of "Keynes and his Contemporaries"', *Journal of Behavioral Economics*, 14:1 (1985), pp. 209–12.
15. Friedman admitted this in private correspondence with Boland: 'Friedman has stated that such characterization of his methodology is "entirely correct"'. W. J. Frazer and L. A. Boland, 'An Essay on the Foundations of Friedman's Methodology', in J. C. Wood and R. N. Woods (eds), *Milton Friedman: Critical Assessments. Routledge Critical Assessments of Contemporary Economists, Vol. III* (London: Routledge, 1990), pp. 458–80, on p. 458.
16. 'Conjunctive type of argument: Because statement A1 is true, and A2 is true, and A3 is true, and ... one can conclude that the statement C1 is true'. L. A. Boland, *Critical Economic Methodology: A Personal Odyssey* (London and New York: Routledge, 1997), p. 17.
17. 'A mode of reasoning from a hypothetical proposition according to which if the antecedent be affirmed the consequent is affirmed (as, if A is true, B is true; but A is true; therefore, B is true)'. *Merriam Webster Dictionary*, at http://www.merriam-webster.com/dictionary/modus%20ponens [accessed 21 February 2014].
18. 'Disjunctive type of argument: Because statement R1 is true, or R2 is true, or R3 is true, or ... one can conclude that the statement C2 is true'. Boland, *Critical Economic Methodology*, p. 17.
19. See note 17, above.
20. L. A. Boland, 'A Critique of Friedman's Critics', *Journal of Economic Literature*, 17:2 (1979), pp. 503–22.
21. See W. Hands, 'Did Milton Friedman's Positive Methodology License the Formalist Revolution?', in Maki (ed.), *The Methodology of Positive Economics*, pp. 143–64, on p. 153.
22. Maki (ed.), *The Methodology of Positive Economics*, p. 94.
23. Mises, *Human Action*, p. 92.
24. J. M. Keynes, 'Professor Tinbergen's Method', *Economic Journal*, 49 (1939), pp. 558–68.
25. R. M. O'Donnell, 'Keynes on Mathematics: Philosophical Foundations and Economic Applications', *Cambridge Journal of Economics*, 14:1 (March 1990), pp. 29–47, on p. 29.
26. See T. Lawson, *Economics and Reality* (London and New York: Routledge, 1997), p. 59. Also, V. Chick, 'On Knowing One's Place: The Role of Formalism in Economics', *Economic Journal*, 108 (1998), pp. 1859–69.
27. J. Jespersen, *The Methodology of Macroeconomics: A Post Keynesian Perspective* (Chelham: Edward Elgar Publising, 2009), p. 178.
28. J. Huerta de Soto, *Money, Bank Credit, and Economic Cycles* (Auburn, AL: Ludwig von Mises Institute, 2006), pp. 418–20.
29. K. Hoover, *Causality in Macroeconomics* (Cambridge: Cambridge University Press, 2001).
30. F. P. Ramsey, 'A Mathematical Theory of Saving', *Economic Journal*, 38:152 (1928), pp. 543–59; D. Cass, 'Optimum Growth in an Aggregative Model of Capital Accumulation', *Review of Economic Studies*, 32:3 (1965), pp. 233–40; T. C. Koopmans, 'On the Concept of Optimal Economic Growth', in *Study Week on the Econometric Approach to Develop-*

*ment Planning* (Vatican City: Pontificia Academia Scientiarum, 1965), pp. 225–87; W. Brock and L. Mirman, 'Optimal Economic Growth and Uncertainty: The Discounted Case', *Journal of Economic Theory*, 4:3 (1972), pp. 479–513.
31. R. Nelson and S. Winter, *An Evolutionary Theory of Economic Change* (Cambridge, MA: Belknap Press, 1982).
32. V. Smith, 'Experimental Methods in Economics', in S. Durlauf and L. Blum (eds), *The New Palgrave Dictionary of Economics*, 2nd edn (London: Palgrave Macmillan, 2008), p. 2, online edition at http://www.dictionaryofeconomics.com/article?id=pde2008_E000186 [14 August 2014].
33. D. Kahneman and A. Tversky, 'Prospect Theory: An Analysis of Decision under Risk', *Econometrica*, 47:2 (1979), pp. 263–92.
34. S. Metcalfe, *Evolutionary Economics and Creative Destruction* (London: Routledge, 1998).
35. Nelson and Winter, *An Evolutionary Theory of Economic Change*, p. 10.
36. G. M. Hodgson, 'Generalizing Darwinism to Social Evolution: Some Early Attempts', *Journal of Economic Issues*, 39:4 (2005), pp. 899–914; G. M. Hodgson, 'Dismantling Lamarckism: Why Descriptions of Socio-Economics Evolution as Lamarckian are Misleading', *Journal of Evolutionary Economics*, 16 (2006), pp. 343–66; G. M. Hodgson, 'The Nature and Units of Social Selection', *Journal of Evolutionary Economics*, 16:5 (2006), pp. 477–89; G. M. Hodgson, 'Why We Need a Generalized Darwinism and why Generalized Darwinism is not Enough', *Journal of Economic Behaviour & Organization*, 61 (2006), pp. 1–19.
37. D. Cervone, 'The Architecture of Personality', *Psycholocial Review*, 111:1 (2004), pp. 183–204, on p. 185.
38. Ibid.
39. Ibid.

## 4 The Meta-Theory at Work: A Case Study in Growth Theory and Real Business Cycle Theory

1. Solow, 'A Contribution to the Theory of Economic Growth'.
2. See Harrod, 'An Essay in Dynamic Theory' and Domar, 'Capital Expansion, Rate of Growth, and Employment'.
3. Kaldor's and Kalecki's models, for instance.
4. Solow, 'A Contribution to the Theory of Economic Growth'; Swan, 'Economic Growth and Capital Accumulation'; P. Aghion and P. Howitt, 'A Model of Growth through Creative Destruction', *Econometrica*, 60:2 (March 1992), pp. 323–51.
5. A very good survey is the *Handbook of Economic Growth* (P. Aghion and S. Durlauf, *Handbook of Economic Growth Vol 1A and 1B* (Amsterdam: North-Holland Elsevier, 2005)). In addition, another useful reference is R. Barro and X. Sala-i-Martín, *Economic Growth*, 2nd edn (Cambridge, MA: MIT Press, 2004).
6. From this point on we will only refer to Robert Solow.
7. R. Solow, 'Technical Change and the Aggregate Production Function', *Review of Economics and Statistics*, 39:3 (August 1957), pp. 312–20.
8. G. Mankiw, P. Romer and D. Weil, 'A Contribution of the Empirics of Economic Growth', *Quarterly Journal of Economics*, 107:2 (May 1992), pp. 407–37.
9. Solow, 'Technical Change and the Aggregate Production Function'.

10. R. E. Lucas, 'On the Mechanics of Economic Development', *Journal of Monetary Economics*, 22 (1988), pp. 3–42.
11. P. Romer, 'Endogenous Technological Change', *Journal of Political Economy*, 98:5 (October 1990), pp. 1002–37.
12. Aghion and Howitt, 'A Model of Growth through Creative Destruction'.
13. Solow, 'A Contribution to the Theory of Economic Growth'.
14. Since Solow has made many addition relevant contributions to growth theory, we will only refer to him, and not to Swan, from this point onwards.
15. Solow, 'A Contribution to the Theory of Economic Growth'.
16. See the chapters on growth accounting in the *Handbook of Economic Growth* mentioned on p. 178, in note 5.
17. Barro and Sala-i-Martín, *Economic Growth*.
18. K. J. Arrow, 'The Economic Implications of Learning by Doing', *Review of Economic Studies*, 29:3 (June 1962), pp. 155–73.
19. A. Maddison, *Phases of Capitalist Development* (Oxford: Oxford University Press, 1982).
20. R. Summers and A. Heston, 'A New Set of International Comparisons or Real Product and Price Levels Estimates for 130 Countries, 1950–1985', *Review of Income and Wealth*, 34:1 (March 1988), pp. 1–25.
21. P. Romer, 'Increasing Returns and Long-Run Growth', *Journal of Political Economy*, 94:5 (October 1986), pp. 1002–37.
22. P. Romer, 'Crazy Explanations for the Productivity Slowdown', in S. Fisher (ed.), *NBER Macroeconomics Annual 1987, Vol. 2* (Cambridge MA: MIT Press, 1987), pp. 163–210, on pp. 163–202.
23. Romer, 'Endogenous Technological Change'.
24. Lucas, 'On the Mechanics of Economic Development'.
25. G. Grossman and E. Helpman, 'Trade, Innovation and Growth', *American Economic Review*, 80:2 (May 1990), pp. 86–91. See also G. Grossman and E. Helpman, *Innovation and Growth in the Global Economy* (Cambridge, MA: MIT Press, 1991), ch. 4.
26. C. Jones, 'Time Series Tests of Endogenous Growth Models', *Quarterly Journal of Economics*, 110:2 (May 1995), pp. 495–525; C. Jones, 'R&D-Based Models of Economic Growth', *Journal of Political Economy*, 103:4 (1995), pp. 759–84.
27. R. Barro and X. Sala-i-Martín, 'Technological Diffusion, Convergence and Growth', *Journal of Economic Growth*, 2 (1997), pp. 1–26.
28. J. Braun, 'Essays on Economic Growth and Migration' (PhD dissertation, Harvard University, 1993).
29. P. Weil, 'Overlapping Families of Infinitely Lived Agents', *Journal of Public Economics*, 38:2 (March 1989), pp. 183–98.
30. R. Levine, 'Finance and Growth: Theory and Evidence', in P. Aghion and S. Durlauf, *Handbook of Economic Growth*, pp. 866–934.
31. A typical case study is Korea. After the war in 1953 South Korea and North Korea exhibited a very similar per capita GDP. Fifty years later, the differences are huge and cannot be explained without taking into account the economic institutions of both countries.
32. D. Acemoglu, S. Johnson and A. Robinson, 'Institutions as a Fundamental Cause of Long-Run Growth Evidence', in Aghion and Durlauf, *Handbook of Economic Growth*, pp. 386–471.
33. Kydland and Prescott, 'Time to Build and Aggregate Fluctuations', p. 1.
34. Ibid.
35. T. Sargent, *Macroeconomic Theory* (New York: Academic Press, 1979).

36. Kydland and Prescott explicitly discarded the role of money in the article 'Business Cycles: Real Facts and a Monetary Myth', *Federal Reserve Bank of Minneapolis Quarterly Review*, 14:2 (Spring 1990), pp. 3–18.
37. E. Prescott, 'Theory Ahead of Business Cycle Measurement', *Federal Reserve Bank of Minneapolis Quarterly Review*, 10:4 (Fall 1986), pp. 9–22, on p. 9.
38. Ibid., p. 22.
39. G. D. Hansen and R. Wright, 'The Labor Market in Real Business Cycle Theory', *Federal Reserve Bank of Minneapolis Quarterly Review*, 16:2 (Spring 1992), pp. 2–12.
40. G. D. Hansen, 'Indivisible Labor and the Business Cycle', *Journal of Monetary Economics*, 16:3 (1985), pp. 309–27.
41. L. Christiano and M. Eichenbaum, 'Current Real Business Cycle Theories and Aggregate Labor Market Fluctuations', *American Economic Review*, 82:3 (1992), pp. 430–50.
42. J. Benhabib, J. Rogerson and R. Wright, 'Homework in Macroeconomics: Household Production and Aggregate Fluctuations', *Journal of Political Economy*, 99:6 (1991), pp. 1166–87.
43. T. Cooley and G. Hansen, 'The Inflation Tax in a Real Business Cycle Model', *American Economic Review*, 79:4 (September 1989), pp. 733–48.
44. Kydland and Prescott, 'Business Cycles'.
45. Prescott, 'Theory Ahead of Business Cycle Measurement', p. 12.
46. J. Galí, 'Technology, Employment, and the Business Cycle: Do Technology Shocks Explain Aggregate Fluctuations?', *American Economic Review*, 89:1 (1999), pp. 249–71.
47. Ibid., p. 265.
48. C. Burnside, M. Eichenbaum and S. Rebelo, 'Labor Hoarding and the Business Cycle', *Journal of Political Economy*, 101:2 (1993), pp. 245–73.
49. C. Burnside, M. Eichenbaum and S. Rebelo, 'Sectoral Solow Residuals', *European Economic Review*, 40 (1996), pp. 861–9.
50. B. S. Bernanke, M. Gertler and S. Gilchrist, 'The Financial Accelerator in a Quantitative Business Cycle Framework', in J. Taylor and M. Woodford, *Handbook of Macroeconomics, v. 1C* (Amsterdam: North-Holland Elsevier, 1999), pp. 1341–93.
51. See Chapter 3 for a broader discussion.
52. We are not going to discuss here the legal and political issues that underlie the differences between EU and US economic policy. It is correct to say that these issues account for 80 per cent of the differences because the institutional framework matters a lot. We just want to focus on the effects of economic policies in the Eurozone and in the US as far as GDP and unemployment are concerned.

## 5 Governments and the Financial Crisis: Making Economic Policy in the Dark

1. D. Focarelli and A. Pozzolo, 'Banking Industry', in Durlauf and Blum (eds), *The New Palgrave Dictionary of Economics*, 2nd edn, 2008, online edition [accessed 14 August 2014].
2. T. Adrian and A. Ashcraft, 'Shadow Banking: A Review of the Literature', in S. Durlauf and L. Blum (eds), *The New Palgrave Dictionary of Economics* (London: Palgrave Macmillan, 2012), online edition at http://www.dictionaryofeconomics.com/article?id=pde2012_S000552 [accessed 11 June 2014].
3. E. Dorrucci and J. McKay, 'The International Monetary System after the Financial Crisis', *ECB Occasional Paper Series*, 122 (2011), pp. 1–62.

4. H. Nguyen and L. Servén, 'Global Imbalances Before and After the Global Crisis', *World Bank Policy Research Working Paper*, 5354 (2010).
5. M. Dooley, P. Garber and D. Folkerts-Landau, 'An Essay on the Revived Bretton-Woods System', *National Bureau of Economic Research, Working Papers 9971* (2003).
6. B. S. Bernanke, 'The Global Saving Glut and the US Current Account Deficit', 2005, at http://www.federalreserve.gov/boarddocs/speeches/2005/200503102/default.htm [accessed 11 August 2014].
7. Caballero, 'On the Macroeconomics of Asset Shortage'.
8. R. J. Caballero, 'Macroeconomics after the Crisis: Time to Deal with the Pretense-of-Knowledge Syndrome', *Journal of Economic Perspectives*, 24:4 (Fall 2010), pp. 85–102.
9. S. Dunaway, 'Global Imbalances and the Financial Crisis', *Council on Foreign Relations Special Report*, 44 (2009), pp. 1–56; B. Eichengreen, 'The Financial Crisis and Global Policy Reforms', *Federal Reserve Bank of San Francisco Asia Economic Policy Conference* (2009), pp. 18–20.
10. Dorrucci and McKay, 'The International Monetary System after the Financial Crisis'.
11. Ibid., p. 17.
12. C. Borio and P. Disyayat, 'Global Imbalances and the Financial Crisis: Link or not Link?', *BIS Working Papers*, 346 (2010), pp. 1–37.
13. T. Bracke, M. Bussière, M. Fidora and R. Straub, 'A Framework for Assessing Global Imbalances', *ECB Occasional Paper Series*, 78 (2008), pp. 1–51.
14. Dorrucci and McKay, 'The International Monetary System after the Financial Crisis', p. 14.
15. B. Eichengreen, *Exorbitant Privilege: The Rise and Fall of the Dollar and the Future of the International Monetary System* (Oxford: Oxford University Press, 2011).
16. E. Dorrucci, G. Pula and D. Santabárbara, 'China's Economic Growth and Rebalancing', *ECB Occasional Paper Series*, 142 (2013), pp. 1–54, on p. 10.
17. X. Zhou, 'Reform of the International Monetary System', Website of the People's Bank of China, 2009, at http://www.pbc.gov.cn [accessed 11 August 2014].
18. Ibid.
19. Dorrucci and McKay, 'The International Monetary System after the Financial Crisis', p. 24.
20. Dorrucci, Pula and Santabárbara, 'China's Economic Growth and Rebalancing', p. 24.
21. Z. Pozsar, T. Adrian, A. Ashcraft and H. Boesky, 'Shadow Banking', *Federal Reserve Bank of New York Staffs Reports*, 458 (2010), pp. 1–35, on p. 10.
22. Briefly described in Adrian and Ashcraft, 'Shadow Banking', pp. 5–9 and more detailed in Pozsar et al., 'Shadow Banking'.
23. T. J. Fitzpatrick IV and J. B. Thomson, 'Lehman Brothers Bankruptcy, What Lessons can be Drawn?', in Durlauf and Blum (eds), *The New Palgrave Dictionary of Economics*, 2012, online edition.
24. US Financial Crisis Inquiry Commission, *Final Report of the National Commission on the Causes of the Financial and Economic Crisis in the United States* (Washington, DC: US Government Printing Office, 2011), p. 22.
25. Fitzpatrick and Thomson, 'Lehman Brothers Bankruptcy, What Lessons can be Drawn?', p. 3.
26. US Financial Crisis Inquiry Commission, *Final Report of the National Commission on the Causes of the Financial and Economic Crisis in the United States*, p. xxi.
27. Bernanke, 'The Global Saving Glut and the US Current Account Deficit'.
28. Borio and Disyayat, 'Global Imbalances and the Financial Crisis'.
29. Adrian and Ashcraft, 'Shadow Banking', pp. 4–5.

30. Pozsar et al., 'Shadow Banking', p. 9.
31. T. Mayer, 'Euroland's Hidden Balance-of-Payments Crisis', *Reports on European Integration, EU Monitor*, 88 (2011), pp. 1–8, on p. 2.
32. Ibid.
33. Dorrucci and McKay, 'The International Monetary System after the Financial Crisis'.
34. M. Camarero, J. L. Carrion-i-Silvestre and C. Tamarit, 'External Imbalances in a Monetary Union. Does the Lawson Doctrine Apply to Europe?', *Department of Applied Economics II, University of Valencia Working Papers*, 1006 (2010), pp. 1–33.
35. O. Blanchard, 'Current Account Deficits in Rich Countries', *IMF Staff Papers*, 54:2 (2007), pp. 191–219.
36. Ibid.
37. International Monetary Fund, *Minutes of Executive Board Meeting 07/42-1*, 2007, at http://ep00.epimg.net/descargables/2014/03/30/76d620a70db1bb4d5d4af4b07b887055.pdf [accessed 11 August 2014].
38. C. Bowdler and A. Radia, 'Unconventional Monetary Policy: The Assessment', *Oxford Review of Economic Policy*, 28:4 (2012), pp. 603–21, on p. 604.
39. The data is available on the Federal Reserve's web page, at http://www.federalreserve.gov/monetarypolicy/bst_recenttrends.htm [accessed 11 August 2014].
40. D. Andolfatto, 'Is the Fed Monetizing Government Debt?', in *Economic Synopses*, Federal Reserve of Saint Louis, 5 (2013), pp. 1–2.
41. J. Williamson, 'Washington Consensus', in Durlauf and Blum (eds), *The New Palgrave Dictionary of Economics*, 2nd edn, 2008, online edition [accessed 14 August 2014].
42. http://www.treasury.gov/resource-center/data-chart-center/tic/Documents/mfh.txt [accessed 11 August 2014].
43. http://www.federalreserve.gov/releases/h41/20140130/ [accessed 11 August 2014].
44. B. Bernanke, 'Five Questions about the Federal Reserve and Monetary Policy', 2012, at http://www.federalreserve.gov/newsevents/speech/bernanke20121001a.htm [accessed 11 August 2014].
45. ECB *Financial Stability Review*, November 2013, in the foreword.
46. Bowdler and Radia, 'Unconventional Monetary Policy'.
47. Mayer, 'Euroland's Hidden Balance-of-Payments Crisis'.

## 6 Explaining More Complex Phenomena: The Financial System

1. We are not going to review the literature on this issue because we do not want to compare different financial crises. An excellent recent survey is C. M. Reinhart and K. Rogoff, *This Time is Different: Eight Centuries of Financial Folly* (Princeton, NJ: Princeton University Press, 2011).
2. Data from Global Financial Survey Database (World Bank), at http://econ.worldbank.org/ [accessed 4 June 2014].
3. A. Haldane, S. Brennan and V. Madouros, 'What is the Contribution of the Financial Sector: Miracle or Mirage?', in A. Turner et al., *The Future of Finance: The LSE Report* (London: The London School of Economics and Political Science, 2010), pp. 87–120, annex.
4. Ibid.
5. Markowitz and Sharpe outlined the basic theory. See H. M. Markowitz, 'Portfolio Selection', *Journal of Finance*, 7:1 (March 1952), pp. 77–91, and R. Merton, 'An Analytic

Derivation of the Efficient Portfolio Frontier', *Journal of Financial and Quantitative Analysis*, 7:4 (September 1972), pp. 1851–72.

6. It is the same hypothesis that we have discussed extensively in Chapter 1. Without this hypothesis the required calculations are very difficult to perform.
7. The preceding assumed that there was no uncertainty.
8. Kydland and Prescott, 'Time to Build and Aggregate Fluctuations'.
9. The neo-Keynesian DGSE modelling starts with Rothemberg's and Woodford's model of 1997.
10. This is Bernanke's and Gilchrist's model.
11. The financial accelerator model is only one exception, and it is not critical in any way.
12. R. Solow, 'Oral Statement', in *Building a Science of Economics for the Real World* (Washington, DC: Committee on Science and Technology, House of Representatives, 2010), pp. 12–15, on p. 12.
13. J. Stiglitz, 'Macroeconomics, Monetary Policy, and the Crisis', in O. J. Blanchard, D. Romer, M. Spence and J. E. Stiglitz (eds), *In the Wake of the Crisis: Leading Economists Reassess Economic Policy* (Cambridge MA: MIT Press, 2012), pp. 31–42.
14. Ibid., p. 39.
15. G. Kenny and J. Morgan, 'Some Lessons from the Financial Crisis for the Economic Analysis', *ECB Occasional Paper Series*, 130 (October 2011), pp. 1–30.
16. Ibid., p. 17.
17. Ibid.
18. R. Freeman, 'The Great Doubling: The Challenge of the New Global Labor Market', in J. Edwards, M. Crain and A. Kalleberg (eds), *Ending Poverty In America: How to Restore the American Dream* (New York: New Press, 2007), pp. 55–65.
19. C. Borio, 'The Financial Crisis of 2007–?: Macroeconomic Origins and Policy Lessons', *G20 Workshop on the Global Economy Mumbai*, India, 24–6 May 2009, at http://17g20.pa.go.kr/Documents/g20_workshop_causes_of_the_crisis.pdf [accessed 11 August 2014].
20. M. Obstfeld, 'The Immoderate World Economy', *Journal of International Money and Finance*, 29:4 (June 2010), pp. 603–14, on p. 603.
21. Friedman, 'The *Methodology of Positive Economics*'.
22. L. Ohanian, 'The Economic Crisis from a Neoclassical Perspective', *Journal of Economic Perspectives*, 24:4 (2010), pp. 45–56, on p. 46.
23. Ibid., p. 51.
24. See Caballero, 'Macroeconomics after the Crisis'.
25. R. J. Caballero and A. Krishnamurthy, 'Global Imbalances and Financial Fragility', *National Bureau of Economic Research, Working Papers 14688* (2009), pp. 1–12, on p. 3.
26. R. E. Lucas, 'Why doesn't Capital Flow from Rich to Poor Countries?', *American Economic Review*, 80:2 (1990), pp. 92–6.
27. J. M. Keynes, 'Alternative Theories of the Rate of Interest', *Economic Journal*, 47:186 (1937), pp. 241–52, on p. 246.
28. H. P. Minsky, 'Can it Happen Again? A Reprise', *Challenge*, 25:3 (1982), pp. 5–13, on p. 5.
29. As Minsky called it. See H. P. Minsky, *Can It Happen Again?: Essays on Instability and Finance* (Armonk, NY: M. E. Sharpe, 1982), p. 121.
30. Minsky, 'Can it Happen Again? A Reprise', p. 9.
31. Ibid., p. 10.

32. R. Koo, 'Balance Sheet Recession as the "Other Half" of Macroeconomics', *European Journal of Economics and Economic Policies: Intervention*, 10:2 (2013), pp. 136–57, on p. 142.
33. Huerta de Soto, *The Austrian School of Economics*, p. 65.
34. Ibid., p. 70.
35. See Huerta de Soto, *Money, Bank Credit, and Economic Cycles*, ch. 9.
36. G. Shmueli, 'To Explain or to Predict?', *Statistical Science*, 25:3 (2010), pp. 289–310, on pp. 305–6.
37. H. Dewachter and R. Wouters, 'Endogenous Risk in a DSGE Model with Capital-Constrained Financial Intermediaries', forthcoming, *Journal of Economic Dynamics & Control*, 2014, at http://dx.doi.org/10.1016/j.jedc.2014.03.004 [accessed 11 August 2014].
38. Austrian economics shares this approach as well, but from a different point of view. Many circumstances lead the economy out of equilibrium, but agents grasp the opportunities for profit that disequilibrium generates. In so doing they drive the economy back to equilibrium. The Keynesian approach focuses much more on disequilibrium. In fact, Keynesian economies seldom are in equilibrium.
39. P. Mirowski, *Never Let a Serious Crisis Go to Waste: How Neoliberalism Survived the Financial Meltdown* (London: Verso, 2013).

# WORKS CITED

Acemoglu, D., S. Johnson and A. Robinson, 'Institutions as a Fundamental Cause of Long-Run Growth', in P. Aghion and S. Durlauf, *Handbook of Economic Growth, Vol 1A* (Amsterdam, North-Holland Elsevier, 2005), pp. 386–471.

Adrian, T. and A. Ashcraft, 'Shadow Banking: A Review of the Literature', in S. Durlauf and L. Blum (eds), *The New Palgrave Dictionary of Economics* (London: Palgrave Macmillan, 2012), online edition at http://www.dictionaryofeconomics.com/article?id=pde2012_S000552 [accessed 11 June 2014].

Aghion, P. and S. Durlauf, *Handbook of Economic Growth, Vol 1A and 1B* (Amsterdam: North-Holland Elsevier, 2005).

Aghion, P. and P. Howitt, 'A Model of Growth through Creative Destruction', *Econometrica*, 60:2 (March 1992), pp. 323–51.

Amoroso, L., *Lezioni di Economia Matematica* (Padua: CEDAM Casa Editrice Dottore Antonio Milani, 1921).

Andolfatto, D., 'Is the Fed Monetizing Government Debt?', in *Economic Synopses*, Federal Reserve of Saint Louis, 5 (2013), pp. 1–2.

Arrow, K. J., 'The Economic Implications of Learning by Doing', *Review of Economic Studies*, 29:3 (June 1962), pp. 155–73.

Arrow, K. J. and G. Debreu, 'Existence of an Equilibrium for a Competitive Economy', *Econometrica*, 22:3 (1954), pp. 265–90.

Baker, D., B. DeLong and P. Krugman, 'Asset Returns and Economic Growth', *Brooking Papers on Economic Activity*, 1 (2005), pp. 289–330.

Barro, R. and X. Sala-i-Martín, 'Technological Diffusion, Convergence and Growth', *Journal of Economic Growth*, 2 (1997), pp. 1–26.

—, *Economic Growth*, 2nd edn (Cambridge, MA: MIT Press, 2004).

Benhabib, J., J. Rogerson and R. Wright, 'Homework in Macroeconomics: Household Production and Aggregate Fluctuations', *Journal of Political Economy*, 99:6 (1991), pp. 1166–87.

Bernanke, B. S., 'The Global Saving Glut and the US Current Account Deficit', 2005, at http://www.federalreserve.gov/boarddocs/speeches/2005/200503102/default.htm [accessed 11 August 2014].

Bernanke, B. S., 'Five Questions about the Federal Reserve and Monetary Policy', 2012, at http://www.federalreserve.gov/newsevents/speech/bernanke20121001a.htm [accessed 11 August 2014].

Bernanke, B. S., M. Gertler and S. Gilchrist, 'The Financial Accelerator in a Quantitative Business Cycle Framework', in J. Taylor and M. Woodford, *Handbook of Macroeconomics, v 1C* (Amsterdam: North-Holland Elsevier, 1999), pp. 1341–93.

Bezemer, D., '"No One Saw this Coming": Understanding Financial Crisis through Accounting Models', *Munich Personal RePec Archive*, 15892 (2009), pp. 1–50.

Blanchard, O., 'Current Account Deficits in Rich Countries', *IMF Staff Papers*, 54:2 (2007), pp. 191–219.

Boland, L. A., 'A Critique of Friedman's Critics', *Journal of Economic Literature*, 17:2 (1979), pp. 503–22.

—, *Critical Economic Methodology: A Personal Odyssey* (London and New York: Routledge, 1997).

Borio, C., 'The Financial Crisis of 2007–?: Macroeconomic Origins and Policy Lessons', *G20 Workshop on the Global Economy Mumbai*, India, 24–6 May 2009, at http://17g20.pa.go.kr/Documents/g20_workshop_causes_of_the_crisis.pdf [accessed 11 August 2014].

Borio, C. and P. Disyayat, 'Global Imbalances and the Financial Crisis: Link or not Link?', *BIS Working Papers*, 346 (2010), pp. 1–37.

Bowdler, C. and A. Radia, 'Unconventional Monetary Policy: The Assessment', *Oxford Review of Economic Policy*, 28:4 (2012), pp. 603–21.

Bracke, T., M. Bussière, M. Fidora and R. Straub, 'A Framework for Assessing Global Imbalances', *ECB Occasional Paper Series*, 78 (2008), pp. 1–51.

Braun, J., 'Essays on Economic Growth and Migration' (PhD dissertation, Harvard University, 1993).

British Academy, 'The Global Financial Crisis – Why Didn't Anybody Notice?', July 2009.

Brock, W. and L. Mirman, 'Optimal Economic Growth and Uncertainty: The Discounted Case', *Journal of Economic Theory*, 4:3 (1972), pp. 479–513.

Burnside, C., M. Eichenbaum and S. Rebelo, 'Labor Hoarding and the Business Cycle', *Journal of Political Economy*, 101:2 (1993), pp. 245–73.

—, 'Sectoral Solow Residuals', *European Economic Review*, 40 (1996), pp. 861–9.

Caballero, R. J., 'On the Macroeconomics of Asset Shortage', *National Bureau of Economic Research, Working Papers 12753* (Cambridge, MA: NBER, 2006).

—, 'Macroeconomics after the Crisis: Time to Deal with the Pretense-of-Knowledge Syndrome', *Journal of Economic Perspectives*, 24:4 (Fall 2010), pp. 85–102.

Caballero, R. J. and A. Krishnamurthy, 'Global Imbalances and Financial Fragility', *National Bureau of Economic Research, Working Papers 14688* (2009), pp. 1–12.

Camarero, M., J. L. Carrion-i-Silvestre and C. Tamarit, 'External Imbalances in a Monetary Union. Does the Lawson Doctrine Apply to Europe?', *Department of Applied Economics II, University of Valencia Working Papers*, 1006 (2010), pp. 1–33.

Cass, D., 'Optimum Growth in an Aggregative Model of Capital Accumulation', *Review of Economic Studies*, 32:3 (1965), pp. 233–40.

Castañeda, J., *Lecciones de Teoría Económica* (Madrid: Aguilar, 1968).

Cervone, D., 'The Architecture of Personality', *Psycholocial Review*, 111:1 (2004), pp. 183–204.

Chari, V. V., 'Nobel Laureate Robert E. Lucas, Jr.: Architect of Modern Macroeconomics', *Federal Reserve Bank of Minneapolis Quarterly Review*, 23:2 (1999), pp. 2–12.

Chick, V., 'On Knowing One's Place: The Role of Formalism in Economics', *Economic Journal*, 108 (1998), pp. 1859–69.

Christiano, L. and M. Eichenbaum, 'Current Real Business Cycle Theories and Aggregate Labor Market Fluctuations', *American Economic Review*, 82:3 (1992), pp. 430–50.

Cooley, T. and G. Hansen, 'The Inflation Tax in a Real Business Cycle Model', *American Economic Review*, 79:4 (September 1989), pp. 733–48.

Crotty, J., 'Are Keynesian Uncertainy and Macrotheory Compatible? Conventional Decision Making, Institutional Structures, and Conditional Stability in Keynesian Macromodels', in G. Dimsky and R. Pollin (eds), *New Perspectives in Monetary Macroeconomics* (Ann Arbor, MI: University of Michigan Press, 1994), pp. 105–39.

Davidson, P., *International Money and the Real World* (New York: St. Martin's Press, 1992).

Davis, J. B., 'Keynes's Later Philosophy', *History of Political Economy*, 27:2 (1995), pp. 237–60.

De Grauwe, P., *Economics of Monetary Union*, 9th edn (Oxford: Oxford University Press, 2012).

Debreu, G., *Theory of Value: An Axiomatic Analysis of Economic Equilibrium* (New Haven, CT, and London: Yale University Press, 1959).

Dequech, D., 'On Some Arguments for the Rationality of Conventional Behaviour under Uncertainty', in P. Kriesler and C. Sardoni (eds), *Keynes, Post Keynesianism and Political Economy: Essays in Honour of Geoff. Harcourt, Volume Three* (London: Routledge, 1999), pp. 179–98.

Dewachter H. and R. Wouters, 'Endogenous Risk in a DSGE Model with Capital-Constrained Financial Intermediaries', forthcoming, *Journal of Economic Dynamics & Control*, 2014, at http://dx.doi.org/10.1016/j.jedc.2014.03.004 [accessed 11 August 2014].

Domar, E., 'Capital Expansion, Rate of Growth, and Employment', *Econometrica*, 14:2 (1946), pp. 137–47.

Dooley, M., P. Garber and D. Folkerts-Landau, 'An Essay on the Revived Bretton-Woods System', *National Bureau of Economic Research, Working Papers 9971* (2003).

Dorrucci, E. and J. McKay, 'The International Monetary System after the Financial Crisis', *ECB Occasional Paper Series*, 122 (2011), pp. 1–62.

Dorrucci, E., G. Pula and D. Santabárbara, 'China's Economic Growth and Rebalancing', *ECB Occasional Paper Series*, 142 (2013), pp. 1–54.

Dunaway, S., 'Global Imbalances and the Financial Crisis', *Council on Foreign Relations Special Report*, 44 (2009), pp. 1–56.

Edgeworth, F. Y., *Mathematical Psychics: An Essay on the Application of Mathematics to the Moral Sciences* (London: Macmillan and Co., 1881).

Eichengreen, B., 'The Financial Crisis and Global Policy Reforms', *Federal Reserve Bank of San Francisco Asia Economic Policy Conference* (2009), pp. 18–20.

—, *Exorbitant Privilege: The Rise and Fall of the Dollar and the Future of the International Monetary System* (Oxford: Oxford University Press, 2011).

European Commission, *Economic Crisis in Europe: Causes, Consequences and Responses* (Luxembourg: European Commission, 2009).

Fisher, I., *Mathematical Investigations in the Theory of Value and Prices* (New York: August M. Kelley, 1892).

Fitzgibbons, A., *Keynes's Vision: A New Political Economy* (Oxford: Clarendon Press, 1988).

Fitzpatrick IV, T. J. and J. B. Thomson, 'Lehman Brothers Bankruptcy, What Lessons can be Drawn?', in Durlauf and Blum (eds), *The New Palgrave Dictionary of Economics*, 2012, online edition.

Focarelli, D. and A. Pozzolo, 'Banking Industry', in S. Durlauf and L. Blum (eds), *The New Palgrave Dictionary of Economics*, 2nd edn (London: Palgrave Macmillan, 2008), online edition at http://www.dictionaryofeconomics.com/article?id=pde2008_B000309 [accessed 14 August 2014].

Frazer, W. J. and L. A. Boland, 'An Essay on the Foundations of Friedman's Methodology', in J. C. Wood and R. N. Woods (eds), *Milton Friedman: Critical Assessments. Routledge Critical Assessments of Contemporary Economists, Vol. III* (London: Routledge, 1990), pp. 458–80.

Freeman, R., 'The Great Doubling: The Challenge of the New Global Labor Market', in J. Edwards, M. Crain and A. Kalleberg (eds), *Ending Poverty in America: How to Restore the American Dream* (New York: New Press, 2007), pp. 55–65.

Friedman, M., 'The *Methodology of Positive Economics*', in M. Friedman, *Essays in Positive Economics* (Chicago, IL: University of Chicago Press, 1953), pp. 3–43.

—, *Essays in Positive Economics* (Chicago, IL: University of Chicago Press, 1953).

Galí, J., 'Technology, Employment, and the Business Cycle: Do Technology Shocks Explain Aggregate Fluctuations?', *American Economic Review*, 89:1 (1999), pp. 249–71.

—, *Monetary Policy, Inflation and the Business Cycle* (Princeton, NJ: Princeton University Press, 2008).

Global Financial Survey Database (World Bank), at http://econ.worldbank.org/ [accessed 4 June 2014].

Grossman, G. and E. Helpman, 'Trade, Innovation and Growth', *American Economic Review*, 80:2 (May 1990), pp. 86–91.

—, *Innovation and Growth in the Global Economy* (Cambridge, MA: MIT Press, 1991).

Grossman, S. and J. Stiglitz, 'Information and Competitive Price Systems', *American Economic Review*, 66:2 (1976), pp. 246–53.

Haldane, A., S. Brennan and V. Madouros, 'What is the Contribution of the Financial Sector: Miracle or Mirage?', in A. Turner et al., *The Future of Finance: The LSE Report* (London: London School of Economics and Political Science, 2010), pp. 87–120, annex.

Hammond, J. D., 'Early Drafts of Friedman's Methodology Essay', in U. Maki (ed.), *The Methodology of Positive Economics: Reflections on the Milton Friedman Legacy* (Cambridge: Cambridge University Press, 2009), pp. 68–89.

Hansen, G. D., 'Indivisible Labor and the Business Cycle', *Journal of Monetary Economics*, 16:3 (1985), pp. 309–27.

Hansen, G. D. and R. Wright, 'The Labor Market in Real Business Cycle Theory', *Federal Reserve Bank of Minneapolis Quarterly Review*, 16:2 (Spring 1992), pp. 2–12.

Hands, W., 'Did Milton Friedman's Positive Methodology License the Formalist Revolution?', in Maki (ed.), *The Methodology of Positive Economics*, pp. 143–64.

Harrod, R. F., 'An Essay in Dynamic Theory', *Economic Journal*, 49:193 (1939), pp. 14–33.

Hodgson, G. M., 'Generalizing Darwinism to Social Evolution: Some Early Attempts', *Journal of Economic Issues*, 39:4 (2005), pp. 899–914.

—, 'Dismantling Lamarckism: Why Descriptions of Socio-Economics Evolution as Lamarckian are Misleading', *Journal of Evolutionary Economics*, 16 (2006), pp. 343–66.

—, 'The Nature and Units of Social Selection', *Journal of Evolutionary Economics*, 16:5 (2006), pp. 477–89.

—, 'Why We Need a Generalized Darwinism and why Generalized Darwinism is not Enough', *Journal of Economic Behaviour & Organization*, 61 (2006), pp. 1–19.

Hoover, K., *Causality in Macroeconomics* (Cambridge: Cambridge University Press, 2001).

Hudson, M., 'Saving, Asset-Price Inflation, and Debt-Induced Deflation', in L. Randall Wray and M. Fostater (eds), *Money, Financial Instability and Stabilization Policy* (Cheltenham: Edward Elgar, 2006), pp. 104–24.

—, 'The Road to Serfdom: An Illustrated Guide to the Coming Real Estate Collapse', *Harper's Magazine* (2006), pp. 39–46.

Huerta de Soto, J., *Money, Bank Credit, and Economic Cycles* (Auburn, AL: Ludwig von Mises Institute, 2006).

—, *The Austrian School of Economics* (Aldershot: Edward Elgar, 2008).

Hutchison, T., *The Significance and Basic Postulates of Economic Theory* (New York: Augustus M. Kelley: 1938 reprint).

International Monetary Fund, *Minutes of Executive Board Meeting 07/42-1*, 2007, at http://ep00.epimg.net/descargables/2014/03/30/76d620a70db1bb4d5d4af4b07b887055.pdf [accessed 11 August 2014].

—, *World Outlook* (Washington, DC: IMF, October 2007).

—, *World Outlook* (Washington, DC: IMF, October 2008).

—, *Fiscal Implications of the Global Economic and Financial Crisis. Staff Position Paper* (Washington, DC: IMF, June 2009).

—, *World Economic Outlook, Global Prospects and Policies. Spring 2009* (Washington, DC: IMF, June 2009).

Jespersen, J., *The Methodology of Macroeconomics: A Post Keynesian Perspective* (Cheltham: Edward Elgar Publishing, 2009).

Jevons, W. S., *The Theory of Political Economy* (London: Macmillan and Co., 1871).

Jones, C., 'R&D-Based Models of Economic Growth', *Journal of Political Economy*, 103:4 (1995), pp. 759–84.

—, 'Time Series Tests of Endogenous Growth Models', *Quarterly Journal of Economics*, 110:2 (May 1995), pp. 495–525.

Kahneman, D. and A. Tversky, 'Prospect Theory: An Analysis of Decision under Risk', *Econometrica*, 47:2 (1979), pp. 263–92.

—, *Choices, Values and Frames* (Cambridge: Cambridge University Press, 2000).

Keeley, B. and P. Love, *From Crisis to Recovery: The Causes, Course and Consequences of the Great Recession* (Paris: Organization for Economic Cooperation and Development, 2010).

Keen, S., 'Why did I See the Financial Crisis Coming and "They" Didn't?', *Analysis*, 2008, at http://www.compareshares.com.au/keen04.php [accessed 11 June 2014].

Kenny G. and J. Morgan, 'Some Lessons from the Financial Crisis for the Economic Analysis', *ECB Occasional Paper Series*, 130 (October 2011), pp. 1–30.

Keynes, J. M., *A Treatise on Probability* (London: Macmillan, 1921).

—, *The General Theory of Employment, Interest and Money* (London: Macmillan, 1936).

—, 'Alternative Theories of the Rate of Interest', *Economic Journal*, 47:186 (1937), pp. 241–52.

—, 'Professor Tinbergen's Method', *Economic Journal*, 49 (1939), pp. 558–68.

—, *The General Theory and After: A Supplement, Collected Writings, Vol. XXIX* (London: Macmillan, 1972).

—, *The Collected Writings of John Maynard Keynes: Vol. VIII. A Treatise on Probability* (London: Macmillan, 1972).

—, 'The General Theory of Employment', in J. M. Keynes, *The Collected Writings of John Maynard Keynes, Vol. XIV* (London: Macmillan, 1972), pp. 109–23.

King, J. E., *A History of Post Keynesian Economics since 1936* (Cheltenham: Edward Elgar, 1993).

Kirzner, I., 'Ludwig von Mises and Friedrich von Hayek: The Modern Extension of Austrian Subjectivism', in S. Littlechild (ed.), *Austrian Economics I.* (Aldershot: Elgar, 1990), pp. 342–65.

Kolakowski, L., *The Positivist Philosophy* (London: Penguin, 1972).

Koo, R., 'Balance Sheet Recession as the "Other Half" of Macroeconomics', *European Journal of Economics and Economic Policies: Intervention*, 10:2 (2013), pp. 136–57.

Koopmans, T. C., 'On the Concept of Optimal Economic Growth', in *Study Week on the Econometric Approach to Development Planning* (Vatican City: Pontificia Academia Scientiarum, 1965), pp. 225–87.

Kregel, J. A., 'Aspects of a Post Keynesian Theory of Finance', *Journal of Post Keynesian Economics*, 21:1 (October 1988), pp. 111–33.

Kydland, F. and E. Prescott, 'Time to Build and Aggregate Fluctuations', *Econometrica*, 50:6 (November 1982), pp. 1345–70.

—, 'Business Cycles: Real Facts and a Monetary Myth', *Federal Reserve Bank of Minneapolis Quarterly Review*, 14:2 (Spring 1990), pp. 3–18.

Lachmann, L. M. 'From Mises to Shackle: An Essay in Austrian Economics and Kaleidic Society', *Journal of Economic Literature*, 14:1 (1976), pp. 54–62.

Lawson, T., 'Probability and Uncertainty in Economic Analysis', *Journal of Post Keynesian Economics*, 11:1 (1988), pp. 38–65.

—, *Economics and Reality* (London and New York: Routledge, 1997).

Levine, R., 'Finance and Growth: Theory and Evidence', in Aghion and Durlauf, *Handbook of Economic Growth, Vol 1A*, pp. 866–934.

Lindbeck, A., 'New Keynesianism and Aggregate Economic Activity', *Economic Journal*, 108:446 (1998), pp. 167–80.

Lucas, R. E., 'Methods and Problems in Business Cycle Theory', *Journal of Money, Credit and Banking*, 12:4 (1980), pp. 696–715.

—, 'On the Mechanics of Economic Development', *Journal of Monetary Economics*, 22 (1988), pp. 3–42.

—, 'Why doesn't Capital Flow from Rich to Poor Countries?', *American Economic Review*, 80:2 (1990), pp. 92–6.

McCann, C., *Probability Foundations of Economics* (New York: Routledge, 1994).

Maddison, A., *Phases of Capitalist Development* (Oxford: Oxford University Press, 1982).

Maki, U. (ed.), *The Methodology of Positive Economics: Reflections on the Milton Friedman Legacy* (Cambridge: Cambridge University Press, 2009).

Mankiw, G., P. Romer and D. Weil, 'A Contribution of the Empirics of Economic Growth', *Quarterly Journal of Economics*, 107:2 (May 1992), pp. 407–37.

Marchionatti, R., 'On Keynes' Animal Spirits', *Kyklos*, 52:3 (2001), pp. 415–39.

Markowitz, H. M., 'Portfolio Selection', *Journal of Finance*, 7:1 (March 1952), pp. 77–91.

Mas-Colell, A., M. D. Whinston and J. R. Green, *Microeconomic Theory* (New York: Oxford University Press, 1995).

Mayer, T., 'The Influence of Friedman's Methodological Essay', in Maki (ed.), *The Methodology of Positive Economics*, pp. 119–42.

—, 'Euroland's Hidden Balance-of-Payments Crisis', *Reports on European Integration, EU Monitor*, 88 (2011), pp. 1–8.

Menger, C., *Principles of Economics* (Auburn, AL: Ludwig von Mises Institute, 1976).

—, *Investigations into the Method of the Social Sciences* (Grove City, PA: Libertarian Press, 1996).

*Merriam Webster Dictionary*, at http://www.merriam-webster.com/dictionary/modus%20 ponens [accessed 21 February 2014].

Merton, R., 'An Analytic Derivation of the Efficient Portfolio Frontier', *Journal of Financial and Quantitative Analysis*, 7:4 (September 1972), pp. 1851–72.

Metcalfe, S., *Evolutionary Economics and Creative Destruction* (London: Routledge, 1998).

Minsky, H. P., 'Can it Happen Again? A Reprise', *Challenge*, 25:3 (1982), pp. 5–13.

—, *Can It Happen Again?: Essays on Instability and Finance* (Armonk, NY: M. E. Sharpe, 1982).

—, *Stabilizing an Unstable Economy* (New Haven, CT: Yale University Press, 1986).

Mirowski, P., *More Heat than Light: Economics as Social Physics, Physics as Nature's Economics* (Cambridge: Cambridge University Press, 1989).

—, *Never Let a Serious Crisis Go to Waste: How Neoliberalism Survived the Financial Meltdown* (London: Verso, 2013).

Mises, L. von, *The Ultimate Foundation of Economic Science* (Princeton, NJ: D. Van Nostrand Company, Inc, 1962).

—, *Human Action* (Auburn, AL: Ludwig von Mises Institute, 1998).

—, *Epistemological Problems of Economics*, trans. G. Reisman (Indianapolis, IN: Liberty Fund, 2013).

Moss, S., 'The History of the Theory of the Firm from Marshall to Robinson and Chamberlin: The Source of Positivism in Economics', *Economica*, 51:203 (1984), pp. 307–18.

Muñoz, F. and M. Encinar, 'Intentionality and the Emergence of Complexity: An Analytical Approach', *Journal of Evolutionary Economics* (2014), forthcoming.

Muñoz, F., M. Encinar and C. Cañibano, 'On the Role of Intentionality in Evolutionary Economic Change', *Structural Change and Economic Dynamics*, 22 (2011), pp. 193–203.

Nelson, R. and S. Winter, *An Evolutionary Theory of Economic Change* (Cambridge, MA: Belknap Press, 1982).

Nguyen, H. and L. Servén, 'Global Imbalances Before and After the Global Crisis', *World Bank Policy Research Working Paper*, 5354 (2010).

Obstfeld, M., 'The Immoderate World Economy', *Journal of International Money and Finance*, 29:4 (June 2010), pp. 603–14, on p. 603.

O'Donnell, R. M., 'Keynes on Mathematics: Philosophical Foundations and Economic Applications', *Cambridge Journal of Economics*, 14:1 (March 1990), pp. 29–47.

Ohanian, L., 'The Economic Crisis from a Neoclassical Perspective', *Journal of Economic Perspectives*, 4:2 (2010), pp. 45–56.

Pareto, V., *Cours d'Économie Politique II* (Geneva: Droz, 1897).

Passmore, J., *A Hundred Years of Philosophy* (London: Penguin, 1968).

Pozsar, Z., T. Adrian, A. Ashcraft and H. Boesky, 'Shadow Banking', *Federal Reserve Bank of New York Staffs Reports*, 458 (2010), pp. 1–35.

Prescott, E., 'Theory Ahead of Business Cycle Measurement', *Federal Reserve Bank of Minneapolis Quarterly Review*, 10:4 (Fall 1986), pp. 9–22.

Prychitko, D. L., 'Competing Explanations of the Minsky Moment: The Financial Instability Hypothesis in Light of Austrian Theory', *Review of Austrian Economics*, 23 (2010), pp. 199–221.

Rajan, R., 'Has Financial Development Made the World Riskier?', *National Bureau of Economic Research, Working Papers 11728* (Cambridge, MA: NBER, 2006), pp. 313–69.

Ramsey, F. P., 'A Mathematical Theory of Saving', *Economic Journal*, 38:152 (1928), pp. 543–59.

*Reinhart*, C. M. and K. *Rogoff*, *This Time is Different: Eight Centuries of Financial Folly* (*Princeton*, NJ: Princeton University Press, 2011).

Richebächer, K., *The Richebächer Letter: Monthly Analysis of Currencies and Credit Markets*, July 2006; August 2006.

Robbins, L., *An Essay on the Nature and Significance of Economic Science* (London: Macmillan, 1935).

Rodríguez, A., 'Austrian Economics as a Progressive Paradigm: Explaining More Complex Economic Phenomena', *Review of Austrian Economics*, 15:4 (2002), pp. 335–57.

Romer, P., 'Increasing Returns and Long-Run Growth', *Journal of Political Economy*, 94:5 (October 1986), pp. 1002–37.

—, 'Crazy Explanations for the Productivity Slowdown', in S. Fisher (ed.), *NBER Macroeconomics Annual 1987, Vol. 2* (Cambridge, MA: MIT Press, 1987), pp. 163–210.

—, 'Endogenous Technological Change', *Journal of Political Economy*, 98:5 (October 1990), pp. 1002–37.

Rotemberg, J. and M. Woodford, 'An Optimization-Based Econometric Framework for the Evaluation of Monetary Policy', in B. Bernanke and J. Rotemberg, *NBER Macroeconomics Annual 1997, Volume 12* (Cambridge MA: MIT Press, 1997), pp. 297–361.

Rotheim, R., 'New Keynesian Macroeconomics and Markets', in R. Rotheim (ed.), *New Keynesian Economics/Post Keynesian Alternatives* (London: Routledge, 1998), pp. 51–70.

Rubio de Urquía, R., 'Ética y Procesos de Asignación de Recursos', *Información Comercial Española*, 691 (1991), pp. 7–16.

—, 'Acerca del Lugar de las Concepciones Antropológicas en la Constitución y Progreso de la Teoría Económica', *Boletín de la Real Sociedad Bascongada de Amigos del País*, L-2 (1994), pp. 457–81.

—, 'A Short Note on the Anthropological Foundations of Economic Science', in J. P. Pham (ed.), *Centessimus Annus: Assessment and Perspectives for the Future of Catholic Social Doctrine* (Vatican: Libreria Editrice Vaticana, 1998), pp. 165–73.

—, 'La Naturaleza y Estructura Fundamental de la Teoría Económica y las Relaciones entre Enunciados Teórico-Económicos y Enunciados Antropológicos', in R. Rubio de Urquía, E. M. Ureña and F. F. Muñoz (eds), *Estudios de Teoría Económica y Antropología* (Madrid: IIES de Vitoria-AEDOS-Unión Editorial, 2005), pp. 23–198.

Sargent, T., *Macroeconomic Theory* (New York: Academic Press, 1979).

Shiller, R., *Irrational Exuberance*, 2nd edn (Princeton, NJ: Princeton University Press, 2001).

Shmueli, G., 'To Explain or to Predict?', *Statistical Science*, 25:3 (2010), pp. 289–310.

Smith, V., 'Experimental Methods in Economics', in Durlauf and Blum (eds), *The New Palgrave Dictionary of Economics*, 2nd edn, 2008, online edition.

Solow, R., 'A Contribution to the Theory of Economic Growth', *Quarterly Journal of Economics*, 70:1 (1956), pp. 65–94.

—, 'Technical Change and the Aggregate Production Function', *Review of Economics and Statistics*, 39:3 (August 1957), pp. 312–20.

—, 'The State of Macroeconomics', *Journal of Economic Perspectives*, 22:1 (Winter 2008), pp. 243–9.

—, 'Oral Statement', in *Building a Science of Economics for the Real World* (Washington, DC: Committee on Science and Technology, House of Representatives, 2010), pp. 12–15.

Stadler, G. W., 'Real Business Cycles', *Journal of Economic Literature*, 32:4 (1994), pp. 1750–83.

Stanley, T. D., 'The Cambridge Circus and Other Influences upon Keynes: A Review of "Keynes and his Contemporaries"', *Journal of Behavioural Economics*, 14:1 (1985), pp. 209–12.

Stiglitz, J., 'Macroeconomics, Monetary Policy, and the Crisis', in O. J. Blanchard, D. Romer, M. Spence and J. E. Stiglitz (eds), *In the Wake of the Crisis: Leading Economists Reassess Economic Policy* (Cambridge MA: MIT Press, 2012), pp. 31–42.

Summers, R. and A. Heston, 'A New Set of International Comparisons or Real Product and Price Levels Estimates for 130 Countries, 1950–1985', *Review of Income and Wealth*, 34:1 (March 1988), pp. 1–25.

Swan, T., 'Economic Growth and Capital Accumulation', *Economic Record*, 32:2 (1956), pp. 334–61.

Thaler, R. and C. Sunstein, 'Human Frailty Causes this Crisis', *Financial Times*, 12 November 2008.

US Financial Crisis Inquiry Commission, *Final Report of the National Commission on the Causes of the Financial and Economic Crisis in the United States* (Washington, DC: US Government Printing Office, 2011).

Walras, L., *Éléments d'Économie Politique Pure au Théorie de la Richesse Sociale* (Paris: R. Pichot et R. Durand Auzias, 1874).

Weil, P., 'Overlapping Families of Infinitely Lived Agents', *Journal of Public Economics*, 38:2 (March 1989), pp. 183–98.

White, W., 'Is Price Stability Enough?', *Bank International of Settlements Papers* (Basel: BIS Papers, 2006), p. 9.

Williamson, J., 'Washington Consensus', in Durlauf and Blum (eds), *The New Palgrave Dictionary of Economics*, 2nd edn , 2008, online edition.

Winslow, E. G., 'Keynes and Freud: Psychoanalysis and Keynes's Account of the "Animal Spirits" of Capitalism', *Social Research*, 53:4 (Winter 1986), pp. 549–78.

Zhou, X., 'Reform of the International Monetary System', Website of the People's Bank of China, http://www.pbc.gov.cn:8080/publish/english/956/2009/20091229104425550619706/20091229104425550619706_.html [accessed 11 August 2014].

# INDEX